PRAISE FOR *RETURN TO SOURCE*

'*The veil is being lifted. We are now experiencing what I call an African Renaissance. A rebirth of art, fashion, food, writing, myth, magic and wisdom teachings. What was once deemed primitive is finally recognised for the Healing power and wellness it induces. Araba Ofori-Acquah's book* Return to Source *is part of the wave that is returning us to Africa. And in these pages, you will find a helpful reworking of wellness tools for black people direct from the Source.*'

Caroline Shola Arewa, author of *Opening to Spirit* and *Energy 4 Life*

'Return to Source *is a very important book. It makes African Spirituality accessible to the reader. [Araba] returns us to the Original Principles of the Culture, those ideas that can be found everywhere. She recounts the challenges the culture has endured and clarifies the gifts that have come out of that struggle. And most important, she returns to those Principles and provides the reader with guidelines to apply that wisdom to the requirements of contemporary life. It is an easy read, a pleasurable read and a very necessary one. Enjoy and be enriched.*'

Yeye Luisah Teish, author of *Jambalaya: The Natural Woman's Book of Personal Charms and Practical Rituals*

'With Return to Source, *Araba Ofori-Acquah gifts us with sacred ancestral medicine on the page. At this very moment the majority of our human brothers and sisters are crying out for reconnection – to ourselves, to each other, to the Source of All That Is. I am proud and excited to add this book to my favorite inspirational offerings. I highly recommend that you do the same. This is wellness custom-made for us. And for this sacred offering, I am so very grateful.*'

Abiola Abrams, award-winning author of *African Goddess Initiation* and *African Goddess Rising Oracle*

T0049868

RETURN
TO
SOURCE

ARABA OFORI-ACQUAH

RETURN TO SOURCE

UNLOCK THE POWER OF AFRICAN-CENTERED WELLNESS

HAY HOUSE

Carlsbad, California • New York City
London • Sydney • New Delhi

Published in the United Kingdom by:
Hay House UK Ltd, The Sixth Floor, Watson House, 54 Baker Street
London W1U 7BU
Tel: +44 (0)20 3927 7290; Fax: +44 (0)20 3927 7291; www.hayhouse.co.uk

Published in the United States of America by:
Hay House Inc., PO Box 5100, Carlsbad, CA 92018-5100
Tel: (1) 760 431 7695 or (800) 654 5126; Fax: (1) 760 431 6948 or (800) 650 5115
www.hayhouse.com

Published in Australia by:
Hay House Australia Ltd, 18/36 Ralph St, Alexandria NSW 2015
Tel: (61) 2 9669 4299; Fax: (61) 2 9669 4144; www.hayhouse.com.au

Published in India by:
Hay House Publishers India, Muskaan Complex, Plot No.3, B-2,
Vasant Kunj, New Delhi 110 070
Tel: (91) 11 4176 1620; Fax: (91) 11 4176 1630; www.hayhouse.co.in

The information given in this book should not be treated as a substitute for professional medical advice; always consult a medical practitioner. Any use of information in this book is at the reader's discretion and risk. Neither the author nor the publisher can be held responsible for any loss, claim or damage arising out of the use, or misuse, of the suggestions made, the failure to take medical advice or for any material on third-party websites.

A catalogue record for this book is available from the British Library.

Tradepaper ISBN: 978-1-4019-6828-1
E-book ISBN: 978-1-78817-796-2
Audiobook ISBN: 978-1-78817-791-7

Interior images: www.shutterstock.com
'Cowry' icon by Amos Kofi Commey from Noun Project

10 9 8 7 6 5 4 3 2 1

Printed in the United States of America

This book is dedicated to Mothers. My mother, my biggest support and inspiration, and the mothers who came before her who continue to guide me as Ancestors. The Divine feminine energy within me and within all of us (of all genders) that fuels creativity, and that has allowed me to birth this book.

CONTENTS

WHY THREE COWRIES?

On the front cover of this book, there is an image of three cowrie shells. The cowrie shell is a symbol of heritage and abundance for Black people. These seashells were once used as currency in parts of Africa. In fact, the currency of Ghana today, the cedi, derives its name from 'sideε', the Akan word for cowrie shells. These shells have traditionally also been used for divination and other spiritual purposes, and can today be seen in art, fashion and decor that aims to celebrate African pride.

The number 3 is an auspicious number in many spiritual traditions across the world. It is a number of completion and harmony. For me, it most significantly reflects the three relationships: relationship with self, relationship with others and relationship with the Divine.

OPENING INCANTATION

I give thanks for the opportunity to read this book. I ask the Most High, my Higher Soul and my Ancestors to protect and guide me in my reading so that I may overcome my conditioning, my fear, my doubts and my attachments to see clearly. I ask for discernment so that, seeing clearly, I may take what is for me and leave what is not. And I ask for compassion: for myself, for the author, for the Future Ancestors, for my community and for the world. Ameen/Amen/Àṣẹ/And so it is!

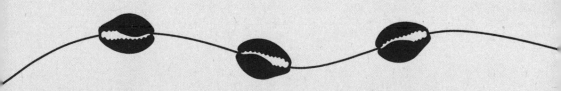

INTRODUCTION

Akwaaba! Welcome! I'm honoured that you've made it to the first page of this book, and I hope I can keep you both informed and entertained until the last. This isn't your typical wellness book, and that's exactly why I had to write it. On my journey of healing through depression and anxiety, I read Louise Hay's *You Can Heal Your Life*. It was the kind of thing I would have considered woo-woo nonsense and rolled my eyes at a mere two years prior, but after a year of antidepressants, therapy, yoga, personal development videos and the beginning stages of a meditation practice, I was willing to give it a try – especially as I was still struggling with insomnia, one of the conditions covered in the book. Far from being nonsense, Louise Hay's book opened the door for me to connect with more metaphysical content, and where better to do that than with Hay House? I read more of their books, listened to podcasts with their authors, watched their videos; Rebecca Campbell, Dr Michael Beckwith and Gabby Bernstein were my faves. I kept consuming content and attending events – I even went to a Tony Robbins seminar and walked across hot coals like Oprah (caveat: it was paid for by my employer; I don't condone 'investing' your last thousand pounds on celebrity coaching). And together, all of these things plus the love of an incredible support network helped me get back to being me.

And once I was back to being me, I said to myself: 'Why are all these teachers and healers white?!'

Aside from Oprah (obvs), Dr Michael Beckwith and Mooji, all the healers I was listening to were white, with a smattering of Asian teachers nowhere near representative of how much of the knowledge being shared was of Asian origin. I decided to be intentional about searching for more Black teachers, including at yoga classes in London – and also decided that I would myself train to be a yoga teacher and, one day, I would write a book with Hay House.

When I returned from my yoga teacher training in India, I wanted to deepen my knowledge in healing sciences. I was thinking about going back to study Ayurveda when a voice in my head said, 'Why are you going to learn their ways when your Ancestors have their own ways to teach you?' I said, 'Chiiiiile, you are right, and also, who said that?' There began my search for African wellness and spiritual teachings. Long story short, the accessibility of such knowledge leaves a lot to be desired, whether you're on the continent or not, for reasons that I hope will become clear as you read on. I have to shout out Mike, a psychic and card reader based in Glastonbury. Just as I was writing off this town – one that was supposedly the UK's centre of spirituality – off as another whitewash, I met this huge (somewhat in size but more so in personality), very white man who turned out to know an awful lot about African spirituality. He put me on to these books: *Jambalaya* by Yeye Luisah Teish and *Opening to Spirit* by Caroline Shola Arewa. I also purchased from him *The New Orleans Voodoo Tarot* (sounds scarier than it is, as we'll also touch on later), which I used mainly for the huge book that comes with it rather than the cards themselves. I'm thankful for these teachings and the few others that can accurately be called books on African wellness and spirituality – but almost all of them focus either on a specific religious path (like Vodun or Ifá) or on a restrictive, very specific path of healing, often with a huge focus on (alkaline or vegan) diet. Also, aside from Shola's book, they are all written by African-Americans and feel like they are *for* African-Americans. Some of them limit their African teachings only to those from ancient Egypt (otherwise known as Kemet). Basically, there was no African wellness book out there for people who don't want to change religion, aren't super into the spiritual stuff and don't identify with the African-American experience.

Enter... me! Now let me be clear. The books and teachers I've mentioned above were integral for me on my journey of healing. Whether I followed the teachings or not, whether I felt like they were speaking to me or not, they each unlocked something new inside me and encouraged me on my path. I benefited from every single piece of content in one way or another. There is a difference between who a book is for and who can benefit from reading it.

Most books in the wellness space – most *everything* in the wellness space – is for middle-class white women. I read books, attended classes, went to festivals, bought yoga pants... that were definitely made *for* white women. While being aware that these things weren't for me, I took what I could take and left what I couldn't. And I benefited greatly from all of them, even the yoga pants. This book is *for* Black people. Who can benefit from reading it? Everyone. If you are white and you read this book, you may feel like I'm not talking to you. And that will give you a microtaste of what Black, Indigenous and people of colour experience every blessed day. But, if you're reading with the right intentions, you will most definitely benefit. If you're not Black but you're Indigenous, a person of colour, Irish, Eastern European, or from any other heritage with a strong traditional culture, you'll probably read this and recognise elements of your tradition within the African practices, which I hope will be a comfort and an inspiration for you to reconnect with or share those practices. This book will be especially beneficial for any healers or educators who want to create safe, inclusive spaces for Black people to heal. If you are Black and you're African-American, South- or Central-American or Caribbean, there may be instances where you feel I'm not representing you, and that is simply because I don't know your experience and it would be wrong to approximate speaking to something I have no intimate knowledge of. I've done my best to speak to you without speaking for you.

I am a Ghanaian-British woman and spent my childhood in London (okay, okay, Bromley – which I will defend as being part of London as well as Kent 'til my dying breath), save for my preteen years spent trying to lose my accent and gain weight in Accra. I made my transition from Londoner to Ghana 'returnee' in 2019 and now live between the two. This is the experience I'll be writing from – Accra via London – because this is the experience I know. I imagine it shares a lot with other on-the-continent Africans and second- or third-generation Africans abroad. Like I said, this book is for all Black people, and so I've tried my best to incorporate, or at the very least, be cognisant of other Black experiences through research and the involvement of my excellent Future Ancestors.

Community is at the heart of African life, and I wanted to reflect that in this book. In each chapter of Parts II, III and IV, you will meet a Future Ancestor: a healer, educator or cultural leader who is doing the good work of keeping our knowledge and traditions alive. I encourage you to connect with them beyond this book; they are all truly inspirational.

This is a book that practises Sankɔfa – looking back in order to move forward. I share the traditions and knowledge that can help us as individuals and as a global Black community. By no means do I wish to imply that everything about our ancestors' lives was better and that we need to go back in time. Clearly they didn't get everything right. But this book isn't a critical examination of all tradition, so I won't be discussing all the ills of their times. It is, indeed, a one-sided view of things, and that is entirely intentional – this is a book about wellness, after all. Equally, I do not wish to imply that everything about the West is evil (although that is up for debate). But this isn't a book about all the great things the West has done for the world. At the time of writing, a book called *The War Against the West* is enjoying a long stint in the bestseller lists – if you want to reflect on how wonderful the West is, I suggest you read that.

What this book *is*: a discussion on (Black) African identity in these modern times, an exercise in decolonisation of the mind, an expression of love and respect to the teachings of our Ancestors, an invitation for Black people around the world to connect to a wellness practice that (finally) is for them.

In Part I of the book, I set the context. Why has African knowledge been demonised and dismissed, often by its own people? Why are we so disconnected from our roots? What would it look like to start repairing that relationship? And what does this have to do with wellness?

Parts II, III and IV of the book deal with the three seeds of African-centred wellness. These seeds give you a framework to help you incorporate ideas rooted in African wisdom into your self-care routine. In each of the chapters within these parts, I will answer these questions: How did this topic show up in traditional African life? What does it look like today? How does it relate to wellness? How can we take inspiration from tradition and turn this into a modern wellness practice? In the wellness sections, you'll notice two themes coming up consistently: belonging and self-esteem. These are absolutely essential to our wellbeing, and even more so for marginalised and minoritised groups, and this is why I basically won't shut up about them.

In Part V, we'll bring it all together and ask ourselves: Now that I have this knowledge, what am I going to do differently?

You'll notice that the last subheading in each chapter is a musical reference. I hope this will create an enjoyable soundtrack for you as you read. I've also left some recommendations of individual Instagram accounts, teachers, apps and other resources throughout the book. We're going to cover so many topics that honestly this is like three books in one, so I encourage you to grab a notebook and pen. Let me know that you're reading by tagging me in your photos on Instagram @araba.oa and if you want to get in touch, email me at araba@arabaoa.com.

Happy reading!

Araba xx

READER NOTES

You'll notice that the word 'ancestor' is sometimes capitalised and other times not. When written as 'ancestor', I'm referring to the biological definition of those who came before us. When written as 'Ancestor', I'm specifically referring to great leaders and changemakers who we honour and revere.

There are some Akan words throughout the text, so here's a quick pronunciation guide: the letter ɔ is pronounced like the *o* in 'frog' and ɛ is pronounced like the *e* in 'egg'.

Part I
WAKING UP

Hwehwɛ mu dua – 'Measuring rod'

Knowledge can only be gained through critical examination. By critiquing our thoughts, our beliefs, our reality, we can understand the past, wake up to the present and act for the future.

Chapter 1

WHAT DOES IT MEAN TO BE AFRICAN?

'It is, of course, true that the African identity is still in the making. There isn't a final identity that is African. But, at the same time, there is an identity coming into existence... I think it is part of the writer's role to encourage the creation of an African identity.'

Chinua Achebe

Identity is a funny thing. There are certain non-negotiable markers that should tell us – and others – whether we are or aren't something. But it's possible to be something technically and yet not *feel* like that thing. If you're reading this book then it's quite possible that, at one point in your life, you've questioned whether you are African enough or Black enough. Perhaps the experience of being surrounded by people speaking your mother tongue and not having a clue what they were saying made you doubt your authenticity. Maybe growing up in a predominantly white environment caused others to ask you why you 'sound white'. Or maybe even a simple change of environment shook your perception of yourself from proud African to shameful impostor in an instant.

If your skin is melanated and your ancestry is African, then you are, undoubtedly, Black and African. My interpretation of the term 'African' includes all people of African descent; whoever else you are – Australian, American, Brazilian, Arab, St. Lucian, biracial, multiracial – you are, in my eyes, African. With such a tangible marker then, how do we end up in situations where our identity is up for debate? At the heart of this is our understanding of what it means to be Black and what it means to be African. At this juncture, let me state plainly that my focus for this book is Black Africans, Indigenous Africans. The question of other African identities, like white Africans, is one for another book, and I think that's a book I have no business writing.

THE DARK CONTINENT

Until the late 19th century, Africa was relatively unknown to the average Westerner beyond the coast, where their activities are well known. As a result, an element of mystery surrounded the land in the eyes of outsiders, forming a void that was ripe for filling with lies and propaganda from those who were seen as experts – 'explorers'. Henry Morton Stanley, a Welsh-American explorer dubbed Africa 'the dark continent' in one of his essays on the area. This term was intended to refer to the supposed savagery and uncivilised nature of Africans, but its implications were far-reaching. This idea of a largely unexplored mass of land filled with strange people served to erase centuries of African history pre-slavery, an atrocity that has stayed with us even to this day. The idea that nothing of note occurred in Africa until Westerners started shipping us overseas is inaccurate, insulting and, unfortunately, pervasive. Even as these untruths were being spilled, it was well documented that African kingdoms had been trading with Europe for centuries prior. However, positioning the continent as a fearsome place where the natives needed to be tamed was much more convenient for the interests of those who wished to conquer and colonise. This was a starting point of the demonisation of Africa and Africans, which has continued to this day.

The trans-Atlantic slave trade served to shatter the identity of Africans in the 'new world', ripping them from their home physically, mentally and emotionally. We must remember, however, that those on the continent were not simply left to live as normal. The enslavement and destruction of African people was also taking place on their own soil. Far from Africans 'selling their brothers and sisters', they found themselves pawns in a game they didn't know they were playing. Indigenous slavery, while unrecognisable in comparison to trans-Atlantic slavery, had existed on the continent for centuries. It's a deep and nuanced subject that I won't be able to do justice to here, but following are a few quick facts about indigenous slavery that show the vast difference between these enterprises. In indigenous slavery:

- People were enslaved for a set amount of time, like a prison sentence.

- Their status as slaves was not passed on to children.

- Enslaved people were often seen as members of the family and could marry into the family, thereby revoking their slave status.

- Enslaved people could climb the social ladder and even be enstooled (the equivalent of holding a parliamentary seat in Western lingo).

- People usually became enslaved as a result of punishment for crimes, unpaid debts and warfare.

A large proportion of these slaves were actually prisoners of war and, recognising this, Western powers actively incited war among the kingdoms on the continent (a tactic they use to this day) in order to up the supply of slaves that they could purchase and carry away with them. Add to this the tactic of Western traders threatening enslavement on any African contact who didn't keep the supply high, and we see that the Western influence on the slave trade started much earlier than the point of purchase. In addition, the idea of Africans who remained on the continent being largely complicit in the kidnap of those who were stolen is an unforgivable insult to the memory of the millions who fought against it. Yes, there were a small minority of collaborators, as there are in any war. But let's not forget that the first 'slave rebellions' happened in Africa. As trading in enslaved peoples neared abolition, colonialism emerged as a way for the West to continue pillaging Africa and her people but with a shiny new label. Without physical enslavement, how could the colonialists control Africa and Africans? Aside from the literal genocides that took place on the continent at the hands of Europeans, the more widespread tool in the colonial arsenal was the corruption and shattering of indigenous belief systems. Regardless of your spiritual beliefs, it is clear that Christianity played a huge role in the mental and emotional enslavement of the African people. As Okot p'Bitek puts it, 'The Christian mission to Africa was double-edged. The missionaries came to preach the gospel as well as to "civilise", and in their role as "civilisers" they were at one with the colonising forces; indeed they were an important vehicle of Western imperialism, which readily lent to the churches its wealth, power and influence.' Anyone who has visited one of the slave dungeons on the coast of West Africa has seen this symbiotic relationship brought to life all too clearly.

I have personally visited a number of slave dungeons in Ghana and Senegal. In every single one, at one point in the tour, I found myself standing in a room that was the place of worship for the relevant European powers. And every single time, the floorboards under my feet doubled as a ceiling for a dungeon below. A dungeon that will have been filled to the brim with bodies. Confused, scared, stolen bodies, festering in excrement – some theirs, some not – waiting but with no idea what it was they were waiting for. Bodies whose screams, cries and prayers were being drowned out by... songs of worship. Sermons. Hymns. Prayers. Heaven above, hell below.

Colonialism was put forward as a mission to 'civilise' Africans and 'develop' the continent. Democracy, Christianity and Western education were some of the tools used. As these powers were fully aware, Africans already had fully functioning political systems, spiritual systems and education systems. They were not coming to teach us anything we didn't know but rather to usurp what was already established – all to further their economic and imperial interests. In other words, the true mission of colonialism was to destroy Africans' belief systems in order to break their spirit and their self-confidence, leading to submission. After that, resources would be ripe for the picking.

This mission is at the heart of the demonisation of African traditional beliefs and practices, and its results stand today. As will become clear throughout this book, the traditional African way of life was holistic; that is, every aspect of life intertwined. As John Mbiti puts it, 'There is no formal distinction between the sacred and the secular, between the religious and non-religious, between the spiritual and material areas of life.' As a result of this, in embracing Christianity and, to a lesser extent, Islam (which seems better able to coexist with aspects of tradition), many Africans did then and do now reject, not just traditional religion, but every aspect of traditional life. This has created a situation today where many Africans, whether on the continent or in the Diaspora, feel ignorant of their culture and find their elders, traditionally the teachers, at a loss to shine any meaningful light on it.

With this intentional assault on African practices and beliefs, it's no wonder that many Black people today might feel a sense of fear or shame around even *thinking* about exploring African wellness and spirituality. It might seem like an all-or-nothing kind of thing. As a Christian, you might feel that any kind of foray into African traditional practices makes you a defector. As an atheist, you might dismiss African practices as supernatural. But as an African, it is your birthright to access the knowledge and healing practices left for you by your Ancestors, without fear or guilt. Wellness and spirituality often intermingle, and it's important for us to unlearn the lies we've accepted about African spirituality. For example, 'voodoo' is a term that has become synonymous with 'black magic', when in fact Voodoo, or more accurately Vodou, is an African Diasporic religion derived from Vodun of West Africa. It is a religion that deserves respect just as any other religion does and whose devotees often also follow Christian doctrine. But my focus for this book is wellness over spirituality – this isn't about us all converting to African religion. It's about us having access to unbiased, relevant information on the many ways to practise wellness in an African-centred way – and then having the choice to take what we want to take and leave what we want to leave. That's why this book exists, and that's why you're reading it.

REDEFINING AFRICA

When I was at school, it was cool to be Caribbean. Sure, people would just say you were from Jamaica, even if you were from elsewhere, but at least they *kind of* knew where you were from and found it interesting. The coolest kind of Black was the African-American variety. When I was in Year 9 at school, and the only Black girl in my class, a new girl joined, taking me from a solo act to a duet…and she was from the States! She was legit an upgraded version of me. I was apparently okay-looking 'for a Black girl', but she was beautiful. I was funny, but she was hilarious. I could sing, but she could SANG! My dear friend Bianca was effortlessly cool. To be from Africa was not cool…not at all. Growing up, all being from Africa meant was that your parents were strict, and people were surprised if you didn't have an accent. And that there was always rice and stew at home. The only holidays to Africa people could conceive of were safaris and even then, they expected that, unless you went luxury, you'd be sleeping in a tree or a mud hut.

But now? The external image of Africa is undergoing a rebrand. In the last five years, elements of our culture have transitioned from something that the Diaspora enjoy at family gatherings to worldwide phenomena. Afrobeats music, jollof wars, African superfoods, box braids – these and many other aspects of who we are have officially crossed over into the mainstream. Travelling to Africa has gone from a safety concern to a truly Instagrammable experience. Celebrities have been retracing and reclaiming their African roots, and African art, food, startups, fashion and investment opportunities seem to be more attractive to outsiders than ever before (a double-edged sword for sure, but we won't get into that).

Ghana's Year of Return campaign in 2019, though considered a depthless money grab by some, formalised a sentiment that had been bubbling among the Diaspora – especially those with questions around their exact heritage – for decades, if not longer. Black people around the world were invited to return home to Africa, with Ghana acting as a sort of entryway. Purely by coincidence, my own return to Ghana was in January 2019. I met fellow British-Ghanaians, African-Americans, Caribbeans and even Africans from elsewhere on the continent who had made their way to Ghana for the same reason as I had. A calling. A pull. A nudge from the Ancestors.

A far cry from the memories I had of living in Ghana as a child, I went to Accra to meet parties, brunches, galleries, festivals, and a diverse mishmash of people trying to find their place. I also met culture shock, dumsor (power outages), Diasporan privilege and heartbreak, and came face to face with the question of my Africanness pretty much every day, courtesy of almost every Uber driver inevitably saying, 'Are you sure?' when I told them I was Ghanaian. But the most surprising discovery for me, which sounds painfully obvious in hindsight, was that simply moving to an African country isn't the answer to reconnecting with African tradition.

AFRICAN-ISH

Thanks in no small part to colonialism, most African countries are actually pretty Westernised. Because I'm British and Ghanaian, I had been somewhat blind to just how pervasive the former colonial powers' presence is in Ghana – that is, until I went to Senegal. I don't speak French, and my experience of France as a country is just a few short trips, so French culture is obvious to me in a way that British culture simply isn't. In 2018, after a couple of weeks in English-speaking Gambia, I hopped into a friendly stranger's car, onto a ferry and, in a few hours, found myself in Dakar. In the three hours it took me to leave the ferry station, find my ('international') hostel, check in (with a receptionist who didn't speak English), walk around the local area trying (and failing) to get a SIM card for my phone, get lost, and find my hostel again, I was convinced I had made a terrible mistake.

France is the only country I've been to where all my painstakingly practised local language phrases were of absolutely no use. Each time I attempted to speak, a French person would cut me off before I could finish and tell me they could speak English. Even when I explained I'd like to practise my French, they would give me a look that was somehow utterly disgusted and disinterested all at once, and continue the conversation in English, as if the words I'd spoken had disintegrated into dust before they'd reached my receiver's ears. Years later, in Senegal, I was met with the same disdain, only this time neither my French nor my Wolof phrases were entertained. Even when I pointed at the bright 'Orange' logo posted in many shops' windows, they shook their head no to my request for a SIM card or simply ignored me altogether. Needless to say, I was not enjoying my first Francophone African adventure. And to be fair, the unsuspecting locals probably weren't enjoying yet another gormless backpacker in harem pants butchering their language.

Before travelling to Senegal, I had arranged to cover a yoga class for a fellow teacher who was out of town. I took a taxi from a pretty normal-looking part of town into a very fancy part of town, took a lift up to a penthouse, and found myself teaching yoga to a group of almost exclusively white French people. As my time in Senegal continued, I saw more and more this stark contrast between the life of locals and the life of the – seemingly millions – of French expats. I asked one of my local friends if he had ever been to France and he laughed so hard he nearly fell off the wall we were sitting on. Apparently the chances of having a visa approved are next to none. I asked a French expat what she had to do to be able to move to Senegal, and she looked at me as if I had asked 'Is water wet?' So finally I asked myself – did the coloniser ever really leave?

Being faced with such obvious French influence and privilege in Senegal helped me open my eyes to the very same in my home country. Our president speaks with an accent that would give half the royals a run for their money. Our judges still wear those ridiculous grey wigs. Many children are actively punished for speaking local languages instead of English at home and in school. Locals love the late queen as if she didn't oversee decades of our oppression. 'Making it' to the UK is still seen as the dream for so many. White Jesus is everywhere... everywhere!

All this is to say that most African countries are not simply African. The effects of colonisation and, subsequently, globalisation have created countries whose culture, beliefs and way of life have been diluted and muddied, so the work of reconnecting may go much deeper than we think.

AFRICAN WELLNESS

The global wellness industry has exploded over the last decade or so. According to the Global Wellness Institute (GWI), from 2015 to 2019, the industry grew by roughly 6.5 per cent per year. Due to COVID, the industry faced an 11 per cent decline in 2020 – but it still sits at $4.4 trillion.[1] As the quest for wellness has become a higher priority, the paths to wellness put forward by the industry have multiplied in number. Yoga and other Eastern traditions have been gaining popularity in the West since the late 19th century. But now practices from a range of other traditions have entered the mainstream. South American and Indigenous American shamanism. Celtic paganism and Wicca. Traditional Chinese Medicine. Despite this huge diversity and appreciation for knowledge and practices from around the world, somehow, Africa is still missing. In my hometown of London, I can get acupuncture, see an Ayurvedic practitioner, practise shamanic dance or even attend a Mexican sweat lodge ceremony. But as soon as I start looking for African wellness practices, my choices are few and far between. In the global wellness conversation, Africa's voice is missing. This is not a surprise, because it's reminiscent of, well, everything. Whether in literature, art, music or philosophy, African experiences and knowledge have continually been underestimated and underrepresented, or lumped into a separate category of their own, often with the prefix 'ethno'. But this has an extra sting when it comes to wellness because so many of the ideas that are put forward as 'New Age' are, in fact, ancient African concepts. We must remind ourselves that Africa is the birthplace of humanity. And so is it not also the birthplace of wellness? Herbal healing, the law of attraction, oracle cards, ecstatic dance – these and many more popular wellness practices and ideas have their roots in Africa. So where is the acknowledgement? Why is it that the only knowledge attributed to Africa on the global wellness stage lies in the religions such as Vodun and Ifá, which are maligned and demonised? These questions and more led me to Ghana.

When I came to Ghana, I (very naively) expected to find African wellness at my fingertips. Instead, I found a very Western approach to wellness. Exercise and healthy living are exploits of the well-off, and so I found gyms, spas and yoga classes. As a yoga teacher myself I was, of course, keen to do my part in the wellness community while learning what I came to learn. But was (again, naively) surprised to see mostly white faces in many of the classes I taught. So not only was the wellness scene seemingly reflective of the industry in the West, but it was also mainly benefiting those from the West and the local elite. For someone who had essentially come to Ghana to 'do' African wellness, this was quite the shock.

What I now know is that it all comes back to the African worldview, which will be discussed in detail in the next chapter. But basically I was approaching this with my Western mindset of separation, when there is, in fact, no separation. As Chukwunyere Kamalu puts it in his book *Person, Divinity and Nature*, 'African religions include cosmology, science (medicine/healing science in particular), art, psychology, philosophy, etc. all integrated into a holistic system of thought.' In which case I would argue that, with the conception we have of religions these days and all the baggage that comes with it, referring to them as 'African religions' isn't quite accurate. It's simply African life – or at least *traditional* African life. With this in mind, wellness is not something we 'do'. Wellness is not a yoga class or a smoothie or a massage. Wellness is infused in every aspect of our lives: in our relationships, our approach to challenges, our rituals, our art, our work. So in my quest to (re)discover African wellness, my major finding is that there is no such thing as African wellness.

This realisation didn't come to me in an instant. In my desire to be truly African in my approach to wellness, I looked to African religion, I studied Pan-Africanism and I even became part of a community dedicated to 'ReAfrikanisation'. As we debated whether real Africans were allowed to eat pasta or not, I realised that the path I was eyeing up was one of dogma and separation – exactly what I wanted to avoid *and*, ironically, exactly what the African worldview transcends. Also, I really like pasta. Reflecting on my learnings from each of these experiences, and conversations with friends on a similar journey, I came to understand the truth. Just as there is no one way to be African, there is no one way to practise wellness as an African. But we can all practise African-*centred* wellness. My definition for this is *'a wellness practice rooted in African wisdom that promotes the healing and empowerment of the global Black community'*.

I want to dissect this real quick:

Wellness practice: The word 'practice' is defined by the Cambridge Dictionary as 'action rather than thought or ideas' and 'something that is usually or regularly done, often as a habit, tradition, or custom'. A wellness practice should be embedded into how you live, not just a theory or an occasional exploit.

Rooted: This is about the foundations of the practice, not the manifestation of it. You don't need to only do 'African' practices, whatever that means, but rather be guided by African thought and values.

African wisdom: There are many different cultures, beliefs and practices across the continent. But as we'll discuss, at their core lie some shared values.

Healing: Meant in the holistic sense; physical, mental, emotional and spiritual growth.

Empowerment: Again from the Cambridge Dictionary, 'the process of gaining freedom and power to do what you want or to control what happens to you'.

Community: This does not negate your need – and right – for individual wellness but rather puts it in the context of community. Ancestor and first president of Tanzania, Mwalimu Julius Nyerere, said, 'In our traditional African society we were individuals within a community. We took care of the community, and the community took care of us.'[2] We can, and we must, heal together.

Many of us wishing to practise African-centred wellness simply don't have the knowledge of what that really means. We might have experienced the fear and demonisation of traditional practices from our parents, denying us the opportunity to learn. Or we might (like me) have found ourselves on the dogmatic path, where in our desire to be African, we reject all else. There's a huge gap left in between these two states of being. A space where those who want to connect with their heritage but also exist in this global, modern world are left to wonder whether they're simply not African enough unless they convert to Ifá or get initiated into a traditional path. My intention is for this book to fill that void, starting with an understanding of the African worldview and building into the specifics of practising African-centred wellness. I hope to guide you in creating a wellness practice that feels authentic, transformational and, most importantly, achievable.

WHO AM I?

So, we find ourselves returning to this ultimate question – am I African (enough)? What it means to be African has undoubtedly changed. You are not African because you eat fufu and soup. You are not African because you wear batik. You are not African because of where you live, what you read or the work you do. All of these things are cosmetic. You're not African because you speak Hausa or Zulu. Although it is a powerful means for connecting with and gaining a deeper understanding of your heritage, language as a marker for being African disintegrated when the first slave ship left the shores. I believe that to be a modern African requires three things: education, energy and intention.

Education

An African educates themself on their people, their culture and their community. This doesn't mean you have to know every major historical event or even how to cook your local dishes. It means you take an active interest in your people and your heritage. This could be in the form of political activism, consuming Black literature, tracing your family roots, travelling to other Black and African countries, or even reading this book.

Energy

Energy never dies. As an African, the energy of your ancestors lives within you. If your Ancestors are those who knew the Motherland before the white man 'discovered' it, if your Ancestors are those who carried secrets of Africa with them to the 'new world', if your Ancestors are those who fought the oppressor to realise independence for African nations, if your Ancestors are those who built communities that feel like home despite being in foreign lands, if your Ancestors are those who never knew Africa but sang songs, cooked food and told tales that were like celebrations of a life long forgotten yet still coursing through their veins, then you are African. As freedom fighter, Pan-African, and first president of Ghana Kwame Nkrumah said, 'I am not African because I was born in Africa but because Africa was born in me.'

Intention

It is possible to be African in education and energy but not in intention. The shackles of mental slavery grip many an African mind and soul. In fact, growing up in this age, it requires an active rejection of the information presented to us through the education system and the media to undo the anti-Blackness that is woven into us, bit by bit, from birth. To connect fully and deeply with our African identity, we must do the work to recognise and heal the self-hatred that is so insidious to us as individuals and as a people. Our intention must be to restore pride and power to Africans, which might sound like a lofty task but can be made manifest through teaching our kids Black and African history (not through the white gaze), economic empowerment through buying Black, challenging the stereotypes we hold about ourselves and other Black people, ending colourism in our communities and learning to love the complexity of our complexions, the fullness of our forms and every kink or curl that protrudes from our crowns.

Just like every element of your being, your Africanness is dynamic. You may have once held problematic views about your African brothers and sisters. You may still have insecurities about your physical appearance. You may feel like leaving the continent for the West is the only route to success. You may feel ignorant about your culture. You may be at preschool level in speaking your local language. None of these things make you any less African. They simply mean you're still growing. And aren't we all? So my friend, what is the answer to the question? Are you African?

Chapter 2

THE AFRICAN WORLDVIEW

*'For the master's tools will never dismantle the
master's house. They may allow us temporarily
to beat him at his own game, but they will never
enable us to bring about genuine change.'*

Audre Lorde

The concept of a worldview was introduced by philosopher (and African slavery advocate) Immanuel Kant in the 18th century, and subsequently popularised by Nietzsche, Kierkegaard, Hegel and a ton of other dead white men. The concept has many other names – within this book, I'll also refer to it as 'belief system'. There isn't one agreed definition, but it is essentially a person's – or a society's – conception of life, the universe and everything in it. A worldview is all-encompassing and drives every thought, feeling and action. Religion in itself is not a worldview: two people of the same religion can have differing belief systems, which cause their faith to manifest in different ways. However, it is your worldview that determines which religions you will be open to, if any. Worldview is heavily influenced by your culture: the history, beliefs, values and practices of your people. This is why leading thinkers in the Black community generally agree that there is an African worldview, one that differs from the Western worldview.

As Africans, even if our family's feet have not touched African soil for generations, it's unlikely that we are completely disconnected from our worldview, a driving force in our people's way of thinking, feeling and living for centuries. However, in working to live and thrive in Western-dominated environments – both on the continent and in the Diaspora – this belief system has been under attack, leaving us conflicted and perhaps even a bit lost, moving within a system of beliefs that doesn't feel authentic or freeing.

A worldview is not necessarily fixed. If we think of the worldview as a set of beliefs, these beliefs both determine and are fed by our thoughts, which determine our actions. If we consciously change our actions and our thoughts, our beliefs eventually follow suit. The booming industries of cognitive behavioural therapy (CBT), neuro-linguistic programming (NLP) and other forms of coaching or personal development wouldn't exist unless this were the case. Taking time to understand the African worldview, reconnect with it, and reawaken it within us is, I believe, the first step towards wellness. We cannot find true wellness without an unshakeable sense of self, and this starts with our worldview.

DECOLONISATION

Colonisation can be understood partly as the imposition of a Western worldview onto our realities. The process of colonisation didn't require us to 'convert' to the Western worldview; it simply created a world in which that belief system was the driving force behind everything, leaving us no option other than to assimilate. It's not my intention to go into great detail about the Western worldview, but here are some descriptors I've come across: individualistic, dominion-oriented and cerebral, indiscriminately prioritising logic over emotion and spirit, and the physical over the subtle. We'll see later how this is at odds with the African worldview. I want to take a moment to note that the Western worldview does not cover every culture within the West ('the West' isn't even a real place, so who is and isn't included is dynamic and open to interpretation anyway). Notably, the Irish and communities within Eastern Europe have traditionally quite contrasting worldviews that align more closely with the African and other indigenous belief systems. Regardless, it's the Western worldview that dominated throughout the colonial period and has since.

Decolonisation as an idea has morphed over the decades, according to the context at the time. It first came about as a purely political phenomenon – the exiting of colonial powers from their territories. Independence. Freedom. As is plain for all to see, for majority Black countries in Africa and the Americas, this has been quite the disappointment. As writer Patrick Gathara puts it, political decolonisation simply became 'a tool to transform Africans from being the objects of colonial subjugation into partners in their own exploitation'. This is because colonisation wasn't an exclusively political exercise. The economic benefits were huge, and were, for the most part, retained by Western powers with neocolonial policies. As George Sefa Dei and Chizoba Imoka state in their paper, 'Colonialism: Why Write Back?', 'oppressed communities continue to find themselves inserted in very hostile politico-economic conditions that reproduce dependency and imperial savior complexes'.[3] In addition, colonialism was an assault on the minds, bodies and souls of the colonised, an assault on our worldview. Ancestor, first president of Senegal and a leader in the Négritude movement, Léopold Sédar Senghor, understood that true decolonisation had to be 'the abolition of all prejudice, of all superiority complex, in the mind of the coloniser, and also of all inferiority complex in the mind of the colonised'. But, focusing on the colonised, this is not simple work. Ngũgĩ wa Thiong'o, Future Ancestor and writer who predominantly writes in Gĩkũyũ, referenced a 'cultural bomb', which continued to detonate in the lives of the colonised well after the oppressors had physically left, and which continues to detonate today. As he puts it, 'The effect of a cultural bomb is to annihilate a people's belief in their names, in their languages, in their environment, in their heritage of struggle, in their unity, in their capacities and ultimately in themselves…

Amidst this wasteland it has created, imperialism [submitting to the Western worldview] presents itself as the cure.'

To defuse this cultural bomb in recent times, there seems to have been a resurgence in the commitment to decolonisation and, with it, a gross overuse – and sometimes, misuse – of the phrase, applying it to all manner of things. In today's context, where we have the language for so many aspects of 'the work' that needs to be done to create a better world for everyone, I don't believe Senghor's definition of decolonisation remains entirely accurate. While the work of antiracism, for example, is for everyone, I believe that the work of decolonisation is for the colonised, past and present. And as such, it looks different for different groups of colonised peoples. The experience of Black and African people cannot be likened to the settler colonial experience that the Indigenous American people continue to face today; however, I share Eve Tuck and K. Wayne Yang's view that decolonisation is not a metaphor. It is not 'a philanthropic process of "helping" the at-risk and alleviating suffering; it is not a generic term for struggle against oppressive conditions and outcomes.'[4]

Therefore, it's not everything that can, or should, be decolonised. And when we use this word for every initiative, it loses its meaning and its power. Let's take the movement to decolonise museums in the West as an example. The modern concept of a museum in itself is a Western idea that doesn't align with African ideas of art (more on this in Chapter 6) or archiving. In addition to this, the museum industry as we know it is rooted in colonialism. The Ashmolean, the first public museum in the UK, states on its website, 'The Ashmolean came into existence in 1682, when the wealthy antiquary Elias Ashmole gifted his collection to the University… the uncomfortable truth is that much of the collection was inevitably selected and obtained as a result of colonial power.' Uncomfortable, indeed. So the solution is to decolonise museums, right? An article by Greer Valley reports that one such incidence of 'decolonising' involves a German museum returning stolen artefacts to Namibia. Great! On a three-year loan, with the Namibian museum being entitled to 'apply' for a permanent loan after that period. Wait, what? Oh, and the Namibian government foots the bill for the return and any restoration work done, including the removal of toxic chemicals previously used to preserve the articles. Again, uncomfortable, indeed. Is this repatriation? Not at its finest but sure. Is it decolonisation? I'll leave that to you to decide (it's not). I maintain my assertion that decolonising is not the work of the West. Museums in the West should repatriate, they should diversify their staff, they should rethink their exhibitions with antiracist sentiment. But you can't decolonise something that is rooted in the colonial template; otherwise, afterwards, what is left?

Moving to museums in Black spaces, in Africa or elsewhere, these can and should be decolonised and, in this process, what is left should be the indigenous template or at least a modern rendering of it. As Valley states, the conversation around repatriation should be 'one that asks not whether African museums have the conditions to preserve and exhibit such objects but, rather, how to create spaces that don't operate with colonial logics'. Africans archive through ritual, performance, artwork, storytelling – these are the tools that can help us to preserve artefacts and knowledge our way. To summarise my point, something that is the fruit of Western thought, systems and structures, cannot be decolonised because it was never colonised in the first place – it is *of* the coloniser. That thing can be indigenised, reimagined, diversified and many other things, but it cannot be decolonised. This is not to discredit all the incredible work being done around the world to decentre white supremacy nor is it to give white people a free pass from doing the work. I simply put forward that we stop using the word 'decolonise' when we mean something else, and that the work white people and Western institutions need to do is plentiful, but none of it is accurately described as decolonising. The decolonisation movement is about the colonised people.

For Indigenous Americans, decolonisation is the complete 'repatriation of Indigenous land and life'. For Black people, it is slightly more complicated since the face of colonialism has morphed, becoming less place-based and more insidious over the decades, reaching its tentacles into facets of our lives we don't even recognise. The definition that resonates most for me is that of Dei and Imoka, who describe decolonisation as 'both a process and set of practices aligned with the body/mind/spirit interface and a politics of healing ourselves from the psychological scars, physical and cultural dislocation, and wounds of colonial mimicry'. For Black people, decolonisation is, at least in part, a rejection of the Western worldview and a reclamation of the African worldview.

I think it's important to discuss religion briefly here. There is a rhetoric – one that I myself briefly accepted – that a truly decolonised Black person could never be Christian or Muslim due to the history of the religions on the continent. Clearly that is untrue – those atrocities were enacted by people, not a religion. In the *name* of a religion, yes, but by people all the same and their particular interpretation of that religion. Equally, as we'll see later, these and other major religions fit easily within the African worldview. However, I do believe, as renowned philosopher and recently transitioned Ancestor Kwasi Wiredu states in his book *Decolonising African Religions*, that the process of decolonisation requires a critical examination of whatever faith you have, up until the time of decolonisation, ascribed to. Because I believe it requires a critical examination of *all* the core beliefs that have shaped you and determined your movement in the world. That critical examination may lead you to discard religion entirely, it may lead you to convert to a different path or it may lead you to change the way you practise – for example, looking to the Ethiopian roots of Christianity instead of the Western rendering. If it leads to absolutely no change, it probably wasn't quite critical enough.

This book is an exercise in decolonisation for Black people. It replaces falsities and fear with education and understanding. It celebrates African thought, tradition and tools for healing. And it, very intentionally, is for all Black people, of all religious beliefs. This book, and my work in general, is not decolonising the wellness industry. The wellness industry is part of the capitalist system, just like every industry. So by engaging in it I'm taking part in the (neo)colonial system. However, I am – I hope – *diversifying* the industry and giving Africa an authentic voice in the global wellness conversation.

THE AFRICAN WORLDVIEW

Africa is not a monolith, especially when we include the Diaspora in our understanding of Africa. My intention here is not to reduce the complex and diverse cultures, experiences and ideas of Africa and her children into one generalised, oversimplified mess. But just as we celebrate the range and scope of Black people and Black culture, we must also celebrate the threads that unite us. We must celebrate the unity in our diversity. In the same way that we can speak of Western phenomena with the understanding that they do not relate to every single individual across the West in the same way, I will talk about African tradition, culture and concepts.

So, about this worldview. How do we define something so vast? While a worldview incorporates more than just our values, I feel that they are a critical factor, and allow us a framework with which to understand a worldview without making our heads explode. I'm going to introduce you to the three values I believe form the foundation of the African worldview.

These three values, in my opinion, are at the core of what it means to be African but have been consistently and systematically suppressed in our – first forced and then self-preservatory – attempts to assimilate to Western values and the Western worldview. While his views on Africa leave a lot to be desired, psychologist Carl Jung's theory of the shadow (interestingly, a similar concept of the shadow can be found in a number of African traditions) gives us a route to understanding how this suppression has affected us as a global Black community.

If you frequent the spaces on the internet filled with wellness and self-improvement content, you've undoubtedly been told you need to do your shadow work. But what actually is this shadow that everyone's talking about? In his mapping of the human psyche, Jung put forward that each of us has a shadow, an unconscious space where our repressed traits live. It's important to note that our shadow isn't filled with only negative traits – it is filled with *repressed* traits. Generally, since we all want to be loved, the parts of ourselves we repress tend to be the ones that would get us shunned or, you know, arrested or killed. But there are also other traits that we push down; for example, a child who was told they ask too many questions might grow to repress their curiosity or a person who experienced abuse may repress their sexuality. These parts of us that live in our shadow don't lie dormant. In fact, they're begging for us to recognise them. Since we're actively doing everything in our power to deny their existence, we often end up projecting onto other people. So that inquisitive child may snap at people when they ask questions, or the survivor of abuse may engage in slut shaming. One of the keys to self-actualisation, according to Jung, is first to become aware of the shadow, and then assimilate it so that it no longer has power over you.

Mostly what you'll find in your shadow is an energy that, expressed productively, can be hugely beneficial for you and your community. But in denying this energy for fear of its darkness, you're also banishing its light. In this context, we can use the term 'shadow' to refer to the negative side of a trait rather than the entirety of a person's shadow, which, remember, can include positive aspects. Let's visit the inquisitive child again. If we conceptualise the energy as that of curiosity, it absolutely can have a shadow, or negative, side. We all know that curiosity killed the cat – although it's unclear whether it took just one of its lives or all nine. But, if recognised, accepted, celebrated and channelled, that same energy could allow this cat, sorry, *child* to grow up to be a badass private investigator like Jessica Jones. Let's look at another example with a trait that we can all agree is bad: manipulation. It's not nice to play with people's lives as if they're characters in a game of 'The Sims'. But what is the energy behind manipulation? It could be argued that the energy is empathy. In order to manipulate someone, you have to be tuned in to what they are thinking and feeling, and how they will respond to certain stimuli. Expressed in a productive way, this same energy could make you an extremely effective counsellor or educator.

The values I'm going to present to you have been repressed in the global Black community, and they're trying to escape the shadows through projection and negative manifestations. To free ourselves, we need to harness the energy of these values, direct them towards productive means and welcome them into the light.

THE 3 AFRICAN VALUES

In my work with clients, whether in groups or as individuals, I find the exercise of identifying core values one of the most impactful. Our core values give us an understanding of why we behave the way we do, why we place importance on some things above others, and how we relate to those around us. They also act as a reminder of who we want to become, who we already are at our core. One of the most challenging parts of this exercise for people is that they are allowed to select only three to five values. They often get to seven or eight and insist they can't cut any more. But regardless of what we might think, it is only a handful of values that truly drive our thoughts, beliefs and actions. They override other, secondary values when it comes to crunch time. When we examine the shadow side of our values, we recognise where we might be prone to step out of line and this awareness enables us to recognise and correct these behaviours. Referring again to Jung, 'Just as an individual must recognise projections of the shadow to achieve greater consciousness, so… must the culture as a whole'.

I read somewhere that great Pan-African leader W.E.B. DuBois said that there is no path to the universal except through the particular. Through my research, reflection and discussions I've identified three core values that I believe represent the traditional African worldview, presented here with examples from Kemetic (Ancient Egyptian), Yoruba, Akan and Bantu philosophies, chosen because, collectively, they cover the majority of the continent geographically through time but also due to the wealth of source material or first-hand knowledge I've been able to gain in these traditions. So here goes. The three African values are community, destiny and harmony.

Community

The African concept of community:

- includes the unborn and the Ancestors

- includes the land, driving home the importance of humans acting as custodians of the land

- does not deny individuality; the gifts of the individual are nurtured and celebrated by the community

- values the hierarchy within community, with elders given due respect

- recognises and honours interdependence.

In *Self-Healing Power and Therapy*, Dr Kimbwandènde Kia Bunseki Fu-Kiau explains that 'the Bantu concept of a human being's influence upon the environment, society, and his fellow human beings is very clear: nothing is isolated in the universe... human beings, living or dead... are all related to each other'.

By contrast, the Western worldview values individualism over communalism. As Dr Fu-Kiau states, 'Africans live in a collective system with close family ties. The land, the source of everything to sustain life, is a collective ownership. The Westerner, on the contrary, lives in a very individualistic system where family ties are easily broken.

Everything is individually owned; even children, between parents, are objects of controversy.'

Even in wellness, the main narrative in the Western world favours individual enlightenment over community healing or sometimes, more disturbingly, as a path to collective healing by raising the 'collective consciousness' while entirely disengaging from community and social issues.

Through repression of this value, some shadow manifestations and negative projections are:

- the belief that community needs – or sometimes mere wants – should come at the expense of individual safety, agency or joy

- the belief that your community should take care of you even if you won't lift a finger to take care of yourself or anyone around you

- the expectation from elders of unearned respect, encapsulated in the agitated refrain, 'Am I your age, mate?'

- the conviction that all ills are a result of someone else's wrongdoing rather than your own. Not every mother-in-law is a witch, okay?!

We see these shadows in parents trying to force a career, partner, business or anything else on their children and in entitled, lazy individuals relying on their family for income and tyrannical teachers demanding respect from students they themselves treat like animals.

Destiny

The African concept of destiny:

- is assigned or chosen before a being manifests in this reality

- is unique and personal

- does not negate free will – there are many paths to get from A to B – but acknowledges that life will attempt to direct you to the path of your destiny

- can be intuited through divination but doesn't need to be consciously known in order to be fulfilled.

For example, in Akan cosmology, destiny is encapsulated by the concept of Nkrabea (pronounced nn-KRA-be-YA), which is safeguarded by the kra or okra (soul). The kra can be reincarnated, returning to continue its path to fulfilling its Nkrabea.

Chukwunyere Kamalu notes that 'in traditional Africa as in ancient Africa, the purpose of human existence is the same: for the person to fulfil his or her destiny, bestowed even before birth, and thus attain the highest level of self-realisation possible – that of divinity or Godhood within human personhood', what Eastern traditions might refer to as Christ consciousness or enlightenment. He goes on to say that the keeper of destiny – kra for the Akans, ka in Kemet, ori for the Yorubas – is 'the part of ourselves associated with an unrealised future and the unfolding of a "higher" or "better" self'.

The Western worldview focuses on free will and logic, with destiny being left to the afterlife if believed in at all. It parrots the power of 'sensible' choices and hard work to shoot you all the way to the top in a meritocratic society, conveniently leaving out the makeup of the scorecard that deems whiteness and maleness, among other things, valid reasons for extra points.

The idea of destiny can be quite overwhelming but, for me, a destiny is not the same as a purpose, or what I call your soul's purpose. Your soul's purpose keeps you on the path to fulfilling your destiny. Also, your destiny is fixed, while your purpose can change throughout your life. I like to think of destiny as the end point, the overarching achievement you'll realise you've made as you ready yourself for a transition to the Ancestral realm. Your soul's purpose is more like a scavenger hunt, taking you in different directions to collect various gems and, ultimately, leading you to the final destination. By staying balanced or in harmony, we are guided – by our intuition, the Ancestors, God – to ensure that we live a purpose-led life, one that will help us get the prize at the end.

Through repression of this value, some shadow manifestations and negative projections are:

- a resignation that invites life to push you in whatever direction it wants
- a lack of accountability, attributing everything to fate or destiny
- the belief that tragedies falling on others are their destiny (if not witchcraft)
- dismissal of the idea of 'purpose' with a belief that decisions should be based only on logic.

We see these shadows in a lack of support and compassion for those experiencing mental health, marital or other challenges; the push to select 'good' careers instead of those that channel your passion; and my most loved and most hated phrase, 'Let's see what God will do' – a wonderful expression of hope and faith in situations where there is nothing more to be done, a frustrating shunning of responsibility and accountability when said in response to 'So when will you complete this work/pay me back/ pass on this message/[other time sensitive task that is way below God's pay grade]?'

Harmony

While they are not exactly the same, balance, order and oneness interweave with the idea of harmony. The African concept of harmony:

- is driven by a belief in the Divine order of things, and it is only by respecting this order that harmony can be achieved

- constitutes harmony on many levels: within the individual, within the family and community, with nature and natural cycles, with God and the spirit world.

At the individual level, Fu-Kiau states that the Bantu understanding of health is 'to be *mu kinenga*, "in balance" – with ourselves, our environment, and the universe'. Mbiti says that 'it is considered that the universe is orderly. As long as this order is not upset there is harmony... Man is not the master in the universe... he has to live in harmony with the universe, obeying the laws of natural, moral and mystical order.'

The Kemetic concept of Ma'at – often personified as a goddess – has variously been translated as cosmic order, balance, justice, truth and harmony. Analysing these and other ideas, activist, professor and creator of the holiday Kwanzaa, Maulana Karenga, decides on the definition 'an interrelated order of rightness'.

The Western worldview values dominion over harmony. Dominion over the self, with endless 'hacks' and productivity tips that deny our natural cycles, dominion over nature dressed up as technological advancement, dominion over others and dominion over the cosmos (they're colonising Mars next?!). The overarching theme is, to use influential American management theorist Mary Parker Follett's wording, 'power over' instead of 'power with'.

In moving to a mindset of harmony, we need to remember that the only constant in life is change. Therefore, harmony should be understood on a dynamic scale. All things won't be in balance at all times but rather, as we flow – within ourselves, with others, with nature, with Spirit – we can cultivate an overall pattern of harmony. We see this dynamism reflected in nature – harmony isn't achieved through stasis; it is achieved because after some plants in the forest wither and die, they provide space and nutrients for other plants to flourish.

Through repression of this value, some shadow manifestations and negative projections are:

- extreme dogma about the perceived order of things, often focused on control over minute details of life; usually mistaken for order or harmony when in fact harmony involves flow and is focused on the bigger picture

- an attachment to 'the way we do things' without considering whether the existing template is correct

- toxic positivity, refusing to acknowledge challenges and struggles so that they can be properly addressed.

We see these shadows in the proposed anti-LGBTQ+ bill in Ghana supposedly based on what is 'right' according to the Bible while the societal ills of (government) theft, adultery and greed are apparently fine; the desire to retain harmony or 'keep the peace' by ignoring family issues like abuse and generally trying to enforce order on individuals based on man-made rules rather than alignment with nature.

LV N ATTN

In compiling this list of African values, there were others that made the shortlist. Ethics is a huge theme across African belief systems, the idea that a person is measured by their actions. This, for me, is representative of both the importance of community – do our actions matter if there is no man or God to see them? – and harmony, the desire to act in a manner that respects natural law. I toyed with selecting faith as a value, but then I wondered, 'Is a society whose spirituality is so practical, action-oriented and steeped in ritual one that values faith over harmony?' They have faith, yes, but it's a faith that says that by performing the right actions, prayers will be answered, which, to me, is more a belief in harmony and the laws of the universe than (blind) faith, and is evidenced by the fact that, in Ghana, people never ask me if I'm a Christian, only if I'm a church-goer. Pride is another value that I not just entertained but really *wanted* to add to the list. As a community taught self-hatred from the jump, rediscovering a sense of pride is key. And pride in culture and customs is evident across pre-colonial Africa. But ultimately I decided that, while pride is definitely an African value, any true sense of pride in culture is driven by love for and commitment to community.

So, these are the core values that underpin the traditional African worldview: community, destiny and harmony. And these are the values that, if we show them the proper love and attention, can guide us in our journey to healing and empowerment as individuals and as a global Black community.

Chapter 3

RECLAIMING OUR POWER

'Your Ancestors have not forgotten you. You still have a home, you still have a name. Always remember that, if you carry this with you, you will always find your home again.'

Shela's Journey by Maïmouna Jallow

For more than 400 years, Africans have been made to feel powerless. Through continued and unrelenting deliberate, strategic assaults on our physical, mental, emotional and spiritual health, the system of white supremacy has muddied our worldview and shattered our self-esteem. The average African, whether on the continent or abroad, has internalised the idea that to be African is to be less than, that Africa is either an uncivilised bushland or a hotbed of wealth and corruption and that true success and happiness can only be achieved through proximity to whiteness – or, if you're lucky, simulating whiteness. Of course if you're reading this you probably think this doesn't describe you. But have you taken the time to really challenge your core beliefs on Blackness and success?

The truth is all of us harbour some level of anti-Blackness. It is impossible not to in this world in which we live. In fact, it is often unsafe not to in this world. Anti-Blackness has become a method of survival for some of us. While we might make jokes about 'sounding white' or being abrofusem (Akan word for a Ghanaian who acts like a Westerner), the truth is some of us don't have the luxury to choose another approach. 'Acting white' is the difference between being employed or not. 'Talking white' is the difference between being attacked or not. You cannot change the system without first understanding the system and being in the system (while avoiding becoming *of* the system). So the solution is not to beat ourselves up for not being Black enough or not policing anti-Blackness enough. The solution is power.

RACE AND POWER

Whiteness is power. Whiteness, as African-American historian and bestselling author Nell Irvin Painter puts it, is also an ideology, not a biological fact. This is why proximity to whiteness or passing as white can bestow on a person of colour some semblance of the benefits of white privilege; the sun never directly shines on you, but you can get close enough, closer than other people of colour, to feel a bit of warmth and perhaps avoid death by hypothermia. And that's before we get into the other power plays decreed by the Western worldview: maleness and wealth, for example. Whiteness was literally invented to maintain and expand power. In the early days of slavery, African enslaved people worked side by side with Irish indentured workers. While slavery was a life sentence that passed on to your offspring, indentured servitude was a fixed-term sentence; however, both groups were treated poorly. Initially, by law, Christians were not allowed to be held as slaves, only as indentured workers. The enslavers faced two challenges: the first, that Africans were being converted to Christianity and the second, successful uprisings were a high possibility with the Africans and Irish working together. To kill two birds with one power-hungry stone, whiteness was invented. The law changed to prevent 'whites' from being held as slaves and the unity between enslaved Africans and (newly) white indentured workers began to fracture, propelled further by benefits given to whites only. And thus, the elite maintained their power and created the foundation for white supremacist ideology to reign. What has followed is centuries of an unrelenting wielding of that power: from the 'mild' (having to tone down Blackness in the workplace) to the extreme (genocide). While some people argue that the more deadly racism on an international scale is largely a thing of the past, they are forgetting the more insidious modern manifestation of whiteness as 'an intricate web of laws and norms that [maintain] disparities of wealth, education, housing, incarceration and access to political power', as writer Robert P. Baird describes it in his Guardian article 'The invention of Whiteness: The Long History of a Dangerous Idea'.

In the face of this power imbalance, one of the most radical things we can do is recognise, protect and parade our power. But this doesn't always look how you might think. We may imagine acts of power as protest, breaking glass ceilings and putting Black people, knowledge and culture on the map. And these things are all, no doubt, powerful. But they are also tiring. Simply living as a member of the global majority drains our ever-depleting energy reserves. And the system of oppression *intentionally* tires us with microaggressions, division, laughable leadership, poverty, sensationalist media, and all the 'little' things that take up more and more space in our minds and energy fields so that we run out of steam and have no power left to... live. And if we spend our lives putting out fires, not only do we miss out on living but we also limit the amount of lasting change we can make. Knowing this, we recognise that one of the most powerful forms of resistance is rest. Remember, one of the values we're channelling is harmony: we do the work, and we balance it with rest and rejuvenation. We inevitably face rage and pain, and we balance it with joy. We strive to make a difference in the community, and we do it while taking proper care of ourselves. While not coined by Audre Lorde, the term 'self-care' was certainly popularised by the radical feminist Ancestor, who wrote, 'Caring for myself is not self-indulgence. It is self-preservation, and that is an act of political warfare.' As André Spicer, a professor of organisational behaviour, writes, 'Lorde's ideas about self-care were picked up by many in queer, feminist and activist circles. Caring for yourself became a way of preserving yourself in a world that was hostile to your identity, your community and your way of life.' In Sarah Taylor's article 'Self-care, Audre Lorde and Black Radical Activism', she reminds us that self-care in the Black community was focused on collective healing, as seen in the Black Panther Party's health clinics and free breakfast programmes. Far from being something rooted in consumerism, she urges us to remember that 'in its origin, self-care is a revolutionary call-to-arms and political act against a white supremacist capitalist patriarchy'. Committing to self-care, community healing and sustained wellbeing is a way for Black people to protect and preserve our power.

PERSONAL POWER

African-centred wellness as presented in this book helps us to preserve our power, and the three African values give us a solid foundation from which to decolonise our thinking. By incorporating these frameworks, we'll be living an African life… but there's still that pesky issue of *feeling* African (enough). Belonging is an essential part of cultivating self-care and wellbeing, so this aspect is a crucial part of the work. As you'll realise the further you get into this book, pretty much everything I suggest is a route to cultivating belonging. This book itself is intended to be an exercise in belonging and, if at any point so far you've nodded your head and seen yourself in my words, then I've succeeded in my goal. But before we get into African-centred wellness practices, I want to share with you some practical tips that helped me find belonging through understanding, accepting and celebrating my identity as an African woman.

Tip 1: Find Home

Some of us have the privilege of knowing our heritage with relative certainty, so we know where our ancestral home is, or we might even have been born and raised there. Many do not have this privilege. Either way, identifying with a community is a good way to build confidence in your identity. Since African countries as we know them have existed for less than 100 years and were created for no reason other than colonial exploits, you might find you identify more with a specific ethnic group or region rather than a country. There are ancestry DNA tests that you can take to get an 'accurate' reading on where your heritage lies. If, like me, you feel uneasy about giving away your DNA to – let's face it – white-owned companies who will do who knows what with it, you can take a less scientific approach. I am a strong believer in intuition, so I suggest spending some time learning about different ethnic groups and see who you feel drawn to. If you have the luxury of being able to travel, remember, your face tells a story. Visit the right part of Africa and locals will be claiming you as their own before you can get a word in. If your heritage is Diasporan from a tradition with strong retention of African culture, like Haiti, for example, you may not even need to look back to the continent to find home. The point is not to craft a new identity or disown your experience thus far but simply to give you a focal point for learning more about a particular culture and identity that resonates with you. For example, I am Fante, which is a subgroup within the Akan ethnic group found mostly along the southwest coast of Ghana. This, for me, is testament to why I am so drawn to Adinkra (an Akan writing system we'll come back to in Chapter 10) and to being by the sea! It also gave me a starting point in my search for wellness and spiritual traditions – but it is not a container for my identity and my growth.

Tip 2: Embrace Pan-Africanism

No matter what specific location our ancestry ties us to, we are united as Africans, as Black people. Division and tribalism have been a catalyst for Africa's downfall for centuries, and we cannot rise with the same approach. Pan-Africanism is an ideal, a push for the unity of the African people at home and in the Diaspora that has its roots in the slave rebellions of the Americas. As explained by Nigerian philosopher and Ancestor Sophie Oluwole, 'The very first efforts to identify the unity of African culture were reactions against racism. [In 1893] Pan-Africanism was launched in London primarily as a political movement.' It was driven forward by leading figures in both the civil rights movement centred on the USA and the independence movement centred on Africa and the Caribbean. Great Ancestors such as Kwame Nkrumah, Malcolm X, Aimé Césaire, Amílcar Cabral, Nina Simone, Marcus Garvey, Maya Angelou and Harold Moody recognised and promoted the need for the global Black community to unite and support each other in overcoming varying manifestations of white supremacy and oppression.

In the times since the height of Pan-Africanism, division has grown. The narrative of separation between Africans and Diasporans, and even different Africans and different Diasporans, has remained prevalent, brought to life by events such as the violence against Nigerians in South Africa and the debate in Hollywood about Black British actors 'stealing' roles that 'belong' to African-Americans, a convenient distraction from the dearth of meaningful Black roles to fight over in the first place.

While both of these events and others like them are nuanced and complex, they hold the same theme of a lack of unity among the global Black population. Pan-Africanism seeks to provide an antidote to this. Black people are not the all the same. We don't all share the same experiences or the same histories. But, for better or worse, we are united in our struggle against white supremacy and our fight to regain agency. There is no single manifesto for Pan-Africanism; it presents in different ways. For me, being Pan-African means taking pride in and working for the elevation of the global Black community. I don't believe it is possible for a Black person to truly defeat the anti-Blackness that is conditioned into us without also becoming Pan-African.

That said, it is important to note that adopting a Pan-African approach or identity doesn't mean that you can disrespect or appropriate from other cultures. For example, identifying as Pan-African doesn't mean that you can rename yourself without fully understanding the context and importance of the name you have chosen – especially if you're going to pronounce it incorrectly. Being Pan-African doesn't mean that you can claim a village, town or city as your own while deriding the people and giving nothing back to the community. However, it's equally important not to place a huge amount of pressure on yourself. Being Pan-African doesn't mean you have to know what's happening in every country on the continent, plus what's happening across the Diaspora at all times. It doesn't mean that you have to become an educator to all ignorant people of the world on all things African.

To be a Pan-African you simply must identify as a member of the global Black community, have interest in and compassion for your brothers and sisters around the world and be invested in the empowerment of Africa and her people.

Tip 3: Put Theory into Practice

This could mean visiting a majority Black country if you have the means, learning a new language or making changes to your community. Whatever it is, these actions will help you to grow conviction in your identity. It is with this newfound grounding, self-assuredness and connection to home that we can fully stand in our power, as individuals and as a community.

For some people, part of doing the work is renaming. In most African traditions, a name is not just a name. Dr Kimbwandènde Kia Bunseki Fu-Kiau captures the importance of naming, saying, 'Your name is the real you. It is a moving power, your moving power towards success. It is a socially given power to you that no one can prevent. Your name is the most important word that you will ever know in your lifetime'. Choosing a name out of a book just because you like the sound of it is something our Ancestors wouldn't understand. A name has power. A name is both a prediction of and prayer for the future. Every time someone says your name, they're uttering a spell. So naming has always been of the utmost importance in many African belief systems. In some cultures, names are a reflection of your Nkrabea, as intuited by the community elders or spiritual leaders. In other cultures, a baby's name is that of the Ancestor whose spirit is believed to be reincarnating in that child. For some, your name reflects your totem animal or the tribe to which you belong. For others, a name expresses the emotional conditions in which a child is born, or even the weather or season. In some places, a child's name is derived from when they were born – for example, a day name, or the place they hold in the family, for example, second-born. To use myself as an example, 'Araba' is the name for a Fante girl born on a Tuesday, and I have another name which is that of an Ancestor in my paternal lineage.

To put it simply, a name isn't just a name. So while it may feel empowering and exciting to rename yourself or name a baby with an African name, this is not a process to be taken lightly. It's important that we show respect by doing research, consulting with people from the community where the name originates if possible, choosing wisely, and learning the proper pronunciation rather than freestyling!

For those of us who were given traditional and 'Christian' names at birth, this process is a little easier but just as powerful. Most young people with a direct connection to an African country whether by birth or parentage will recognise this scenario. My legal documents show a Western first name – sometimes called a 'Christian' name though it's not from the Bible because, at this point, the culture has conflated the two – and a Ghanaian last name. Aside from this, I have two other Ghanaian names, which my family knows and may call me by, but which don't feature on any of my legal documents. Some people might call this a 'house name' – in other words, the name you get called in the house but never in public. One of these 'house names' is Araba, the name that I have now reclaimed to make my primary first name, and which should more accurately be called my 'soul name' according to Akan tradition

If this is you, you might have wanted to reclaim your traditional name but worried about things like whether anyone will be able to pronounce it, whether it sounds professional enough, whether a name change at your big age will be too confusing. This narrative of African names being confusing or difficult to spell and pronounce is yet another lie we need to awaken from. Growing up in the UK, I met people from other cultures whose names might have been considered 'difficult'. But they didn't swap them for 'easier' English names. At the very worst, they might shorten it to a nickname but ultimately, it's up to you to listen and learn the spelling and pronunciation. If we can do that for others, surely we can do it for African names? The truth of the matter is that when the colonisers were doing the busy work of making Africans feel uncivilised and inferior, our names were not spared. Christianity was the only way to be saved, and since the Bible didn't feature Babatunde or Dzifa or Chiedza, God must not have liked our names very much. So we were given Christian names to reflect our coming into the light. This idea that Christian names are more virtuous and desirable than our local names has stayed with us. And this is why rejecting your Christian name in favour of your indigenous name – whether you are Christian in faith or not – can be such a powerful process.

Tip 4: Make a Physical Return

Travelling is a privilege. Being able to pack up your life and relocate is a privilege. Neither of these things are available to everyone. But if they are available to you, remember that 'moving to Africa' is not the solution to dealing with racism, poor mental health, low self-esteem or anything else. It can definitely help, but it's not a silver bullet. When people repatriate, there are push factors and there are pull factors. The push factors from places like the USA and the UK might include systemic racism, lack of opportunities and cold weather. But what are your pull factors? Why Ghana or Egypt or Zimbabwe? 'The president said we should come home' is not good enough. If you choose a country simply because it's easy, then when your rose-tinted glasses are inevitably knocked off your face in the middle of a power outage while your water isn't running and your food delivery is two hours late because the delivery guy doesn't understand your accent, you'll wonder to yourself, 'Why did I move here again?' Pull factors could include a love of or connection with the culture, a great support system* or purpose-driven work opportunities (*moving for love will, 90 per cent of the time, end in heartbreak).

If you've decided to move to the continent, and chosen a new home with good reason, the work is still not done. You need to do something you've probably never had to do before: check your privilege. While in the USA you may have been the triple threat of, for example, a queer Black woman, in many African countries, you're a woman with dollars, access and an assumed credibility based on your accent. Not to mention you're probably more able to live comfortably in your queerness than a local. If you walk around like the country owes you something (it doesn't), all you're doing is assuming the role of the oppressor you fled from. I need to state something here that some of you won't like. Reparations are due all Black people from the former colonisers. Reparations are not due Diasporans from an Africa that itself has been plundered, drained and beaten into a submission from which it is yet to emerge.

Swiftly moving on, since Africa don't owe you zip, be ready for its people on the continent to test you. When I first moved to Ghana, it felt like every other day I was having to justify my identity and my decision to move to Ghana or be tested on my knowledge of the country I was claiming as my own. I'll be honest, it *really* bugged me at first. Can everyone just accept that I'm Ghanaian, okay?! But as I interrogated it, I realised that the reason it cut me so deeply was because I felt I was failing the test. I couldn't (still can't) speak my local language well, I suddenly had all this privilege dripping off me that I didn't know what to do with and I did have the thought in the back of my mind, 'If it doesn't work out, I'll just go back to the UK.' Most people probe and question and joke because they want to understand you; they want to place you. It only becomes an attack when you don't even know where to place yourself. When I spoke to Usifu, a Future Ancestor you'll meet in Chapter 10, he gave a new context to this back and forth between locals and returnees. 'When I went through my fraternity initiation in Sierra Leone as a child, I was tested. So people returning to the continent must expect to be tested. You do not earn acceptance simply by existing. Live with the people, go to the farm with them, learn their dances, learn the language and gradually, you will be accepted.' In traditional African communities, you have to earn your recognition as an adult through rites of passage and initiation. So I guess what I'm saying is you will be tested. By the people, by the environment, by the customs, by the system, by your Western mindset trying to stop you from adapting. It's not so much that the tests are a pass or fail situation but more that the tests themselves are a form of initiation. The whole process is a rite of passage to help you become a true member of your new community.

Coming home to ourselves, our Blackness, our Africanness, our personal power is a never-ending journey. It requires us to continually confront our prejudices and misconceptions. It sometimes asks us to find belonging in a group or place that might at first feel alien. It challenges the attachments we have to our name, our habits and our beliefs. But just like the journey of healing, it is important that we remember that this is an ongoing process, and it will look different every day, week, month, year. The most important thing is that we keep going.

COMING HOME TO AFRICAN-CENTRED WELLNESS

Okay, so we've identified the three African values that can help us reignite our African worldview. We've looked at a few practical tips to help us reaffirm our African identity. From this base, with a strong sense of self and commitment to decolonising our belief system, we can move into the practicalities of an African-centred approach to wellness. I know I've spent part of this book so far hammering home the point that, in the traditional African worldview there is no separation, there is no 'wellness practice', yada yada. But the fact of the matter is, we live in Westernised capitalistic societies where our lifestyles are fragmented, and if we don't come up with a specific wellness practice, we're likely not to be very well at all. In addition, for the majority of us to integrate theory into action, we need a systematic framework that will help us along the way. So, I'll give you two! First, I'll present five principles of African-centred wellness that essentially give us a view of the three African values but specifically from a wellness context. Then, I'll share the three seeds of African-centred wellness, which make up the bulk of this book.

The 5 Principles of African-centred Wellness

Following these principles, you can easily create a wellness practice (or, if you're a healer or educator, a wellness programme) that is African-centred.

African-centred wellness:

- centres Black bodies, Black experiences and Black empowerment
- values community healing over individual enlightenment
- respects elders and Ancestors over modern-day gurus and corporations
- positions ritual as a part of everyday life
- invites us to live as, of and with nature, in reverence of Mother Earth.

Now, if you're already clued up on individual wellness practices (and you hate learning), you could legit stop reading here and just use these five principles to guide you. But if you're ready to get super practical and learn more about African tradition along the way, read on, dear reader, read on!

The 3 Seeds of African-centred Wellness

The three seeds of African-centred wellness provide a framework for choosing individual practices that will make up your wellness routine. Each seed blends into the other. Just as the fruit on a tree is both the result of maturation and the nucleus from which a new tree can spring, each seed is both a natural manifestation of living well as an African and a path to living well as an African. They are all-encompassing – I can't think of a single positive action that doesn't somehow fall under at least one – but at the same time specific enough to help us start, review or reinvigorate our journey of African-centred wellness. The three seeds are:

- Music and Movement – I initially had these as separate, but they are so intertwined, so complementary that it made sense to place them together.

- Mother Earth – called Asase Yaa or Asaase Efua by the Akan people, no conversation around wellness is complete without her.

- Magick – Aleister Crowley (a controversial figure but he dropped a few gems) defined magick with a *k* as 'the Science and Art of causing Change to occur in conformity with Will'. While magic is unexplained, supernatural and only practised by the few, magick is intentional transformational change that is available to us all.

ESSENCE

Over the coming chapters, I'll break down each seed into three examples, share the traditional roots of these practices, and suggest how we can capture their essence in modern-day acts of wellness and self-care. Grab a notebook and pen, top up your water (or wine!) and let's begin.

Part II
MUSIC AND MOVEMENT

Ahoɔden – 'Energy'

Music and movement are manifestations of Divine creative energy flowing through us. Using these tools, we can become master energy manipulators, changing both our internal and external environments and thereby changing our realities.

Chapter 4

DANCE

'Dance is an embodiment of your journey with spirit, with creation and with creating.'

Nangamso 'Mkutaji' Gumbe

Dance is a form of movement that breathes life into rhythm. It is where movement and music meet within our bodies and souls, whether that music is the sound of a drum, the sound of our heartbeat or the thud of our feet on the ground. Like so many things, dance in the African context has always been community focused, whereas dance in the Western context has traditionally been focused on a separation between the performer and the audience. It is only now, with the rise of platforms like TikTok, that dance has in some ways started to reconnect with its communal roots, with people from all corners of the world communicating through shared choreography and challenges. With people roping their whole families in to learn these dances, and the movement to recognise the Black creatives who originated much of the choreography, these challenges have come to be about so much more than just filming a dance. When sangomas – Southern African healers – undergo training, they must learn a set of dances as part of their initiation. In traditional ceremonies from all over Africa, dance can be seen as a central feature. Revered Trinidadian-American dancer and Ancestor Pearl Primus put it best when she said, '[African] people use their bodies as instruments through which every conceivable emotion or event is projected. The result is a hypnotic marriage between life and dance. The two are inseparable. When a child is born, when a person is buried, there is dance. People dance the sowing of the seed and the harvest, puberty rites, hunting, warfare. They dance for rain, sun, strong and numerous children, marriage and play. Love, hatred, fear, joy, sorrow, disgust, amazement, all these and all other emotions are expressed through rhythmic movement.' In traditional African life, dance is so much more than exercise, performance or art. How can we tap into this deeper meaning and dance our way to wellness?

TRADITIONAL DANCE IN AFRICA

Dance is a form of communication between the dancer or dancers and the Divine, as well as communication between the dancers and the watchers, some of whom may transform into dancers before the drumbeat ends. Dance rarely takes place without the backdrop of drumming, chanting or another traditional instrument, so it is often also communication between the dancers and the musicians. Different cultures across the continent have specific dances unique to their people. And within this, they have different dances for different occasions. The Amhara people of Ethiopia have the Eskista, a celebratory dance that centres around movement in the shoulders and is said to be inspired by the movements of a snake. The Shona people of Southern Africa have the Mbira dance, a highly spiritual ritual dance performed to the sound of the Mbira instrument and designed to facilitate communication with Ancestors and spirits. In the traditional African context, *everyone* is a dancer. But then you also have the *dancer* dancers. Far from existing simply for others to marvel and observe, these dancers more typically set the scene at a festival or celebration before drawing fellow dancers to join them from the crowd.

The choreography in traditional African dance is frequently inspired by everyday life. Many of the motions emulate the movements of animals, natural phenomena and the movements of people as they do various types of work. Dance sequences act as a form of archiving, encoding the history and mythology of a people. For example, some dances of the Ewe people emulate the movements of a bird. In their folklore, it is said that their ancestors were led from the kingdom of Dahomey to modern-day Eweland, which exists in Ghana, by the guidance of a bird. Learning the dances of your culture was once a central part of growing up. For some, it happened during their rites of passage. Others learned their cultural dances more informally. Healers-in-training learned healing dances behind closed doors, later administering them as medicine to the sick. Some dances were (and still are) kept exclusively for those going through a form of spiritual initiation. No matter how the dance was learned, its meaning and importance was passed down along with its technique.

Costume is an important part of traditional African dance. The way a traditional dance troupe dresses is an expression and celebration of their culture – for example Asante (or Ashanti) dancers tend to wear kente and lots of gold adornments. There are stilt dancers, found across the continent and the Diaspora, whose outfits cover their wooden stilts to give the illusion that their legs are really, really long. Whenever I see these dancers, with all the jumping and gyrating they do, I'm fearful that they will fall and land on my head. They never fall or even falter, obviously, because they are intensely talented and well practiced, but still, I keep my distance! In Ghana, we also have masquerade dancers. Around the festive season at the end of the year, there are parades in cities across the country, where anyone can rent one of the masquerade outfits and dance in the streets (it's on my bucket list for this year). The outfit is a head-to-toe white suit covered in brightly coloured embroidery and adornments, complete with a mask. While this outfit is available to anyone who wants to wear it, there are also other masked dancers who wear the wooden sculpture masks you might traditionally associate with Africa. Now, in my opinion, traditional wooden sculptures and masks – many of which are believed to be home to a particular deity – are not to be played with. You couldn't *pay* me to wear one of those masks on my face without an express order coming directly from a diviner, my Ancestors or the one true living God. So it makes sense, then, that dances performed with these masks are more selective. In her book, simply titled *African Dance*, recently transitioned Ancestor Kariamu Welsh-Asante said, 'Mask dances performed throughout Africa are used in a variety of ways, including warding off evil spirits; storytelling; suggesting supernatural or mystical powers; spreading good feelings; honouring African deities; and/or embodying animal, human, or spiritual figures.' Now did you see how many times she used a variation of the word 'spirits'? *That* is why dancing with these masks no be small matter.[i]

In some ritual settings, specific dances are performed only by those with the training or calling to perform them. These dances often act as an invitation for a particular spirit to possess the body of the dancer, allowing it to communicate with the ritual attendees. The dancers start out consciously performing the sequence, accompanied by chanting, drumming or another instrument, and essentially work themselves into a trance, at which point the intended spirit takes over. For some, these ritual dances are an annual affair, taking place in conjunction with a particular festival or celebration – for example, a harvest festival or the festival for a particular deity. In discussing the culture of the San people of Southern Africa, professor and Future Ancestor Funso Afolayan states that 'through intense singing and clapping by women and vigorously ecstatic dancing and hyperventilating by men, certain spiritually gifted San healers are able to enter a trance or altered state of consciousness that causes healing or supernatural potency (*nlum*) to boil up within them.... Impacted through a touch to the sick, the *nlum* brings recovery, restoration and rejuvenation to the individuals as well as to the group.' While possession might sound highly mystical or even scary, I think it's a matter of semantics and understanding. If you've ever seen a dancer in their element – or ever *been* a dancer in their element – you've experienced at least a glimpse of what could be

---

i   Pidgin phrase meaning 'it's not a small/insignificant thing'.

called possession. Because I believe that, whether in a ritual setting or not, it is only when we allow the Divine to move through us that we are truly dancing.

Future Ancestor: Nangamso 'Mkutaji' Gumbe

Nangamso is a writer, dancer and entrepreneur of Tsonga and Xhosa heritage, currently living in South Africa. When I spoke to Nangamso about how African dance differs from Western dance, she said, 'In an African setting, every single person contributes to the activity at hand, whether you are playing a drum, stomping your feet or singing or clicking – it is a collective collaboration. Everybody in that space is contributing to that performance. It's not about how great your movement is and how many tricks you can do or how beautiful your voice is – it's about your role in the collective experience. Come as you are and contribute what you can.'

She also shared the importance of dance as an archiving tool, saying, 'Movement is a way of archiving. I recently learned a dance of thunder, and this is used to celebrate, commemorate and give honour to the deity of thunder. There are certain communities, especially in Southern Africa, that use specific movements to ask for rain during drought season. So it's more than just the technical, it's not about you as an individual, it's about the story that you're telling with the people you're collaborating with.'

MODERN-DAY MYTHS

A few years ago my mum went to a work Christmas party. When she came back I asked her about how it was and if people danced. She said only she and the other Black lady danced and then added, 'You know Black people, we don't waste music!' She was being flippant, but there is some truth in what she said. As John J. Ollivier states in his book *The Wisdom of African Mythology*, 'The African is somehow wedded to rhythm. It is an obsession, a second nature to him; dance and music are its most perfect expressions.' While we obviously need to deconstruct the stereotype that all Black people can dance, it is true that rhythm is embedded in our culture, even if some of us can only appreciate it from a distance. One of my favourite things about being in Ghana is that there are always people dancing – everywhere! Sometimes even without any music! Petrol station attendants, street hawkers, security guards, schoolchildren – you can't go a day in Accra without seeing someone somewhere just casually dancing better than I could ever dream to. When we hear music – especially when we hear a drumbeat – we can't help but move. But while the love for dancing doesn't seem to show any signs of slowing in the Black community, traditional African dances are being lost.

Traditional dance used to form a part of everyday life for people growing up on the continent, and for Diasporan communities that retained a strong culture, for example, in the Caribbean. But now, more people move away from their birthplaces, schools place less value on traditional *anything*, and families are intent on modernising but end up Westernising instead. For second- and third-generation immigrants, it falls to parents and family members to teach these dances, yet the first generation are often the ones who have either forgotten or turned their back on such traditions. But there is hope! One of the positives that comes out of a tradition dying away is that it always enlivens a select few to take up the mantle of keeping it alive. If you want to connect with the traditional dances of your ethnic group or of groups across Africa, you will need a teacher who can train you in the specific movements, their meaning, their associated drumbeats or musical accompaniments and their application in ritual and ceremony. There are cultural centres, local initiatives and passionate individuals across the continent who are dedicated to this task if you look in the right places. If you're in the Diaspora or on the continent but not connected to the right people, Nangamso advises taking the academic route. Find a dance or African studies professor at your local university and ask them to point you in the right direction – they are likely to know cultural leaders who can help.

While the light of traditional dance itself may be dimming, the energy of African dance is very much alive! Fuelled by the globalisation of African music, the use of social media platforms for dance and the popularity of groups like DWP Academy,[ii] modern African dance is having a moment, especially Afrobeats dance. Afrobeats music evolved from the high life music of West Africa popularised in the 20th century by artists like Fela Kuti and Ebo Taylor. It stays true to its roots through the use of drums and local languages while drawing inspiration from modern genres such as hip-hop, electronic and dance music. In tandem, Afrobeats dance brings traditional dance elements into the modern age. Key tenets of Afrobeats dance – complex footwork, use of shoulder and arm movements, storytelling through movement – are all familiar features of traditional African dance. So while your parents might screw their face and say, 'Ah, na weyi na wɔ frɛ ni dancing a?' ('Is this the one you call dancing?'), today's dances are truly a continuation of, rather than a deviation from, tradition.

Now, we can't talk about African dance without talking about twerking, right? Right. So here goes. Twerking is yet another aspect of our culture that has been co-opted, demonised, sexualised and basically stripped from its roots. Twerk is not (necessarily) what you see in music videos and on Instagram. While the term originated in New Orleans in the 1980s, the style of dance itself goes way further back. It is a group of dance movements that focus on movement and isolation of the hips, traditionally performed by women from Africa and the Caribbean. If you've grown up in a West African, African-American or Caribbean home, you've almost

ii   It stands for Dance with a Purpose. They are the biggest dance academy in Ghana whose dancers also happen to be an internet sensation, and featured in Beyoncé's 'Black Is King' among other music videos.

definitely seen your aunt, grandma or mother twerking at some point in your life. It is a dance of celebration, beauty, joy and confidence – a dance designed to empower women and excite all who witness it! Makau Kitata, a lecturer at the University of Nairobi says, 'From a Western point of view, twerking is overly sexual and the performers participants in a cultural notoriety… However, in its original context it is primarily a dance for festive celebrations.'[5] I'm not saying that twerking is not sexual. It absolutely can be. Once I do it in a thong to a Cardi B song, fresh from applying a thick coat of shea butter, while a giant fan blows my hair all over my face, sure, it's sexual. But at its core, it is a show of skill (twerking is hard, y'all!) and a celebration of culture. You get to choose what kind of context you want to twerk in. For Black people (of all genders) around the world, twerking can be an affirmation of power, culture and Divine feminine energy, and should be embraced without shame or apology.

DANCE AND WELLBEING

I don't know about you, but for me, dance has always been one of those things that I've loved, but my level of skill has never quite matched my level of adoration. I've danced since I was young – ballet, musical theatre, jazz, cheerleading – but as a lanky girl who grew into a lanky woman, I've always had an insecurity in the back of my mind about not looking quite polished enough. Despite this, whether I'm at a twerk class, in da club or rolling around my apartment in my granny panties, dance leaves me feeling free – it truly is medicine. Of course, we know that exercise or movement is good for us: for the physical body and for our mental health. But the benefits of dance go well beyond that. A 2022 study from Middlesex University, referring to the many existing studies on dance, stated that 'compared with other exercise practices, recreational dance provides additional benefits due to the complex brain functions activated when dancing… improving memory, empathy, and emotional intelligence, while reducing stress levels'.[6] The study also presented dance as more effective than other exercise, reading, writing for pleasure and crossword puzzles for preventing – and even reversing – cognitive decline in older people. Even more reason to get the whole family involved! Here are some other ways dance can be life changing.

Belonging

Belonging is essential to our wellbeing. Doing anything in a group setting cultivates feelings of belonging, but there's a particular magic to moving together in a group. In addition to this, connecting with African dance – whether traditional or modern – can help you build a feeling of belonging with the global Black community or the community from which the dance originates. Learning the traditional dance of your people connects you not just to your fellow Asantes, Dagaras, Hamars, Shonas… it connects you to your grandparents, your great-grandparents, your great-great-grandparents. It connects you to your heritage and your tribe, in the broadest sense of the word. It connects you to home.

Self-esteem

Self-esteem is often thought to be the same as confidence, but there is a slight nuance between the two. While confidence is a feeling of certainty in your ability or skill level, self-esteem is a certainty in your success *regardless* of your ability or skill level. When I lived in the UK, lanky limbs aside, I was pretty confident in my ability to hold my own on a dance floor. One of my best friends, Tiff, and I used to love going dancing, and we didn't mind being the centre of attention at all, especially in our carefree days as uni students. Whether we were dancing in the DJ booth or taking up space with a likkle[iii] synchronised dance, it's safe to say, we were highly (over)confident in our abilities. When I moved to Ghana, where people can reeeeeaaally dance, I quickly recognised that my little

---

iii   Patois, meaning 'little'.

one-two step and skinny girl whine was not going to impress anybody. Safe to say, my confidence in my dance ability has taken a turn. But you will still see me dancing in the DJ booth or doing routines with my friends with the same vim[iv] as I did in my uni days. Why? Because my level of self-esteem has remained stable or maybe even gone up! What does that mean in this context? My goal in going out dancing is to enjoy myself, create a vibe and make memories. I may not be the best dancer, but I *know* I'm a master vibe-creator, and if I want to have a good time, a good time will be had by all. I am 100 per cent certain that, whether I can do footwork or not (I cannot), I will achieve success.

When we practise dance often, it teaches us this same lesson. Whether you're in a class learning choreography or trying to keep up with the latest challenge, you will fall, get moves wrong, forget the choreography, accidentally punch someone in the face (yes, I have done this. In cheerleading. We were both in the air. Credit to the punchee – they somehow didn't fall!) and make a ton of other mistakes. But the practice of dance is continuing to show up. It's doing one move incorrectly two hundred times until something clicks and your body finally gets it. It's practising with your group over and over until finally you move like a unit. It's filming and posting the challenge even though you could keep practising forever, because done is better than perfect. Yes, dance can improve your confidence as you become better at it. But more importantly, it boosts your self-esteem because, whether you become 'better' or not, you do achieve some version of success. The success of bonding with your dance community, the success of creating a new piece of choreography, the success of a performance, the success of feeling joyful, peaceful, free.

---

iv   While not strictly Ghanaian, nowhere else have I heard this word used more. A slang term for energy, also the name of one of my fave DJs in Accra.

Embodiment and Self-love

Have you ever seen a dance move, decided to do it, and then watched as your body did something entirely opposite to what you intended? Yeah, same. When we dance, we engage in a level of self-awareness of the body that we don't often require. When we sit, when we lie, when we walk, when we run – we can pretty much move with little to no conscious awareness and be fine. But when we dance? Suddenly the movements of our fingers matter as much as the movement of our hips. A slight shift in our weight can derail our whole sequence. The direction of our gaze affects the speed of our spin. And these are all things we have to be consciously, intentionally, *intently* aware of as we move.

This sounds simple enough, but in a world where it's an achievement *not* to become disconnected from your body, it can be a big ask. Between unrealistic beauty standards, diet culture, the sexualisation of women's bodies from a young age, bullying, fatphobia, racism, colourism, ableism, transphobia, disordered eating, physical and sexual abuse, and the myriad other traumas each person has to navigate, often before even reaching adulthood, it's no wonder that such a high proportion of us are walking around in a body that doesn't feel safe, beautiful or like home. It's no wonder that so many of us aren't just disconnected from our bodies but might actually go so far as to say we dislike, or even hate, them.

A 2020 report from the UK government[7] found that 61 per cent of adults and 66 per cent of children feel negative or very negative about their body image most of the time. Unsurprisingly, these percentages are higher among women, people with a disability and the transgender community. The same report found that 42 per cent of adults had experienced shame in relation to their body in the last year while only 18 per cent reported having experienced joy.

While dance isn't a quick fix for loving your body, spending more time truly in your body helps to restore your connection to it – and this translates away from the dance studio too. As you reconnect with your body through dance, you'll gradually find yourself better able to hear your body's messages, whether it's becoming more sensitive to your hunger and fullness signals or recognising how anxiety shows up in your body, acting as your personal alarm system for when something isn't right.

Cultivating self-love is a long and difficult journey for many of us. In becoming more and more embodied through dance, and with a conscious intention to move towards a more loving relationship with yourself, awareness of how your body moves can gradually turn into acceptance, amazement and awe at just what it is – you are – capable of.

Energetic Release

It is a generally accepted fact that trauma is stored in the body, a statement no longer relegated to pseudoscience or 'unfounded' spiritual community claims. The experiences we go through in life take form as aches, pains, knots, tightness and other physical manifestations. But the physical body is just one aspect of who we are. There is also a subtle part of us, an energetic part of us that we can't see but we can feel. It's this part of you that picks up on tension when you walk into a room or tells you to stay away from a particular person even though they haven't said or done anything wrong. This concept of an energy body or energy field shows up in many different spiritual traditions and is the focal point of treatments such as acupuncture, acupressure, Emotional Freedom Technique (EFT), energy healing and some breathing exercises. If this is the point where I'm losing you, stay with me for a quick exercise.

EXERCISE FOR ENERGETIC RELEASE

1. Press your right thumb into the centre of your left palm and hold for about 30 seconds, then repeat for the other side. This is to sensitise your palms.

2. As you're doing step 1, take a few deep breaths to relax your body and mind.

3. Rub your palms together for five to 10 seconds.

4. Hold your hands about a foot apart with palms turned towards each other and your fingers closed.

5. Focus all your attention on your palms. Close your eyes if it helps.

6. Slooooowly start to move your hands towards each other, keeping your focus on your palms. Move them slightly away from each other and then back towards each other. Keep repeating this process until you feel what's described in the next step.

7. Notice what sensation you can feel between your palms. It should feel almost as if you're gathering something between your palms. You may even feel some pushback or resistance. This is energy! Don't worry if you don't feel it the first time you try; just keep practising.

In addition to our physical body, we have an energy body. This is what people are talking about when they say you have a great aura or somebody has bad energy. Within this energy body, the life force that travels through our energy channels like blood through veins, is what Chinese philosophy calls qi and the yoga scriptures call prana. It is comparable to the Yoruba concept of àṣẹ[v] and the Akan sunsum.[vi] Trauma, negative thought patterns and unhealthy living can cause this energy to get blocked at different points in our energy body, which is what translates into those aches, pains and other issues in the physical body I mentioned earlier.

---

v   Pronounced ah-SHEH, it's the Yoruba concept of life force or the power to make change. It's also a word of affirmation used in a similar way to 'amen'.

vi   Pronounced SOON-soom, it's the Akan concept of the spirit, one of the many parts of a person.

The physical body and the energetic body are inextricably linked, so when you work on one, you impact the other. This is why people go to energy healers for physical complaints. When we dance, we move not just the physical body but the energy body too. Through dance, we get our àṣẹ moving and we can work through blocks without even realising it. If you've ever noticed a random emotion while dancing – anger, joy, sadness – this is probably why. This kind of energetic release can be so powerful that it is a practice all on its own. Somatic therapists guide their clients to locate memories and experiences stored in the body and practise movements combined with breathwork and talking therapy to help clients work through them. While dancing isn't quite as targeted, it definitely has the potential to help us improve our energetic, emotional and physical health.

Trance and Meditation

This isn't a book on meditation, and thank the Ancestors because there are already so many of those (and yes, feel free to draw my attention to this and mock me to your heart's content in a few years when I inevitably publish a book on meditation). So I don't want to go into too much detail about what meditation is and its benefits because, honestly, that content could fill a whole nother book, and we have a lot to cover. What I will say is that trance and meditation are often highly misunderstood. It can be helpful to think of them as a continuum. Have you ever been so engrossed in something – painting, writing, reading, playing an instrument – and then without warning you 'wake up'? Like you suddenly remember who you are and where you are and that time is a thing that actually matters in this reality? And you're just blinking at the canvas or instrument or book like, 'Wait, what did I just wake up from?' The answer is a trance, or in more palatable language, 'flow state'.

When we get into a state of flow, all other aspects of this reality fall away. The only things that exist are you and the activity you're focusing on. Hours go by and feel like minutes; people call your name, and you genuinely don't hear them; eating, going to the bathroom and other mere mortal activities don't concern you. Remember the last time you experienced this? This flow state is at one end of the continuum.

Around the halfway point we have what most of us experience after some time of having a regular meditation practice. We can call this the 'meditative state'. For most of us, most of the time we're meditating we're actually not meditating. We're focusing on the object of our meditation, or we're being distracted by thoughts and sensations, or we're moving our attention back to the object of our meditation, or we're wondering, 'Is this what meditation is supposed to feel like?' This is why it's called a practice. But when you transcend all that toing and froing, you find yourself in a meditative state. It's something that has to be experienced rather than explained, but if you meditate regularly, you've likely had at least a taste of it. Similar to a flow state, when you 'come back' it's almost like waking up.

And then all the way at the other end of the spectrum, we have possession, which we mentioned earlier. To be clear, I'm not advocating that you, dear reader, use dance as a tool for possession. In fact, I would strongly suggest you avoid doing that at all costs! Possession is something that is best done under the supervision of a trusted spiritual teacher, after the appropriate training and preparation. What I *am* championing is the idea of dance as a moving meditation, especially if you find seated meditation simply doesn't connect with you. Dance can be a powerful meditative tool, allowing you to reap the benefits of meditation without having to sit in lotus pose and chant 'om'. You'll find instructions on how to complete a dance meditation in the next section.

READY TO RETURN?

Pearl Primus said that 'dance in Africa is not a separate art, but a part of the whole complex of living'. If we think of dance as conscious movement, we can bring this understanding of dance as part of life into our wellness practice. You don't have to learn traditional or even modern African dance. You can make any form of conscious movement a part of your daily routine. You can revamp your existing movement practice and make it a community affair. You can learn to use conscious movement as a way to express yourself. You can spend six months learning to zanku only to finally get it once the rest of the world has moved on, like somebody I know (me). Here are some specific movement practices to try out.

DANCE PRACTICES FOR THE MODERN AFRICAN

Befriend Your Body

In the previous section I shared how dance can be a tool for self-love. However, Nangamso advises that some of us might need to focus on befriending our body before we even begin any form of African dance. All of us – especially women – receive messages from a young age that there is something wrong with our body. It's too fat, too thin, too weak, too strong, too dark, too light, too jiggly, not jiggly enough....

When we bring these insecurities with us to dance, especially African dance, we block ourselves from achieving the true goal, which is to allow energy to move through our body. If we are self-conscious about how we look, we will maintain an element of control throughout the dance when the key is to release all control. To start cultivating self-acceptance and self-love before you begin your dance journey, spend time with your body and get to know it. Strip naked and look at yourself in the mirror. The more you cringed at that last sentence, the more you need to do it! When you moisturise, don't slap it on as if you've got 21 seconds to go.[vii] Turn it into a self-massage session, paying attention to each part of your body.

---

vii '21 Seconds' is a classic UK Garage hit by So Solid Crew that was released in 2001. If you're a '90s baby, read that again – 2001! Yes, we are that old.

Do you have a full-length mirror? If not, then get one! I didn't have one until about a year ago, and it's a game changer. Parade yourself in front of it, dance in front of it, perform fashion shows – become intimate with your body so that you come to recognise, acknowledge and eventually love each and every blob and blemish.

Learn the New Dances Coming Out of Africa

Back in the day, I spent so much time watching music videos that my mum cancelled our Sky[viii] subscription so I would focus on my exams. I know what you're thinking. What kind of privileged life was I living that we had a Sky subscription? It absolutely *was* a privilege but one that I was only afforded as a happy outcome of my mama's desire for the African TV channels and the God Channel. Anyway, back then, this was how you could learn all the latest dances. These days, I only become aware of new dances when I see them being performed right in front of my eyes by youths who are in the know. Apparently, TikTok and Instagram Reels (neither of which I have time to scroll through) are where you too can learn all the latest dances coming out of the continent! There are even YouTubers who do full-on breakdowns so you can master the moves technically *and* look good. Which might help you build your confidence enough to....

Attend a Dance Class

If you're on a self-love journey, the style of dance you practise can help you rebuild your perception of yourself. If you struggle to feel sexy, practise kizomba. If you feel powerless, practise hip-hop dance. Match your chosen style of dance with the traits you feel you're lacking (please note, they're not actually lacking but simply struggling to blossom under the weight of your own judgement) and see how your view of yourself

---

viii The UK version of DSTV or Comcast. At the time, in the late '90s, you either had Sky or literally only five channels.

transforms. Dance classes are amazing but can also be intimidating. If you're feeling shy or live in a part of the world where in-person classes are few, there are tons of online options. Twerk After Work, the brainchild of young, fearless entrepreneur Bami Kuteyi, offers online classes every day through their app Bam Bam Boogie. For in-person classes, drag a friend along to help you brave it! But remember, all dance classes are not created equal. Especially if you're looking for a cultural connection, be sure to do your research and select classes based on who is teaching them. I'm going to take this opportunity to plug Twerk Girl Ghana, my friend, publicist, business partner and twerk instructor. As her name suggests, she teaches twerk in Ghana, as well as online via the Bam Bam Boogie app. If you're in Ghana, DWP Academy is the place for Afrobeats dance.

Bring African Energy to Any Conscious Movement Practice

Capoeira is a form of conscious movement rooted in African tradition, so this Brazilian martial art could be an excellent one to try out. But even practices from other cultures like yoga, tai chi, Pilates or even walking/running can be elevated even further by bringing an African dance approach to them. That could mean joining or creating a community and doing the practice together. It could mean introducing music and allowing your movement to become one with the sound. It could mean taking the competitive approach out of your practice and viewing it as a way to commune with your body and with the Divine. If you're looking to join a class and you're in London, look up Run Dem Crew, Swim Dem Crew, Amona Venice (@amona_v on Instagram), Sanchia Legister and Isa Welly. In Manchester? Check out Samuel Nwokeka's studio, Yoga Soul. If you're in Nigeria, check out Michael Ernest Nwah and in Ghana there's Bliss Yoga and The Yoga Studio. Wherever you are, you can follow Jessamyn Stanley and join her yoga subscription service, The Underbelly.

Put on Your Dancing Shoes

Who says partying can't be healing? True wellness should weave through each part of your life, rather than being a thing you do on Sundays, sometimes on Wednesdays. With this in mind, gather your gal dem and the man dem, make a date, wear shoes you can actually dance in and get to stepping out. My friends and I choose where to go almost exclusively based on who is DJing and how much space there is to dance, a tactic I highly recommend. So, yes, people, being outside can be part of your wellness routine! But please, it's the dancing I'm saying is good for you... I can't speak to the other tings you've been doing. And a quick reminder here that, in all things, balance is your friend. Please don't go on a bender and say, 'Araba made me do it.'

Ecstatic or Meditative Dance

Ecstatic dance is a movement/spiritual practice that has gained popularity in the West in recent years, as can be seen by the rise of sober morning raves. Essentially, the idea is to move freely and lose yourself in the music until you reach a state of ecstasy or a trance. Sound familiar? The form of ecstatic dance popularised in the West is usually done with electronic music, but we can reclaim this practice with the soundtrack of drumming, Amapiano – South Africa's most popular creation since Mandela – or whatever your favourite upbeat genre of Black music is. Simply take your shoes off, put on a playlist, set an intention and move your body. You might feel weird and self-conscious at first – ever have that feeling where you know nobody's watching but you still *feel* like someone's watching? – so just start with some simple movements like swaying or a slow walk around the room. You can close your eyes if it will help (and if you won't bump into anything) and just keep moving, no matter how stilted or forced it feels, until gradually you start to get into it, and you'll feel the music moving through you.

Nangamso says, 'The first step is listening. Listen to nature, listen to a drumbeat, listen to music. And then respond with your body. Then practise nonjudgement with no shame – allow your body to move without attachment. Eventually you will stop responding, and it will transcend into a meditation.'

This practice can be powerful if you have limited mobility, as it's less about forcing your body into specific movements and more about allowing your body to lead you into what feels comfortable. If you're in the UK and you want to join a conscious clubbing experience and ecstatically dance with hundreds of other people, I recommend the real OG Morning Gloryville, founded by spiritual entrepreneur Sam Moyo.

SKANKIN' SWEET

The association between dance and performance is one that is deeply entrenched for most of us. The idea of moving freely without attempting to look a certain way can bring up all kinds of fears and emotions. The thought of dancing in public when you know you don't have the best moves can be even scarier. And this is reminiscent of a much broader phenomenon. Western individualism has created a mindset among us where life itself is a performance. We are each the main character in a reality TV show, and we're desperate to come across well so we don't get voted out – or cancelled.

Welsh-Asante says that 'all African dances can be used for transcendence and transformational purposes'. I say that we can apply the energy of African traditional dance to any movement practice to achieve transcendence and transformation. Let's learn to flow with the music, or as the music, instead of moving our bodies for an audience (real or imagined), and dance – or skank – like nobody's watching. In fact, let's apply this sentiment to every area of life: work like nobody's watching, create like nobody's watching, dress like nobody's watching, love like nobody's watching. Let spirit move you. Whether you consider yourself a dancer or not, this embodied practice can become a tool to help us live ecstatically, where being in flow – with our community, with nature, with the Divine – is so much more important than how many shares your latest TikTok challenge gets.

Chapter 5

SOUND

'Song is sound and sound is energy and energy is spirit – so for us to ascend to a higher dimension, music is essential, as it opens the portal to that connection.'

Gogo Dineo Ndlanzi

Sound has been in existence since the dawn of our universe, so it's no wonder that it's a source of such awe, inspiration and healing. Randall McClellan captures the universal significance of sound with this passage in his book *The Healing Forces of Music*:

> *Among many of the world's cosmologies the universe began with a Sound. For the Hopi people this sound was a creating song, for the native peoples of Australia the sound was caused by the beating of the original seas with a reed. The Ethiopians speak of a time when the first humans could only sing but eventually forgot the melodies and had to revert to the speaking of words, while in the language of the Ewe the word lo means both 'to sing' and 'to weave'.*

In some African and Indigenous cosmologies, the sound of the creation of the universe is the deep, forceful, echoing vibration of a drum. It's a sound that can be found elsewhere in nature too: the sound of a coconut falling to the ground or the sound of our own heartbeats. What is the sound of Africa if not the beat of a drum? Sound and, specifically, music – just like dance – have been an ever-present force in the lives of African people. Building on this history while taking inspiration from modern sound healing, we can isolate sound and music as a tool to promote wellbeing.

SOUND HEALING IN TRADITIONAL AFRICA

The drum in traditional Africa is much more than an instrument. It is a status symbol, a tool for communication and a work of functional art. While it's important to note that not *all* societies across the continent hold the drum in such high esteem, and not all even use the drum, its place as central to a community is seen across Africa. In his paper on the traditional music of the Ga people,[8] renowned musicologist and Ancestor Dr J.H. Nketia categorises the modes of drumming used as signal drumming, speech drumming and dance drumming. Signal drumming is used to announce chiefs, speech drumming, as it sounds, is intended to imitate speech and dance drumming… well, you know what dance drumming is for! This Ga example illustrates the versatility of the drum and its varying roles within a society. In the traditional African community, drums are perhaps most associated with royalty, storytellers and ritual. They are made from wood and animal skins, and endowed with sacred symbols, proverbs and images. I have a djembe drum, which I bought in Ghana, engraved with one of my favourite Adinkra, Dwennimmɛn.[i] No, I do not know how to play it but, alas, it is a symbol of what could be.

In addition to drums, there are a range of other musical instruments indigenous to Africa. There are string instruments such as the seperewa, wind instruments such as the wooden flute and percussive instruments such as the balafon. The kora is the pride of the Mandinka people, found in the Sahel region of West Africa, and is associated with griot or jali families.

---

i   Pronounced jwi-ni-MEN. This Adinkra represents strength in humility.

Griots are revered keepers of history, storytellers and gifted musicians, and the role is hereditary. This is why you may see many kora players through time with the same last name: Diabaté, Cissoko and Keita, for example. The Mbira is a group of instruments sacred to the Shona people and often used in ritual. Traditional instruments across the continent are made with materials such as wood, gourds and metal.

It is the convergence of these instruments, song, and other elements present in a ritual that promote healing in the traditional African society. Regardless of the purpose of the ritual, it is a healing technology in itself, as will be explored in Chapter 12. Due to the holistic and integrated nature of traditional African life, it is rare to see sound and music isolated, separated from work, ritual or dance. And, therefore, it is difficult to identify a specific sound healing tradition. However, among the many tools at the disposal of the healer, we may find a comparable element.

In my conversations with both Nangamso (Future Ancestor from Chapter 4) and Gogo Dineo Ndlanzi (you'll meet her in Chapter 9), they each drew my attention to the Bantu word 'ngoma'. It is variously translated as drum, dance or music – but also relates to healing, evident in the title healers are given in parts of Southern Africa – sangoma. Traditional healers in Bantu and other societies learn sacred healing songs in their training, which they then use in the treatment of patients. Since this knowledge is mostly guarded and revealed only to those on the priest/ priestess path, it's difficult to know exactly what these healing songs are. However, from my understanding, the voice is the main instrument used in sound healing, and the medicine may utilise the voice of only the healer or the voice of both the healer and the patient.

The healing power of music in the traditional African way of living is largely interwoven in other aspects of life rather than applied in isolation and can still be felt today through ceremonies and performances, as Nketia puts it, 'by those for whom these activities still constitute part of their way of life'.

Future Ancestors: Salma Omar and Ahmed Homaida, Drum Circle Sudan

When Salma Omar and Ahmed Homaida – both of Sudanese heritage – met in 2018, a conversation about drumming and forgotten knowledge led to the creation of Drum Circle Sudan. Discussing why they felt called to begin this movement, they said, *'Sound is the basis of creation. Vibrations create sound. In Africa, drumming is a language, a way of life and a tool of creation. We felt called to reintroduce ourselves to this part of our culture, knowing about the multiple benefits of drumming to brain and body. We believe it is the source of great healing and introspection. It helps us to free the mind and sit in the present which brings about clarity. And communities create joy, understanding, trust, solutions and a new reality. Drum circle is a perfect tool to create a community with clarity, joy and a sense of belonging.'*

On the critical nature of community building, they said, 'With conflict creating a pressure to ignore the past, government efforts to oppress some and uplift others, help some and deny others, we should move with a sense of urgency. To those who feel called, we need to connect, deepen our experience, and share what we learn. We have tools that can help us to connect with something deeper. A stillness and an understanding about the importance of community based in our African roots.'

MODERN-DAY MYTHS

Sound baths are one of my favourite healing practices. When I lived in East London, I used to attend a regular sound healing event at the Round Chapel. There would be a few huge gongs and other instruments set up in the middle of this church, and we would lie around them, like petals on a flower, always with our heads closest to the centre. I used to try to get there as early as possible so I could nab a spot closest to the centre. The sound and the vibrations created by these instruments and amplified by the high dome ceiling were like nothing I'd ever experienced before and have ever experienced since. In my opinion, the practice of sound healing is one of the most underrated therapies in the Black community. This is partly due to simple lack of awareness but also helped in no small part by the image of sound healing as a white woman dressed in all white, perhaps wearing a turban (but not actually Sikh) surrounded by crystal singing bowls that each cost more than a month's worth of rent – and the often high price of attending sound healing sessions.

But what actually *is* sound healing? It is the cliché above, but it's also so much more. According to sound healer Simon Heather, it is 'the therapeutic application of sound frequencies to the body/mind of people with the intention of bringing them into a state of harmony and health'.[9] I think it's important to note here that sound healing is available and effective for the deaf community. As Jessica A. Holmes states in her paper on music and deafness,[10] 'Attitudes to the relationship between music and deafness suffer from two related misconceptions: the enduring assumption that hearing is central to musical experience in conjunction with an extreme impression of deafness as total aural loss.' Since these assumptions are incorrect, sound healing as a practice does not automatically exclude those who may be deaf or hard of hearing. The sound healing therapies inspired by the East utilise vibrational instruments such as gongs and singing bowls. In the modern Western wellness parlance, it's only with the use of these instruments that a sound healing session can be called a 'sound bath', apparently because you're supposed to let the vibrations wash over you. Ei please, don't roll your eyes too hard until you've tried it, oh; it actually makes sense! It's incredible how much movement a sound bath creates in your body when all you're doing is lying still. For general sound healing, other musical instruments, vocals or even recorded music can be used as the therapeutic tool.

If you search for sound healing tracks on your favourite music streaming app, you'll be inundated with songs featuring singing bowls, gongs, binaural beats, piano music and more. Any tracks that feature drumming will use 'shamanic drumming' with a frame drum, native to the Indigenous people of America. I doubt you'll find a single track that uses African instruments – which is no surprise since, as we've established in the previous section, our particular form of healing usually involves dance, not lying down and bathing in sound – but you'll find some ideas on how to Africanise your sound healing practice later in the chapter.

Sound healing in its modern, Eastern-inspired form has been shown to be hugely beneficial for our wellbeing. A 2022 study[11] published in the *Religions* journal found that as well as decreasing tension and depression, the practice can increase spiritual wellbeing. So this style of music therapy may have a lot to offer us. But we must also challenge the notion that all healing has to be silent, slow or passive. While the approach of overriding the body and transcending the mind as a path to wellness works for some, and definitely has a lot to teach us all, we cannot deny the power of loud, joyful and active healing, especially as, for Africans, it's in our blood, it's who we are.

Revisiting the definition of sound healing above, we can find it in many more places than in the vibrational field of a gong. We can find it in the process of learning to play our traditional instruments. We can find it in raising our voices in shouting, chanting or song. We can find it in losing ourselves in feel-good music. We can find it in learning to DJ (that's me!). Sound permeates every facet of our existence, so wherever we can find sound we can find healing.

Future Ancestor: Allen Kwabena (Kobby) Frimpong

Allen, also known as kobby ananse, is a Ghanaian-American artist of Ga and Asante heritage, lineage of Nii Ayinsah Sasraku III of Langma-Kokrobite. He is fascinated by the convergence of sound, art and healing, and is inspired by traditional storytelling and music as manifestations of this. Discussing his personal journey with music, he shared that learning piano as a child paved the way for him to connect with the gyli (xylophone) later in life, saying, '*The gyli as a xylophone, as an instrument, speaks to my soul so deeply in a way that the piano just doesn't. The joy that it brings me to play it is unmatched.*'

On sound healing, he said, '*Sound healing for me is being able to feel the vibrations and frequencies around us, and letting them metabolise in us so that we can harness them, creating new possibilities and opportunities that liberate us from the trauma we've experienced. The trauma that has crystallised within our bodies, keeping us in automated modes of behaviour that reinforce that cycle of trauma. When we allow sound to create new pathways in our minds, hearts and souls, it teaches us to move in the world differently, in ways that encourage us to thrive.*'

SOUND HEALING AND WELLBEING

It's likely that you engage in a level of sound healing already. If, when you're feeling low, you turn to your favourite music, or you play an instrument, or you scream into your pillow, congrats! You've already activated the healing power of sound in your life. Playing an instrument that requires a lot of physical exertion, like the djembe, is great for your physical as well as emotional health. A 2014 study[12] found that it improved participants' cardiovascular health, which, if you've ever tried to play the djembe for more than 10 minutes straight, won't surprise you. Aside from this and the expected benefits of lower stress and improved mood, how else can sound and music heal us?

Belonging

In the throes of the latest romantic disappointment, singing to a certain someone that they ain't sh*t and they weren't special 'til you made them so, as guided by Jhené,[ii] isn't just healing because it reminds you who TF you are. It's also because Jhené gets you. She has *been* you. She is giving word and melody to your internal torture and inviting you to work through it with her. Whether we're experiencing heartbreak, money problems, or a spiritual awakening, listening to lyrics that sound like they were written for us fosters feelings of belonging and self-compassion. Because if even Jhené has to deal with these ruffians, I don't feel so hopeless after all.

Belonging is also cultivated when engaging in community music groups, whether you join a choir or a drumming group. By engaging in sound healing that utilises traditional African sounds, we're finding belonging in our heritage. As much as I love a good sound bath, there's something deeper, something more substantial that is awakened within me when practising sound healing with African drums, flutes and vocals. When you connect deeply with sounds that have held sacred space for your people for centuries, the vibrations don't just course through your body. They course through space and time, through your genetic memory, through the bodies that are encapsulated *within* your body, bringing forth a sense of connection, a sense of community, a sense of home.

---

ii   As in Aiko, the neo-soul queen.

Energetic Release

Sound can be a way for us to release under-expressed or entirely unexpressed emotions and energies. This is why having wailers at funerals can be effective and is the reason you're propelled into shouting or screaming in moments of intense joy or rage. Simply listening to music can promote an energetic release too – sound has the power to move you to tears or help you release stress. Whether through our voice or transferred through an instrument, music gives us the outlet for these energies to flow.

As explored in the previous chapter, the alternative – blocked and trapped energy – eventually manifests into physical health problems such as pain and anxiety. Allowing ourselves the space and permission to release through sound benefits our physical, mental and emotional health.

Healing

You know when people say you should 'raise your vibration'? Aside from being mildly condescending and somewhat self-congratulatory, it may have some basis in science. Everything in the universe has a vibration, a frequency, including us. It has been suggested that when we are unwell our frequency – or vibration – goes down. Most music is tuned at 440 Hz frequency, but there are specific tracks created for the intention of healing that use a range of other frequencies. A quick search on Insight Timer[iii] tells me that I can benefit from different frequencies in the following ways:

- 417 Hz for deep sleep
- 432 Hz for relaxation and meditation
- 528 Hz for DNA healing and repair
- 639 Hz for love and better relationships
- 963 Hz for oneness and connecting to the Divine

---

iii My favourite meditation app. It's free(mium) and filled with meditations, talks, courses and meditation music from tons of healers (including me!).

This might all sound airy fairy, but there is some research to back (some of) it up. A 2018 study published in the *Health* journal[13] found that '528 Hz music has an especially strong stress-reducing effect, even following only five minutes of exposure' while a 2016 study[14] found that 320 Hz improved cognitive capacity (in snails, but still). Even if these different frequencies don't do exactly what they say on the tin, it's clear that listening to lower-frequency music for relaxation and sleep, or higher-frequency music during meditation, or as background music throughout the day, can have healing effects beyond regular music.

Trance and Meditation

Music is an excellent tool to aid entry into a trance or meditative state, especially for people who struggle with silent forms of meditation. Rhythmic drumming can be used to induce a calm, meditative state, as is found in the Indigenous American shamanic healing systems. The idea is that the drumbeat starts out matching your resting heart rate and, as it gradually slows, your heart follows suit, calming you. Entering these states regularly reduces stress and coaxes our bodies into 'rest and digest' mode, where our muscles relax, and systems like our immune, digestive and reproductive systems receive more TLC.

READY TO RETURN?

Sound weaves through every part of our lives, even living within us. McClellan describes the body as 'a virtual symphony of frequencies, sounds, and biological, mental and emotional rhythms in a state of continuous flow which seek to achieve and maintain the state of perfect balance and equilibrium'. By embracing sound healing as a practice, we can help the body in its quest for balance.

SOUND HEALING PRACTICES FOR THE MODERN AFRICAN

Reacquaint Yourself with the Drum

You could, like me, purchase a drum and only play it twice for fear of noise complaints from your neighbours. Or you could utilise this thing called the internet and find drumming tracks to listen to. Salma and Ahmed encourage us to get creative and turn the items around us into drums or percussion: 'There is no right or wrong way to drum, it can be as simple as following the beat to your favourite song, or playing on your lap. Once, we made it a point to invite people and ask them to bring in the popular Sudanese metal drinking cup called Kozz (ironically also the name for the recently overthrown political party) to bang on, a spoon or an empty water drum. Our shakers are made of plastic bottles filled with pebbles or seeds.' Whether you use the drumbeat for dance, meditation, working out or background music when working, it's a powerful, healing sound.

USE AFRICAN MUSIC FOR RELAXATION AND MEDITATION

The traditional instruments and smooth vocals in the songs of artists like Sona Jobarteh, Ayub Ogada and, everyone's fave, Salif Keita are ideal for this practice. As kobby ananse says, 'African sounds and instruments have a poignant rhythm, melody, beat that deconstructs and reconstructs. It takes everything down and puts it back together again in your body in a way that makes you feel so anew.' More contemporary sounds like Lo-Fi and spiritual rap can give you the same result; check out artists like Londrelle and Lavva. You can follow these steps for a meaningful meditation:

1. Make a playlist of songs according to how long you want to meditate for.

2. Create a safe space for healing. That could look like locking your door, putting your phone on Do Not Disturb, lighting a candle or incense or doing whatever else you need to get in the zone.

3. Lie on the floor, a mat or your bed, get comfortable and press play. You can do this practice either with headphones or a speaker – just ensure the music is loud enough to block out other noise.

4. Close your eyes and take some deep breaths. Set an intention for the practice. It could be as simple as 'to relax'.

5. Allow the music to wash over you. Listen to the music with your whole body. Notice how it makes you feel at different points in the meditation. Whenever your thoughts start to wander, come back to the music. Do this as often as necessary without feeling annoyed at yourself – distraction is a normal part of the practice.

6. Once the music stops, stay where you are for a while. Lie in the silence and, again, become aware of how you feel: mentally, physically and emotionally.

7. When you're ready, close the practice out. You might want to journal or voice-record your experience.

Meditate on the Sounds of Your Body

One of my favourite meditations involves resting the thumb of one hand on the inside wrist of the other, where that big vein (that's the scientific term) is and meditating on your pulse. You can also try meditating on your own heartbeat or the sound and sensation of your breath. We all have different levels of interoceptive awareness, that is, some of us can hear/feel our heartbeat and some of us can't. So don't worry if these forms of meditation don't come easily. Also, for some people, focusing on the rhythm of their heart can actually fuel feelings of anxiety and panic, so if this starts to happen, abort the practice immediately. It's not by force!

Sing Your Prayers and Affirmations

When it comes to your spiritual practice – whatever your beliefs – singing raises your energy. This is why you'll see singing and chanting feature in almost every religious or spiritual path. When we sing or chant our prayers, we create a certain resonance that allows us to connect more deeply with the Divine. So whether you're doing your daily affirmations or talking to God, try turning it into a tune. There's no right or wrong, you don't have to use a particular melody and I'm 99.99 per cent sure whoever you're praying to won't mind if you're off-key. Not just this but you'll notice you *feel* better after singing your affirmations, prayers or mantras too.

When I wake up in a bad mood, I sing, 'I'm gonna sing 'til I feel betteeerrrrr,' and it works, y'all! When I'm cooking, I sing for the food to nourish me and taste good and 50 per cent of the prayer is answered 100 per cent of the time. That Frosties kid was on to something.[iv]

Try Out Eastern-inspired Sound Healing or Sound Baths

The traditional sound healing practices of the East include the use of 'Tibetan' singing bowls (although allegedly more likely in Japan than Tibet), the use of gongs in Southeast Asian temples and the chanting of 'om' and other mantras in the Hindu tradition. With the modern manifestation of (definitely not Tibetan) singing bowls, different sizes (and therefore

---

iv In a 2006 advert for the cereal, he insisted it was gonna taste great. In case you fell for the rumours…he is not dead!

notes) are said to align with various chakras[v] in the body, and so you can select what type of healing experience you need; for example, a heart chakra session for when you've had enough of other human beings. You could attend a live group session, like the ones I frequented at the Round Chapel (organised by the Psychedelic Society), arrange a one-on-one with a reputable healer or use recorded tracks, which you can find on YouTube or Insight Timer (Calm Whale is my go-to). For sound healers, check out Junior Valentine or Aisha Carrington if you're in London and Michelle Saudan if you're in Dubai. If you're in Kenya, get in touch with Conscious Kenya to connect with all different types of healers.

Join or Start a Community Music Group

In a 2013 study,[15] Dr David Akombo found that community djembe drumming reduced anxiety and improved academic performance for a group of adolescents. Making music together is an excellent way to boost your wellbeing and find your tribe, and it can take so many forms. You could join a church or secular choir, orchestra or traditional drumming group. If you're a cool kid, you can have jam sessions with your other cool friends. If you're less cool, karaoke. It sounds cringe, but think about it – have you ever *not* had a great time? You could also bring singing or chanting into any community rituals and ceremonies you arrange or take part in, or, at the most basic level, crank up the radio in your car during road trips and sing to your heart's content!

Raise Your Voice

A lot of us go through our days without making a huge amount of noise. We might occasionally raise our voice in an argument or moment of

---

v   Energy centres found in various parts of the body, according to a number of spiritual philosophies. Each chakra relates to different physical, mental and emotional themes – for example, the heart chakra relates to our compassion.

excitement. But pretty much we stay at the same level, and most of what we do is talking. While I'm not going to suggest you start wailing or ululating on public transport or in the middle of the working day, I *do* think we should give ourselves the space to use our voices in a different way. So, next time you're out in nature and won't be too worried about scaring the neighbours, why not try it? Scream, shout, whoop, wail, ululate, make animal noises, whatever! Just use your voice and use it AT THE TOP OF YOUR LUNGS. And notice what a release you feel afterwards.

CHAMPION SOUND

We're constantly engaging in sound healing without realising it. Whether it's screaming to deal with pain or laughing to express joy, sound is always there for us, always ready to make us feel better. By being more intentional about our sound healing practice, we can use it as a way to connect with our heritage, connect with our spirituality and connect with our innate self-healing ability. The sound of the drum, the sound of being alive, the sound of joy, the sound of home — these are what I want to fill the soundtrack of my life. How about you?

Chapter 6

CREATIVITY

'I see my artistry as a priesthood in many
ways as it allows people – including me –
to find their own pathways to healing.'

kobby ananse

The definition of 'creativity' according to the Cambridge Dictionary is 'the ability to use original and unusual ideas'. We can employ creativity in every area of our lives; nowhere have I seen more creative solutions to everyday problems than on the continent! However, viewing creativity through the lens of the arts gives us a, while not absolute, clear image of its presence in our lives and its place in our society. The arts in the African worldview are inseparable from music, as we'll see throughout the chapter. Many of the activities mentioned below – carving, cloth design, pottery – are completed sitting in one spot, with limited movement of the body; however, I think of the creativity itself as a form of movement, as flow. When we enter the flow state, we are completely absorbed in what we are doing. The outside world falls away and all that exists is us and whatever we are creating. Hours feel like minutes and the stresses of everyday life are completely and utterly transcended. So while creativity doesn't always take form as *physical* movement, I view it as an energetic flow through space and time. Creativity is the music of our Divine creative ability flowing to us and through us to manifest in this reality.

In traditional African societies, creativity as expressed through the arts held a central role in the community. In fact, links have been made between the artist and the healer in these contexts, as touched on in the previous chapter. Fast forward to today and, if you grew up in an African household like me, it's highly likely that, far from being revered, the arts were at best a hobby and at worst irrelevant. How did things change so drastically, and how can we tap into the traditional African approach to creativity and the arts to inform our modern lives?

CREATIVITY IN TRADITIONAL AFRICA

What do you think of when you read the words 'African art'? I mean, apart from the words 'stolen' and 'coloniser'. You probably imagine wooden sculptures and masks, bronze figurines, beautiful cloths and the tall, dark and handsome Rasta men who try to force their paintings on you at cultural centres across the West African coast screaming, 'Empress, looking is for free!' But the truth is, in the traditional African context, these things are not simply 'art'. Art, as we think of it today, is a Western concept. The idea of someone making something purely for it to be displayed and admired by others is not in keeping with the traditional African belief system.

The items that we might call art today – sculptures, masks, cloths – were much more meaningful. The term that Anne-Marie Deisser and Mugwima Njuguna use in their book on the cultural heritage of Kenya, 'traditional technologies', feels much more appropriate, acknowledging the skill, process, heritage and significance of these practices. In pre-colonial times, artisans, whether they were woodworkers, brassworkers, weavers or batikers, were held in high esteem in their communities, as it was understood that their abilities were truly a gift. These artisans honed their craft, often coming from a lineage of individuals doing the same work, training with elders and later passing their knowledge on to their juniors, and their creations didn't just hang up on walls or sit in glass display cabinets. They were admired and, perhaps more importantly, *utilised* by the community.

As with everything in traditional Africa, community was at the heart of art and crafting. Though the talented makers may have been celebrated as individuals, their status reflected how their creations were valued by the community. There was also a communal aspect to the actual creation of the art, with artisans gathering to work on their pieces separately but together. In his book *The Healing Wisdom of Africa*, Malidoma Patrice Somé – who transitioned into the Ancestral realm in 2021 – describes how the pottery makers in his village would sit together, singing and chanting in a circle. Music, whether through singing, clapping or rhythmic working, seems to be a natural accompaniment to labour in the traditional African context. This is something that I experience even today in Ghana, although unfortunately it's usually in the form of high-pitched, out-of-tune hymns or pop songs forced upon me while getting my hair done, waiting my turn in one government office or another or travelling in an Uber (in other words, in situations where there is no escape) – not quite as spiritual as the scenes Nana Somé describes in his book.[i] According to his account, it was only when the chanting had whipped up the required creative power that these pottery makers would start moulding their balls of clay into beautiful forms – even if that meant a whole day would go by without the mound of clay being touched. He describes the pieces produced as 'an extension of the collective energy of the circle of women'. This idea of items created by artisans being infused with some kind of spiritual or energetic power is a familiar one – like those masks we mentioned when talking about dance in Chapter 4. Many of these traditional artworks featured some kind of religious or cultural symbolism or imagery. In Ghana, for example, we still see sculptures, carvings and cloths depicting deities, Adinkra symbols and proverbs.

---

i   Nana is a title used as a sign of respect for an elder or Ancestor and is also a given name.

Not only did these pieces typically depict religious and cultural ideas or convey particular messages but they were also often used in rituals and ceremonies or placed in the home with a specific intention. For example, a wooden mask might be worn by an okomfo[ii] as he leads a ritual. Or an Akuaba doll (a traditional fertility doll) may find its way into the arms of a woman who is eager to conceive or is already pregnant and praying for a beautiful child. Adinkra cloths and, subsequently, wax prints (today popularly known as 'African'[iii] or 'Ankara' prints) famously formed a method of communicating a thousand words through only your attire. My favourite story is that of the African print cloth with an image of a bird flying out of its cage, allegedly an allusion to infidelity. Whether women wore this cloth as a threat to their husbands à la 'Date Your Fada' by Ebony (RIP) or as a way to let them know they've been caught à la 'Caught out There' by Kelis, I'm here for the highly fashionable passive aggression.

From these examples, we see that what we would call art today, while certainly admired for its beauty, was given importance because of its utility within the community. Art was functional as well as beautiful, and the artist's role was essential.

MODERN-DAY MYTHS

Like many African kids who grew up in the UK, it was made clear to me from an early age which subjects in school were important and which ones weren't (note: for some reason, A's were still expected in the apparently unimportant subjects), which career paths were accepted and which ones were absolutely out of the question. Unlike a lot of kids, I had the privilege of being encouraged in my artistic exploits by my mum who coughed

---

ii   A traditional priest in the Akan system.

iii The debate rages on about whether or not it's accurate to call these 'African'. But it rages on outside the pages of this book as we have more pressing matters and a limited word count.

up the cash for singing lessons, dance classes and other such luxuries despite us not exactly having the means, bolstering my conviction that, like Taina,[iv] I would one day see my name in lights. Unfortunately this served to make reality hit even harder when the time came to enter sixth form and not only did mother dearest refuse to sign my BRIT school[v] application (and no I couldn't have just forged it – goodie two-shoes over here) but, after promising I could study A-level drama at a 'proper' school instead, she reneged on this promise at the last minute, leaving me with a decidedly unstarry rota of maths, chemistry, economics and English literature (the one arts subject allowed into the team after much persuading and probably more than a few tears).

Why is this such a typical story in Black and Brown households? One argument is the whole 'twice as hard' thing. If by some miracle you missed that speech, it's the one where your parents tell you that you, as a person of colour, have to work twice as hard as your white peers to get half the recognition. Totally understandable since it's true – but also due to the fact that so many of the 'first-generation' Black immigrants to places like the UK left their countries as doctors, lawyers and businesspeople only to arrive in the West and be seen as unqualified even for the most entry-level roles by virtue of the colour of their skin and the assumed level of intelligence, education and authority that went with it. If that was your experience and that of your friends and siblings, of course you would want to do everything possible to ensure that your children can reclaim those roles, no questions asked.

While this theory holds water, it doesn't explain why this same obsession with children becoming doctors, lawyers and accountants is prevalent on the continent too. My few years of schooling in Ghana effectively constituted an artistic wasteland, where art and drama were entirely

---

iv   The title character in a Nickelodeon TV show that fuelled my wayward dreams.

v   The UK school of choice for future stars, attended by some of your faves like Adele, Amy Winehouse (RIP), Raye, FKA Twigs and Spiderman (Tom Holland)!

missing from the curriculum and 'Music and Dance' was more like a lacklustre pop-up event than an actual subject. Even today, the aunties look extremely unimpressed when I tell them I'm a healer (depending on the auntie, I might have to replace this with 'yoga teacher' or 'I run wellness events') and writer. Sometimes there's a glimmer of hope when they think I might be a journalist for some important establishment like the BBC, but once I clarify that I'm not, that hope dies faster than iPhone batteries when a new model comes out. Since there's no history of immigration and subsequent mismatch between capability and employment opportunities here, what's the story?

Tradition as a whole took a hit in Africa in the days of the coloniser. This is a theme that will continue to come up throughout the book because the damage is so far-reaching. But why should an assault on traditional arts cause the perception of any artist or creative, regardless of medium, to have fallen so far? Deisser and Njuguna explain that 'after the suppression of the traditional industries, the [Western or missionary school] educated took the roles of clerks and teachers and thus, the Africans reinterpreted schools and Christianity to mean non-manual employment, modernity and progress'. In other words, the place of an artist is solidified in the psyche of a whole generation of Africans as bottom of the barrel. As a well-to-do, God-fearing, modern African, it would bring shame on your family to engage in a career as lowly as, for example, storytelling (sorry, family).

This fall from grace of artisans from their standing in African communities has serious implications, and I'm not just talking about the fact that I can't find a woodworker who is both talented *and* able to stick to deadlines. Our present-day frenzied focus on academic achievement and the landing of 'good' jobs is the denigration of the arts among a people for whom the role of the artist was once comparable with the role of a healer, or in today's consciousness, a doctor. There's, of course, nothing wrong with being academic or having the kind of job that makes other people's parents ask them why they can't be more like you. But the arts and, more broadly, creativity are essential to so many aspects of who we are and who we want to become: our wellbeing, our tolerance, our innovation, our ability to make the world a better place. And so it follows that these are the very same things we will lose if we don't restore art and creativity to their former glory.

And what of those families who produced generation after generation of carvers, sculptors, weavers and leather workers? If these technologies are seen as less than, then for how much longer will they be safeguarded? If the products of these technologies continue to be seen as lesser alternatives to Western goods, then how can we hope to restore Indigenous artists to their former economic and social glory? At the time of writing, the Centre for National Culture (colloquially known as the Arts Centre) in Accra, where so many artisans hone their craft and make their living, faces demolition to make space for luxury beachfront apartments. The colonial-era dismissal of the arts continues to have a devastating effect on our culture and our people.

Future Ancestor: Kobina Ankomah Graham

Kobina is a writer, creative and educator of Akan heritage currently living in Ghana. His work is rooted in community and culture and guided by his intended legacy of doing his part to expand our collective empathy and social imagination. Discussing the question of 'what is African art?', Kobina says, *'All the things we describe now as African art weren't designed to be hung on walls; the masks were for ceremonies, the drums were for ceremonies, everything was functional, and so the artist had a role within society that was not just valued, but sacred.'*

In response to the shift in perception of the arts, he says, *'In order to have empathy, people have to be able to imagine themselves in other people's shoes. The thing that feeds imagination is arts and culture. When you take away people's ability to imagine themselves beyond their walls, you kill empathy. One of the things we need to do if we're going to move anywhere close to where we [pre-colonial African communities] were socially is to place incredible value on arts and culture.'*

CREATIVITY AND WELLBEING

The link between creativity and wellbeing is well documented. When patients present with low mood, doctors often advise them to engage in arts and crafts, among other things. There is a whole school of psychology dedicated to art therapy, and creative pursuits like writing and improv have been shown to promote healing.

Crafting is interesting because it is often paired with the arts – arts and crafts – but also requires seemingly less creativity and more process. In fact, one of the reasons that crafting is so good for wellbeing is because of the repetition of the process. As you knead the shea butter or weave the basket, the repetition of the movement lulls you into a sort of trance, almost like a meditative state. Of course, that's not to say that creativity cannot feature in crafting. Basket weavers are constantly coming up with new designs, and it is thanks to creativity that we now have lemongrass-infused shea butter! But unlike with painting or poetry, for example, the creativity involved in crafting tends to be more high level, while the moment-to-moment act of crafting involves process, precision and repetition. Whether through performing arts, crafting or any other form of creativity, there are benefits for us as individuals and as a society.

Belonging

The image of the pottery women sitting in a circle together singing, laughing and creating brings me such joy. If we take this communal approach to creativity, whether in brainstorming business ideas, making music or doing pottery, what we're ultimately doing is joining together to create, to bring something to life. Creativity is already a Divine process when we do it individually – levelling up the energy by working together can not only have a positive impact on whatever you're working on but also create deep bonds and feelings of support among the group.

As I write this chapter, I'm at a writers' residency in Nigeria, the second residency I've had the privilege to attend in recent months. While neither residency has required us to collaborate on a piece together, simply being present with other writers, sharing the process, bouncing ideas off each other, working in silence separately but together – all of these subtle yet impactful events have made this book-writing journey a lot less lonely.

Communication and Self-expression

Creativity allows us to find new ways of expressing ourselves. It gives us the opportunity to present emotions, ideas and knowledge that might otherwise remain buried behind the failings of plain language and non-artistic communication. When we feel heard, seen, understood, it does wonders for our wellbeing. But we cannot be heard, seen or understood if we cannot express ourselves. By cultivating creativity and art in our children, we give them the tools to express what may be too abstract or too painful to state simply. By giving ourselves permission as adults to rediscover creative outlets, experiences that lie dusty and dejected in our subconscious suddenly see a tunnel through which they can crawl into the light of our awareness. Creativity gives us a tool with which to explore our shadow, pull thoughts, feelings and memories out of it and give them the attention we weren't willing or able to give all those years ago. Even if we don't get into all that shadow work, self-expression in itself is healing. And, on a more practical level, the better we are able to express ourselves, the more fulfilled we will be in our relationships, our jobs and our lives.

Empathy

Creativity has been shown to increase empathy, perhaps because it gets us into the habit of thinking differently and helps us imagine life beyond our own personal experience. What kind of society are we left with if empathy goes down the drain? Probably one not too far off the one we have now! Increased empathy is good on a personal level. If we are more empathetic, we will experience more ease in making and keeping friends, and generally find it easier to navigate the world. But, as Kobina stressed to me in our conversation, empathy is good – no, crucial – on a community level too. In a community rooted in empathy, parliamentary bills determining who can love and how wouldn't be entertained, let alone passed. In a community rooted in empathy, children wouldn't be strip-searched in an establishment designed to educate and protect them. In a community rooted in empathy, treatment of refugees would not be adjusted according to the shade of their skin. An empathetic community leaves less room for hate, toxic competitiveness and violence and more room for understanding, care and communal wellbeing.

Self-esteem

The pride, joy and – sometimes – disbelief that accompanies seeing your ideas morph into reality is unrivalled. In 2017, I had an idea for yoga shorts and pants that would be made with African print fabric. In 2018, I had a stall in Spitalfields Market for a day for a Pop Up Africa event, selling these real, physical items that had once simply been an idea in my head. Before then and since then, there are many more crazy ideas I've pulled out of my head and into a reality where other people can see, feel and experience them too, but the novelty never wears off. This book was an idea in my head... and now you're reading it. It's wild!

Whether your creativity leads to a change in process at work, a new logo for a client or an exhibition filled with images that once lived in your head, the knowledge that you have the capacity to bring ideas to life will boost your overall self-esteem, a key factor in overall wellbeing.

Trance and Meditation

As with dance, losing yourself in creativity or crafting can help you to tap out of the stresses of everyday life for a moment of calm. It's no wonder that, in the wake of the COVID-19 pandemic, people across the world turned to activities like knitting and jewellery-making to cope. A 2022 study published in the *Behavioral Sciences* journal[16] found that people who engaged in everyday creative activities during the pandemic experienced higher levels of self-esteem, optimism and positivity. Making time for creative exploits – enough time to get lost in them for a while – will help us better handle whatever life throws at us – from global catastrophes to toxic bosses.

READY TO RETURN?

When the kente weaver sits at his loom, he isn't doing it for his wellbeing. When the shea butter maker starts kneading, she isn't doing it to boost her mood. However, knowing what we know about the link between creativity and wellbeing, we can look to these traditional technologies in our quest to connect with wellness in an African-centred way. In bringing more creativity into our lives, we mustn't underestimate all the areas outside of arts and crafts where we can inject this energy: within your corporate job, in your daily routine, in your spiritual practice. Here are a few ideas.

CREATIVITY PRACTICES FOR THE MODERN AFRICAN

Express Creativity in Your Everyday Life

I read once that making small changes in the mundane, everyday tasks we complete can help us be more creative. Driving a different route to work, sleeping on the opposite side of the bed, writing with the 'wrong' hand. Even though these things sound simple, they require your brain to work a bit harder and get out of autopilot. Taking this idea a bit further, we can learn to express creativity within the confines of our existing tasks and habits. Some ideas are:

- Creativity at work – This could look like improving existing systems, finding creative ways to visualise data and reports or engaging in more cross-team collaboration.

- Creativity at home – You could move the furniture round in one of your rooms (sounds small, but it can transform a space!), get more adventurous in your cooking or simply change how you *use* the space – for example, actually eating at the dining table instead of in front of the TV.

- Creativity in your thinking – Get into the habit of challenging your thinking and seeing things from a different perspective.

Start a New Creative Hobby

If you've been reading this chapter and thinking to yourself, 'Damn, I drank the Kool-Aid!', you're probably not alone. Even if the most creative thing you've done in the last ten years is your accounting, your inner artist is in there somewhere. Think back to what you enjoyed doing as a child and that's probably the answer to your innate creative talent. Otherwise, here are some ideas to get you started:

- Writing – especially great because it's free!

- Jewellery-making – to utilise traditional materials, you could work with beads, wood or cowries.

- Hair styling – another nod to our ancestors, this will give you a creative outlet *and* save you the money and stress of visiting auntie's hair shop. Visit my girl Asia's Instagram profile @wild_moon for mad inspiration.

- Make music – we explored the healing power of sound in the previous chapter. Building on this, you could also use making music as your creative outlet, whether that looks like writing songs, playing an instrument or producing music electronically.

- Upcycle to turn trash into treasure – In today's world where we are facing huge amounts of waste destroying our environment, upcycling is an excellent way to create something new without creating new waste. I've seen people turn plastic water sachets into bags, plastic bottles into pencil cases, old tyres into furniture, glass bottles into vases... the options are endless!

Create with the Community in Mind

When I spoke to Kobina, he said, 'Whenever I think about the thing that Africa can export to the world, I think about communal thinking, and how it shifts the way in which we approach so many things.' Bringing this energy of communal thinking to your creative practice could manifest as:

- creating with friends, family or a physical or virtual group

- creating items that you'll gift to members of your community

- using your creative skills to give back, perhaps through skills-sharing workshops.

Ritualise Your Creative Sessions

Before I sit down to write, I meditate, pray and invite my Higher Soul, my Ancestors or a particular Ancestor/energy to be present with me and support me in my endeavours. Not only does this help me create the right space and state of mind in which to work but it also supports me in creating good content. I know it does because of the many times I've had writer's block or screwed up my face while reading my work back, then realised, *ohhh, I forgot to do my ritual*. Deisser and Njuguna say that, traditionally, the creative process of Kenyan artisans 'always demand[s] that the artisan invokes the intervention of supernatural powers through rituals and sacrifices as forms of prayer in order to have a successful production'. And they ain't lyyyyin'.

Your ritual doesn't have to be anything fancy or long. It might include meditation, prayer, invocation, singing/chanting/humming, breathwork, stretching, intention setting, positive affirmations or preparing your physical space. The most important thing is that it makes you feel inspired and ready for action.

SORE (REMIX)

Creativity is central to progress, and yet we seem to be placing more and more value on logic, obedience, falling in line – especially in our education systems. While this thought system left behind as residue from the colonial virus is an excellent approach to creating a society of cogs that will keep the well-oiled machine of capitalism going, it's not the path to freedom or enlightenment. We need to wake up[vi] to the role creativity has to play in our elevation. As individuals, creativity is our tool for connecting with the Divine within us and we must protect it fiercely. As a community, creativity is the only thing that can save us.

---

vi   Or in Akan 'sore', pronounced sor-RIH.

If we are to restore the arts, our clearest expression of creativity, to the position they once held in our minds and by extension create a more empathetic community – and world – we each have a part to play. We need to make space for creativity to flow through us more often, make music a part of daily life and allow creative expression to move our mind, body and soul – but it goes beyond our own creative exploits. How we engage with creative professionals, how we talk about creativity, how we fight for the return of stolen artefacts, how we nurture (or kill) creativity in our children – these all have an impact on a scale larger than we might realise. It's up to each of us to make a conscious effort to give creativity and the arts the respect and attention they deserve.

Part III
MOTHER EARTH

Asase Yɛ Duru – 'The Earth has weight.'

Mother Earth, Asase Yaa, is the sustainer of life. She has provided us with all we need and continues to support and protect us. Without her, there is no life.

Chapter 7

HERBS

*'Many healing modalities are imported but
herbal healing has been here in Africa from the
beginning. We believe in the power of herbs.'*

Yetunde Fatima Ayeola

Mother Earth has given us everything we need to survive. And yet African traditional medicine is often maligned and tarred as 'backwards' in favour of Western medicine while, simultaneously, Western adoption of naturopathy and its Eastern variants such as Traditional Chinese Medicine and Ayurveda continues to rise. Part of the challenge is that herbal medicine in an African context is usually seen as inseparable from 'witch doctors' and traditional priests, causing many religious Africans of other faiths to shy away from it. True, on the continent, herbal medicine is still widely used and accepted, with as much as 85 per cent[17] of the population consulting traditional medicine practitioners for their ills – but that is often out of necessity rather than choice.

In the global context, African herbalism doesn't enjoy the same recognition as comparable Eastern systems such as Ayurveda from India and Traditional Chinese Medicine, perhaps partly because these systems are much easier to give credence to due to their systematic approach and the wealth of written content available. African traditional medicine on the other hand, like so much of our knowledge, is predominantly passed down through oral tradition and apprenticeships, and is safeguarded (or in some opinions, gatekept) by healers and spiritual leaders. But we don't need to be initiated into a secret society or consult the local priestess to start benefiting from the medicine that Mother Earth provides. And the truth is that herbal healing and Western medicine don't need to be an either-or situation. They can complement each other, and the power of herbal healing can easily be incorporated into your healthy living routine.

TRADITIONAL HERBAL MEDICINE IN AFRICA

Just like the African worldview itself, African healing has always taken a holistic approach. It can be traced back to ancient Egypt, a civilisation that some say produced the first doctors and physicians. Their knowledge and application of herbal medicine can be seen from the records transcribed onto walls and papyrus, such as the Ebers Papyrus. Dated to 1500BC it is believed to be the oldest surviving medical document, detailing the medical application of plant medicines that are familiar to us today such as aloe, cannabis, fennel, opium and thyme. According to accomplished academic, Kofi Busia's (not that Kofi Busia) text *Fundamentals of Herbal Medicine: History, Phytopharmacology and Phytotherapeutics Vol. 1*, the role of traditional healer in Kemet fell to the oracles and seers. When we examine the role of the village healers through time in Africa, we can see that this pattern was – and is – evident across the continent. Whether Southern African sangomas, West African okomfos and babalawos, or East African mugwenus, their services to the community reflect the modern-day doctor, midwife, religious leader and therapist all in one. A person might visit a traditional healer with complaints as far-ranging as headaches, marriage problems, infertility or joblessness. Traditional medicine recognises that, since our ailments are a result of both seen and unseen forces, the solutions require treatment of the mind, body and soul, with application in the physical world and the spirit world. Busia describes an appropriate treatment, in the eyes of a traditional healer, to be one that is 'valued for its therapeutic effect as well as its symbolic and spiritual significance'.

Far from being superstitious nonsense, traditional medicine in pre-colonial Africa was advanced, with surgeries being performed as far back as Ancient Egyptian times. Busia states, 'Africans were also known to practise variolation, a traditional form of inoculation against diseases such as yaws and smallpox, centuries before Jenner (father of immunology)'. He particularly highlights the ancient kingdoms and empires of Asante (modern-day Ghana), Benin (modern-day Nigeria), Borno (modern-day Niger, Cameroon, Chad and Nigeria), Ethiopia (modern-day Ethiopia and Eritrea), Jukun (modern-day Nigeria), Monomotapa (modern-day Zimbabwe and Mozambique), Mali (modern-day Senegal, Mauritania, Mali, Burkina Faso, Niger, Gambia, Guinea-Bissau, Guinea, Ivory Coast and Ghana) Nubia (modern-day Sudan and Egypt), Nri (modern-day Nigeria), Nupe (modern-day Nigeria), Oyo (modern-day Nigeria) and Songhai (modern-day Niger, Mali, Mauritania, Senegal, Nigeria, Guinea, Gambia, Algeria, Burkina Faso and Ivory Coast) for their remarkability in traditional healing. While traditional medicine incorporates more than just herbs, plant medicines have played a central part in this form of healing for centuries. Seeing them as much more than just an ingredient in medicines, traditional healers are in tune with the spirits of the plant world and petition for their support in the healing process. You're unlikely to see a healer simply grab a fistful of leaves and hand them over. Ritual and incantation are vital tools used to transform the herbs from their dormant state into one infused with healing energy specifically targeting the client's concerns. Again, this speaks to the all-encompassing approach of traditional medicine, which looks far beyond just the physical.

Maintaining this theme of holism, plants used in herbal medicine are usually fully utilised; the bark, leaves, flowers, roots and seeds all typically have different applications, ensuring that no part of the plant goes to waste. Despite the moniker 'herbal medicine', the plants used extend far beyond just the herb family – this is why you may find spices, fruits and even salt included in herbal prescriptions. Busia notes that the methods of administering herbal medicines can reflect the practices used in Western medicine – orally, nasally, rectally or topically – but also at times differ greatly, with medicines being 'worn as amulets, necklaces, or as talismans around the waist or ankles... hung on doors and windows or placed under a mat or pillow or some obscure place in the house'. These applications are usually focused on the spiritual aspect of treatment.

Unfortunately, it is this same holistic nature that led to the demonisation of our traditional medicine practices. With the Christianisation of the continent during the slave trade and colonialism, traditional medicine was demonised along with other healer practices – from divination to ritual. Under colonial rule, the derision and, in some cases, outright criminalisation of witchcraft extended to 'witch doctors', with a devastating effect on traditional medicine in Africa. When we think of the Christian assault on African countries, we often centre it on religion, but it was truly an assault on our whole way of being. To be Christian in colonial Africa meant not only to learn to speak English but also to receive a 'proper' education, 'proper' healthcare and access to modern technologies. It meant to be saved, which implies that what our ancestors needed saving from was their demonic religion and its associated barbaric language, lack of education, substandard healthcare and 'backwards' way of living. It seems that, even as Western powers flipped the script on herbal healing in the 20th century, recognising its potential positive impact in developing countries, this public perception of it being inferior to Western medicine has persisted, and perhaps even become more prevalent.

In the Americas, the demonisation of all things African was no less brutal, but it's beautiful to see how, instead of allowing it to entirely overshadow the traditional ways, the Ancestors found a way to syncretise. African Diasporic religions and spiritual paths such as Santería, Umbanda and

Vodou allowed for what may have looked purely Catholic on the outside in order to preserve the spirit of African tradition and beliefs at its core. As well as our traditional religions, kidnapped Africans transported with them seeds and knowledge of herbal healing, and, according to Busia, 'Slaves were allowed or even encouraged to rely on their own healing devices.' It is perhaps due both to the syncretisation of African religions into Diasporic religions, which allowed them to thrive – of course, not without the challenges of demonisation, appropriation and other inevitables of Black and Latinx life in white America – and the ability of displaced Africans to practise herbal medicine openly that, today, botanicas are easily found in certain cities across the States in a way that they simply aren't in the UK. A botanica is a spiritual shop that sells herbs, candles and other spiritual tools, typically associated with the African Diasporic religions. On my hunt for a true botanica in London – not the many white-owned naturopathic shops popping up under this name – I found only one in (where else?) Brixton. If it's still in the same place, you can find it at Market Row, under the arches.

MODERN-DAY MYTHS

In the African belief system, it is important for us to live in alignment with the cosmos, and I believe this includes living a life that recognises and seeks to engage with the globalisation and technological advancement of the world instead of fighting against it. Unlike some other worldviews, the African is not concerned with overtaking, replacing or 'winning' but rather with harmony and dynamism. With this in mind, you won't find me trying to convince you to entirely reject Western medicine in favour of traditional herbal medicine. But we must recognise that, as Black people, Western medicine is failing us.

According to the World Bank, in Sub-Saharan Africa, the ratio of medical doctors to people is two to 10,000 compared to 49 to 10,000 in European Union countries. In an interview Dr Michael Obeng, the cosmetic surgeon who found internet fame after removing Gorilla Glue from Tessica Brown's hair, said that the State of New York has more Ghanaian doctors than the country of Ghana itself. You may think this lack of doctors is due to poor education systems or a small talent pool. And of course, you'd be entirely wrong. The issue isn't that African countries aren't training doctors – they are training plenty! The issue is that these doctors are leaving. According to a 2015 study,[18] in the 10 years between 2005 and 2015, the brain drain equated to one African-educated doctor per day migrating from the continent to the USA, with the majority hailing from Egypt, Nigeria, South Africa, Ethiopia and Ghana. So why are they leaving? As well as pursuing further study and specialisation, a major push factor is what doctors face once they graduate. I can only imagine the trauma of consistently seeing patients deteriorate and perish when you *know* you could save them if you just had this particular machine or these particular conditions or this many more hours of sleep. Many healthcare professionals on the continent working in government-led facilities work in less-than-optimal conditions because they lack the financial and human resources (that pesky brain drain again) needed to provide the level of care they were trained to. To add insult to injury, their pay packet – to put it lightly – isn't worth the stress. So even the doctors most dedicated to making a difference in their communities can eventually find themselves burnt-out and disillusioned, jumping on a flight to countries like the USA or France, where they'll be paid a huge premium for their abilities and have the resources to make their work easier and more effective. So yes, despite nurturing and training enough doctors, Africa has a lack of doctors in the workforce. Add to this lack the fact that medical care is often expensive and concentrated in more urban areas, and it's clear that the medical system is not robust enough to serve all Africans, which is why so many, especially people in lower income brackets or living in rural areas, turn to herbal medicine.

In the Diaspora, the systems are there. You would be forgiven for thinking Black people in Western countries don't need herbal medicine. Doctors, hospitals, and pharmaceutical medicine abound. But so does institutional racism. Black women in Britain are more than four times more likely than white women to die during childbirth,[19] while in the USA, they are three times more likely than white women to die.[20] Black people and people of colour are more likely to be put straight on to medication in instances where lifestyle changes should be – and are for white counterparts – the first port of call. The root of these issues is clear – these institutions are made for and, in the vast majority, run by white people, with people of colour being an afterthought, if not a nuisance. In 2022, my mum – who pours love and labour into a National Health Service (NHS) that does not love her back – became the UK's third-ever Black diabetes nurse consultant. This is the highest level a nurse can get to – one where they can influence strategy and process – while still working directly with patients. Diabetes is a condition that disproportionately affects Black people. So why, out of about 30 nurse consultant positions and more than two decades of the role being in existence, have there only ever been three who are Black: the first appointed in the early 2000s and now retired, the second appointed in 2017 and the latest in 2022?

These challenges are not going to be overcome any time soon. There needs to be a serious shift in how African doctors are incentivised and supported to stay in their home countries, with governments putting their politricks aside to really invest in healthcare systems instead of inviting the Diaspora to return to a home that can only be lived in comfortably with a foreign income. Institutions like the NHS cannot make meaningful change with the horde of (mostly white) dinosaurs that retain their positions at the top while holding the door open only for people who look, sound and act like them. The journey to change – for both the continent and the Diaspora – is a long one, which begs the question, how can traditional healing complement Western medicine to fill in these gaps? To answer this, we first need to understand the correct application of herbal medicine.

Use Case

It's important to note that just as Western medicine isn't always the answer, herbal medicine isn't always the answer either, as set out by the table below.

HERBAL MEDICINE	WESTERN MEDICINE
Preventative – should be used to treat ill health *and* promote good health	Reactive – should be used only to treat ill health
First choice for chronic conditions, i.e., ongoing illnesses that require control rather than cure and minor acute conditions, e.g., headache	First choice for major acute conditions, i.e., severe with a sudden onset, e.g., a broken bone
Tolerance doesn't seem to be a problem, allowing for long-term use without severe side effects	Drug tolerance leads to the constant increase in dosage of medicines, increasing the likelihood of addiction and overdose, along with physical side effects

The World Health Organization defines health as 'a state of complete physical, mental and social well-being and not merely the absence of disease or infirmity'. Herbal healing is an excellent tool for promoting good health. Incorporating different herbs into our wellness routine can help us stave off colds and flus, fatigue, bloating and lots of other regular complaints. For more serious complaints, such as chronic conditions, it is best to consult a herbal medicine specialist. While traditional African healers still hold this knowledge, there are also many specialists who learned herbal healing in a classroom or apprenticeship setting and practise herbal medicine without other aspects of traditional medicine like divination and ritual. So whatever your beliefs, you can find a herbal specialist to suit you.

Research

There is a misconception that just because a treatment is natural it is safe. Herbal medicines are potent and should be approached with the same level of precaution as pharmaceuticals. In fact, many pharmaceuticals are derived from natural ingredients.

- Aspirin is made with salicin, a compound derived from willow bark.

- Morphine and codeine are derived from the opium poppy.

- Oncovin, a chemotherapy drug, is made with vincristine, a compound derived from Madagascar periwinkle.

- Many sedatives and antianxiety medications contain valepotriate, a compound derived from valerian.

If you want to get started with DIY herbal healing, it's important you do your research. Check online the qualities of the herb, its typical uses, any side effects to be aware of and the recommended dosage. While much African herbal knowledge has been confirmed by modern science, some remedies are dismissed by the scientific community as being 'not well researched'. But what better research is there than literal centuries of in-community testing? If you can't find the information you need on a herb, the good news is that testing in small doses is unlikely to cause you any harm. As long as you start small and track the effects, experimenting with herbs can be a great way to come up with your own home remedies.

Dosage

Yes, it is possible to overdose in herbal medicine, causing everything from stomach upsets to insomnia. If you're using herbs for promotion of good health rather than treatment of ill health, you're unlikely to go over the maximum safe dosage. When treating a complaint like a headache, again you're unlikely to use too much, but to be on the safe side, check dosages online or with your local herbalist. Treating more serious complaints like hypertension is best done with the support of an experienced healer.

This issue of dosage is where essential oils can often get people into trouble. They are a highly concentrated product, which is both a blessing and a curse. A blessing because one bottle of lemon essential oil will obviously last you much longer than a tub of fresh lemons would. A curse because it's easy to become too heavy-handed with these oils, which will lead to adverse reactions. Numbers vary, but it's estimated that it takes somewhere between 50 and 75 lemons to create one 15 ml bottle of lemon essential oil. That means there's the power of up to a quarter of a lemon in just one single drop. When using essential oils in herbal healing, always follow the guidance on the bottle or in any recipes you might be following. But as a general rule, for one-time or short-term use, one drop will take you far. For cooking up a batch of something – for example, a tub of infused shea butter to last you a month or so – three to five drops should be fine. It is rare that you'll ever need more than five to 10 drops of an essential oil in one go. It's best to mix your essential oil into a carrier oil like coconut or castor before applying it directly onto your skin, and always do a patch test first.

I've seen that people use essential oils in cooking and there was even a trend a while back of using lemon essential oil in drinking water instead of a slice of lemon. I tend to shy away from taking essential oils internally, again, because of their potency. The closest I get to that is using peppermint and tea tree essential oil in my homemade mouthwash – anything that involves actually ingesting the oils, I would avoid with the same vim I use to avoid doTerra salespeople.

Interactions

Just as some medications shouldn't be taken together, herbal remedies can have negative interactions with some pharmaceuticals. Interactions occur when a medicine causes either enhanced or reduced effectiveness of another medicine being taken at the same time, potentially leading to serious side effects. I remember when I was prescribed antidepressants, grapefruit was not allowed. In fact, avoiding grapefruit was stressed more than avoiding alcohol! It turns out that grapefruit interacts with quite a few medications, causing increased blood levels of the substance, as it affects its ability to break down.[21] This leads to an increase in the efficacy of the medication, causing heightened side effects. There's a lot of information available online about drug and herb interactions, and always be sure to inform your healers of all medication you're taking, including herbal.

Quality

One of the challenges with herbal medicine is that it is a largely unregulated field, leaving room for poor-quality or even harmful products. That's why I prefer to use herbal healing as a DIY tool, purchasing individual food-grade herbs, spices and essential oils and using them to make my own remedies, and growing my own herbs (or at least trying to). With this approach, you have more control in terms of the quality of the ingredients and the strength of the concoction. If purchasing premade herbal remedies, for example, tonics and capsules, be sure to buy from reputable or recommended sources and take note of the dosage advice.

Pregnancy

Again, as with pharmaceutical medicines, always discuss herbal remedies with a healer before taking them if you're pregnant, planning to become pregnant, or if you're breastfeeding.

HERBS AND WELLBEING

Okay, I know what you're thinking. It feels like you need a PhD in herbal healing before you can even think about getting started. With all this wahala,[i] you might be wondering, 'why bother?' If pharmaceuticals are derived from plants anyway, and herbal healing carries many of the same risks and considerations as Western medicine, then what's the point in choosing the natural path? Again, I'm by no means advocating that Western medicine be completely thrown away, but here are the reasons why next time you have stomach cramps, you might reach for peppermint instead of paracetamol.

Avoid Addiction

Some pharmaceutical drugs come with the risk of dependency or addiction, most notably opioids, antianxiety medications, sedatives and stimulants. Herbal alternatives don't carry the same risk.

Avoid Side Effects

As mentioned, herbal medicine does also come with side effects but typically at higher doses, whereas with pharmaceuticals, side effects can kick in after even just one pill. Isolation of the active compound from others in the plant can be the cause of some of the negative side effects associated with pharmaceuticals. For example, while aspirin can cause the lining of the stomach to bleed, this doesn't happen with willow bark, as other compounds in the bark prevent it.

---

i   Pidgin term that means 'trouble'.

Manage Chronic Pain

The National Institute for Health and Care Excellence (NICE) stipulates that paracetamol and opioids such as codeine must not be prescribed to manage chronic pain.[22] In fact, any pharmacological intervention is seen as a last resort, with exercise, lifestyle changes and even acupuncture being recommended first. Herbal remedies can be an excellent tool for managing chronic pain – you'll find examples in the next section.

Overall Wellbeing

When you take a pharmaceutical, the compounds have been isolated to perform a very specific action. So you get relief from your complaint but no other benefits. With herbal medicine, the treatment generally has multiple benefits, giving you an overall boost to your health as well as addressing the original complaint.

Self-Esteem

Feeling unwell inevitably comes with a sense of helplessness and self-pity, and with good reason too! These feelings are only made worse in instances where you have to travel far or wait a long time to see a healthcare professional. Making herbal remedies your first port of call can help you take back control of your health, ensuring that you feel equipped with the tools necessary to get better faster.

Future Ancestor: Yetunde Fatima Ayeola

Yetunde is a naturopath in training whom I had the good fortune to meet while I was in Nigeria for my writers' residency. She was visiting Iseyin, where I was staying, for specialist training. In the 30 minutes I spent with her, aside from crushing me by reading me like a book and telling me I need to reduce my plantain intake, she dropped some major gems! She said, *'Herbal healers don't just treat symptoms – we treat the root cause. There are so many different things that can cause a headache, for example. Instead of just giving paracetamol, we do tests and a consultation, and then put together herbs that will treat the root cause.'*

Her top tips for DIY herbal healing might surprise you:

- Water is the first port of call for herbal healing. Start your day with two glasses of warm water to flush out the toxins produced by your body during its increased healing while you were asleep.

- Our melatonin naturally peaks between 10 p.m. and 2 a.m. for most people, so try to ensure you sleep between these hours for maximum healing.

- If you make a herbal remedy, you probably don't need to drink more than 15 ml (a shot glass) a few times a day. Don't drink mugs and mugs of, for example, Neem tea if you have malaria.

- Blended watermelon (including the seeds) with a thumb of ginger is a quick and easy immune booster you can have up to four times a week.

- Don't boil any herbs for more than 15 minutes; otherwise, it breaks down the chemicals you need.

READY TO RETURN?

Many treatments that have been part of our healing repertoire for centuries – salt baths, yoni steams, fasting, cannabis – are becoming fast favourites in the Western wellness industry, and making (mostly white, mostly male) people millions in the process. Herbal healing is a practice we can and should reclaim and reconnect with for ourselves, for our loved ones and, yes, once you gain the proper knowledge, for going where the money reside![ii] In the following section, I'll introduce you to some herbs and their benefits.

AFRICAN HERBS AND THEIR BENEFITS

It is estimated that there are over 5,000 medicinal herbs being used in Africa – and this is probably a conservative figure. Here, I'll share some of the more popular plant medicines found on the continent and their healing properties (*see table on pages 122–124*). Some of this information you can put to use right away – for example, making a rooibos tea to ease indigestion. However, for more serious treatments, please conduct deeper research and speak with your healer or physician. You'll notice some herbs listed have anticancer properties, which means that studies have shown they are able to inhibit the growth of cancer cells. This doesn't endorse self-medicating but rather advocates for adding these herbs to your diet as a preventative measure, and in the case of potential treatment, making further investigations and having discussions with your medical team, especially if you are already taking any other medication.

OTHER HERBS AND THEIR BENEFITS

Wherever you are in the world, there are herbal remedies that you probably already have sitting in your cupboard or growing in your garden. If you happen to be in the African Diaspora, where it might be more difficult to source some of the herbs in the previous section, here are some of the most widely available herbs and their benefits (*see table on pages 125–127*).

---

ii   A phrase popularised by a viral video featuring the most effective money mantra I've come across and a highly dedicated car salesperson.

AFRICAN HERBS AND THEIR BENEFITS

HERB	PART OF PLANT	PROPERTIES	USE CASE	POTENTIAL SIDE EFFECTS IN SMALL DOSES
Abeduru (Turkey berries)	Leaves, stems and fruit	Analgesic, anti-inflammatory, antimicrobial, antioxidant, expectorant	Anaemia, cough- and phlegm-related conditions, diarrhoea, inflammation, pain, stomachache	Unlikely
African basil (Akoko mesa/Akoko besa)	Leaves	Antibacterial, antioxidant	Common cold and infections	Unlikely
Bay leaf*	Leaves	Antibacterial, anticancer, antimicrobial, antioxidant	Blocked sinuses, upset stomach	Unlikely
Buchu	Leaves	Antiseptic, carminative, diuretic	Common cold, IBS (irritable bowel syndrome), UTI (urinary tract infection)	Stomach upset
Devil's claw	Roots	Analgesic, anti-inflammatory	Back pain, headache, osteoarthritis, rheumatoid arthritis and other inflammatory conditions	Diarrhoea and indigestion

(continued)

AFRICAN HERBS AND THEIR BENEFITS (CONTINUED)

HERB	PART OF PLANT	PROPERTIES	USE CASE	POTENTIAL SIDE EFFECTS IN SMALL DOSES
Ginger	Root	Antibacterial, anticancer, antidiabetic, anti-inflammatory, antioxidant, expectorant	Common cold, constipation, cough- and phlegm-related conditions, fatigue, hypertension, indigestion, menstrual pain, muscle pain, nausea (especially good for morning sickness), osteoarthritis, Type 2 diabetes	Heartburn, diarrhoea, low blood pressure, stomach upset
Hibiscus (Sobolo/ Sorrell/ Wanjo)	Flowers	Antibacterial, antidiabetic, antioxidant	Hypertension, Type 2 diabetes	Low blood pressure
Hwentia (Grains of Selim)	Fruit/pods and seeds	Antibacterial, antimicrobial	Respiratory conditions, toothache	Unlikely
Moringa	Leaves and seeds	Anticancer, antidepressant, antifungal, anti-inflammatory, antioxidant, antiviral	Arthritis, constipation, hypertension, low mood, viruses and infections	Low blood pressure

(continued)

AFRICAN HERBS AND THEIR BENEFITS (CONTINUED)

HERB	PART OF PLANT	PROPERTIES	USE CASE	POTENTIAL SIDE EFFECTS IN SMALL DOSES
Neem	Bark, leaves, flowers and seeds	Antibacterial, anticancer, antifungal, anti-inflammatory, antimalarial, antimicrobial, antiparasitic	Acne, dandruff, gingivitis, malaria	May lower sperm count (unsurprising as it has been studied as a potentially effective natural contraceptive)
Prekese (Oshosho/ Aidan fruit)	Fruit/pods	Antidiabetic, anti-inflammatory, antioxidant, antimicrobial	Common cold, diarrhoea, fever, hypertension, skin infections, Type 2 diabetes, vomiting	Low blood pressure
Rooibos (Red bush)	Leaves and stems	Antidiabetic, anti-inflammatory, antioxidant and antispasmodic	Hay fever, indigestion, Type 2 diabetes	Unlikely
Tiger nut (Chufa)	Tubers	Antibacterial, antidiabetic, antioxidant, aphrodisiac	Constipation, erectile dysfunction, indigestion, low sex drive, Type 2 diabetes	Gas and bloating
Turmeric	Root	Antibacterial, anticancer, anti-inflammatory, antimicrobial, antioxidant	Acne, hay fever, IBS, osteoarthritis, pain, rheumatoid arthritis	Stomach upset, diarrhoea

* I'm not sure if bay leaf is technically African but, as a global Black population, we've definitely embraced it as if it is!

OTHER HERBS AND THEIR BENEFITS

HERB	PART OF PLANT	PROPERTIES	USE CASE	POTENTIAL SIDE EFFECTS IN SMALL DOSES
Cannabis (you would be forgiven for thinking this is African. It's actually native to Asia *but* Africans were the first to smoke it)	Leaves, flowers (buds)	Anticancer, anti-inflammatory, antioxidant	Chronic pain, depression, hypertension, IBS, insomnia, stress and anxiety	Hallucinogenic effects, which can be minimised by taking the isolated compound CBD instead of cannabis
Cloves	Flowers	Anticancer, anti-inflammatory, antimicrobial, antioxidant	Gingivitis, stomach ulcers, toothache, Type 2 diabetes	Low blood sugar
Chamomile	Flowers	Antibacterial, anti-inflammatory, antimicrobial, antioxidant, antiviral, sedative	Diarrhoea, indigestion, insomnia, menstrual pain, nausea, stress and anxiety	Allergic reaction, drowsiness
Eucalyptus	Leaves	Antibacterial, anti-inflammatory, antimicrobial, antioxidant, expectorant	Common cold, cough- and phlegm-related conditions, dandruff, dry skin, pain, stress	Skin irritation
Feverfew	Leaves	Anticancer, antidepressant, anti-inflammatory	Menstrual pain, migraine (long-term prevention rather than immediate relief), pain, rheumatoid arthritis	Mouth ulcers, allergic reaction

(continued)

OTHER HERBS AND THEIR BENEFITS (CONTINUED)

HERB	PART OF PLANT	PROPERTIES	USE CASE	POTENTIAL SIDE EFFECTS IN SMALL DOSES
Ginseng (Asian varieties)	Roots	Antidiabetic, anti-inflammatory, antioxidant,	Eczema, erectile dysfunction, fatigue, low mood, Type 2 diabetes	Low blood sugar, headache, insomnia, stomach upset
Lavender	Flowers	Antifungal, anti-inflammatory, antioxidant, antiseptic, sedative	Acne, athlete's foot, eczema, hair loss, headache, hot flashes, insomnia, low mood, osteoarthritis, pain, rheumatoid arthritis, stress and anxiety, wounds	Allergic reaction, stomach upset
Liquorice	Root	Antibacterial, anticancer, anti-inflammatory, antimicrobial, antioxidant, antiviral, expectorant	Acne, asthma, common cold, cough- and phlegm-related conditions, eczema, heartburn, hot flashes, peptic ulcers, sore throat	Elevated blood pressure
Peppermint	Leaves	Antibacterial, anti-inflammatory, antiviral	Bloating, blocked sinuses, common cold, diarrhoea, fatigue, headache, IBS, indigestion, itching, menstrual pain, muscle pain	Unlikely

(continued)

OTHER HERBS AND THEIR BENEFITS (CONTINUED)

HERB	PART OF PLANT	PROPERTIES	USE CASE	POTENTIAL SIDE EFFECTS IN SMALL DOSES
Rosemary	Leaves	Antibacterial, anticancer, antifungal, anti-inflammatory, antimicrobial, antioxidant, antiviral	Hair loss, indigestion, stress and anxiety, wounds	Unlikely
St John's Wort*	Flowers	Antidepressant	Anxiety, hot flashes, low mood, wounds	Diarrhoea, dizziness, insomnia, skin tingling, allergic reaction
Tea tree	Leaves	Antibacterial, antifungal, anti-inflammatory, antiviral	Acne, athlete's foot, dandruff, eczema, fungal nail infection, gingivitis, psoriasis, underarm odour, wounds	Allergic reaction
Thyme	Flowers and leaves	Analgesic, antibacterial, anticancer, antifungal, antimicrobial, antioxidant, antispasmodic	Acne, anxiety, cough, menstrual pain, oral thrush, sore throat	Headache, stomach upset
Valerian*	Root	Antidepressant, sedative	Anxiety, insomnia, hot flashes, menstrual pain	Headache, stomach upset, drowsiness, dizziness, vivid dreams

* These herbs may have serious interactions with many other drugs. Do not start taking them without first consulting a healer or physician, and be sure to discuss with them any other medication you are on or plan to take.

HERBAL HEALING PRACTICES FOR THE MODERN AFRICAN

Armed with this starter knowledge of herbs and their benefits, there are tons of different ways to apply or consume them. At the most basic level, you can be more intentional about the scented candle or tea purchase you're making. But on the more hands-on side of things, you might like to try making your own home remedies. Here are a few examples, including some of my favourite recipes. Allow me to apologise in advance as, like a typical African, I don't really use specific measurements for a lot of these things (except when it comes to essential oils – very important!). Take that as an invitation to decide on your own quantities and ratios, get creative and see what you come up with!

Make a Home Remedy

Paste

Use Case: Topical (on skin) application. Good for inflammation, pain, cysts, insect bites, etc.

Herb Form: Fresh leaves, flowers, roots (grated) and/or powder

Instructions: For fresh herbs, grind together using a pestle and mortar until they form a paste. You may need to add a carrier agent of water, honey, coconut oil (cooling) or almond oil (warming).

For powdered herbs, mix them with any of the carrier agents mentioned above.

Apply directly onto skin or, for a warm compress (good for inflammation), warm a cloth with hot (not boiling) water and spread the paste onto the cloth before pressing on skin.

Oil

Use Case: Topical (on skin) application. Good for dry skin, rashes, insect bites, etc.

Herb Form: Dried leaves, flowers, roots or essential oils

Instructions: See 'Infused Love Oil' below.

Elixir*

*At the risk of sounding like I work for Goop, I'm using the word 'elixir' to describe a highly concentrated medicinal drink to differentiate it from tea, a less concentrated drink that can be enjoyed for preventative health. Both are prepared in similar ways; it's the quantity of herbs that differs.

Use Case: Oral. Good for urgent complaints such as malaria, headache, stomach upset, etc.

Herb Form: Fresh leaves, flowers, roots or dried herbs

Instructions: Check online or with a specialist for correct dosage.

Place (fresh or dried) herbs in water and set on medium heat for 15 minutes, then sieve.

OR

Place water on the heat. While water is heating, grind the (fresh) herbs with a pestle and mortar. Add ground herbs to the water and heat for 15 minutes, then sieve.

NB: Consume only a shot glass of the liquid up to three times daily.

Tea

Use Case: Oral. Good for preventative health or less urgent complaints like bloating, fatigue, etc.

Herb Form: Fresh leaves, flowers, roots, dried herbs or powder

Instructions: See 'Morning Boost Tea' below.

Food addition

Use Case: Oral. Good for preventative health or less urgent complaints like bloating, fatigue, etc.

Herb Form: All forms

Instructions: Add herbs into soups, stews, smoothies or juices.

Brew Up a Caffeine-free Tea

We're all familiar with herbal teas but often underestimate just how effective they can be. A herbal tea is usually my first port of call for any minor issues – from stomach cramps to fatigue – and it's sometimes surprising how quickly and effectively they can work! Of course, you can buy herbal tea bags, which typically state the use case and benefits on the labels, but I think the teas always taste better and are more effective when you make them yourself. Teas are typically made with either fresh or dried herbs, or a combination of both. You can also add fruits like pineapple or lemon for extra flavour and benefits. Herbal teas are almost all naturally caffeine-free, with green tea being a notable exception.

MORNING BOOST TEA

This tea is great for fighting fatigue, aiding digestion and generally making you feel ready for the day! For extra digestive action, use more ginger and add a teaspoon of ground turmeric.

Ingredients

Ginger
Pineapple (fresh or dried)
Pineapple rind (if using fresh pineapple)
Prɛkɛsɛ (optional)
Honey (optional)

Method

1. Wash ginger thoroughly and do not peel. Cut each bulb in half lengthways. How many pieces? The more ginger you use, the stronger and spicier it will be, so use your judgement.

2. Cut pineapple into chunks or slices small enough that you can add a few to your mug and eat them when your tea runs out. If using pineapple rind, be sure to wash thoroughly.

3. Place all items, including prɛkɛsɛ if using, in a medium-sized pot of water and place on low to medium heat.

4. Leave to infuse for 15 minutes.

5. Take off the heat and add honey to taste.

6. Enjoy! Place the extra in the fridge to enjoy as ice tea later in the day.

Make an Infused Oil Blend

Infused oils are for more than just cooking. You can create your own infused oils to use in skincare and haircare too. It's best to use dried herbs and/or essential oils as opposed to fresh herbs, and a tinted glass container, as clear glass can allow UV rays from the sun to affect the composition of the oils, reducing their therapeutic efficacy.

INFUSED LOVE OIL

My favourite is this luxurious massage oil that looks divine, smells divine, feels divine and is actually great for your skin.

Ingredients

Hibiscus flowers or rose petals/rosebuds
Sweet almond oil
Rosehip seed oil
Rose essential oil

Method

1. Drop your dried hibiscus flowers or rose petals into the glass container. How much you use is at your discretion, but it shouldn't come more than about a quarter of the way up the container.

2. Fill the container halfway with sweet almond oil and then top it up with rosehip seed oil.

3. Add five to eight drops of rose essential oil.

4. Take the container outside and place it somewhere it will get lots of sun. Leave it for three to five days and allow the sun to work its magic!

Note: if you live in a not-so-sunny country, firstly, sorry wai.[iii] Secondly, you can achieve the infusion by warming the ingredients together veeeerrrrryyyy gently for about 10 minutes. The mixture should never get hot, just slightly warm. You can do this in a glass dish over hot water.

---

iii 'Wai' is pronounced like the letter *y*. A somewhat condescending, not entirely sympathetic, almost always humorous phrase that translates to 'sorry, okay'.

Make a Spray or Mist

These are a quick and easy way to bring some aromatherapy into your life. They're especially good if you don't like the smoke of incense. I also use homemade sprays for skincare and cleaning products. Here's my favourite calming room mist recipe.

RELAX ROOM/FACE/BODY/ MEDITATION/SLEEP MIST

Yes, this mist can really be used for all those things! The main point is that it's a calming mist (calming for the skin too!) so can be used on any occasion when you want to wind down. Again, try to find a tinted spray bottle for best results.

Ingredients
Alcohol
Lavender essential oil
Chamomile essential oil
Water

Method

1. Place a capful (yes, I know this isn't a real measurement, but this is what I do) of alcohol into your spray bottle. Alcohol helps the water and oil to mix effectively.

2. Add five to 10 drops of lavender oil and five to 10 drops of chamomile oil, depending on how strong you want the fragrance to be and the size of your container.

3. Swill the mixture around in the bottle to combine the liquids.

4. Top the mixture up with water to the top of the bottle.

5. Voila!

Use Herbs to Cleanse Negative Energy

Herbs have spiritual uses as well as physical uses. One of the most common spiritual uses for herbs is cleansing the body or a space of negative and harmful energy. There are many different ways to do this; here are a few of my favourites.

- Leave half an onion by the door – Onions are a powerful ingredient in traditional medicine. They are known for drawing out toxins from the body and negativity from surroundings. Slice an onion in half and leave the halves near doorways to capture bad vibes. This is also why you should never cook with an onion that has been previously cut and left out – it will have absorbed all kinds of nasties from the air around it.

- Salt – Salt is an excellent cleansing tool. You can put it in a bucket and bathe with it to cleanse your energy field, add it to your water when mopping the floor to cleanse your space, leave a pile in corners around the house to attract negative energy and sweep it away (disposing of it outside your home) the next day. Use natural sea or rock salt rather than iodised salt.

- Burn herbs – Some great herbs to burn in an incense burner for cleansing energy are prɛkɛsɛ, basil, dragon's blood (a plant resin) and frankincense.

SWEET MOTHER

In his work on self-healing power, Dr Kimbwandènde Kia Bunseki Fu-Kiau states plainly that 'in the eyes of the African people, especially those in touch with the teachings of the ancient African schools, the earth, our planet is *futu dia n'kisi diakânga Kalûnga mu diâmbu dia môyo* – a "sachet" (parcel) of medicines tied up by Kalûnga [the All Powerful, God] for life on earth'. It's time we made more use of this gift. Herbal healing isn't something to reach for only when we're ill – it can become an important part of our daily self-care routine, helping us on our journey to optimal health. Be (more) intentional about your use of herbs; for example, spraying a peppermint and ginger-scented mist when you need to focus and drinking teas with digestive properties after meals. Find your local herbalist or a Black-owned botanica and consider making that your first port of call for minor complaints. Mother Earth has truly given us all the things we need to live our best life – let's start using them!

Chapter 8

FOOD

'We have all the ingredients we need for a thriving healthy lifestyle, right here on the continent.'

Bryanne Hackman

When you think about eating healthily, you probably don't imagine yourself savouring your favourite cultural dish and, even worse, you might picture food that makes you screw your face up in disgust. We've been sold a lie that healthy eating involves either salads, quinoa, raw food and Western flavours, or the extreme making-over of our local dishes. On the one hand, African and other indigenous foods are painted as fatty, unhealthy, heavy and only for consumption by those who don't care about their health. On the other hand, the changes to the way we cook our local foods are making this narrative kind of true.

Neither disowning our cultural foods for the Western version of healthy food nor ignoring health altogether and just eating what we like is good for us. In both scenarios, there is a disconnect. Food is medicine that Mother Earth has provided to us, and we should treat it as such. But not all medicine is supposed to taste bad. The cultural, communal and pleasure aspects of food are medicine too! A truly healthy diet has to be about more than counting calories and achieving body goals. How can we reimagine healthy eating to be as much about nutrition as it is about enjoyment?

THE TRADITIONAL AFRICAN DIET

You can learn a lot about a culture by looking at – and of course, eating – their food. In fact, that's one of my favourite and most important pastimes when I visit a new country. Advancements in agriculture, industrialisation and globalisation have changed diets around the world, making a discussion on a 'traditional' diet of any peoples somewhat tricky. But despite these massive changes, the spirit of a people's cuisine seems to live on. Nothing illustrates this quite as clearly as the similarities among the foods of South American, Caribbean, African-American and African people. A Haitian friend invited us to a traditional dinner once and I was like, 'Girl, apart from the bashed-up plantain, this is a Ghanaian feast.' Our common roots truly do shine through our food!

With this in mind, my conception of a traditional African diet will be less about going far back in time and more about looking at the traditions that have lived on, even if they might be slowly dying out. It will be less about individual ingredients or recipes and more about the cooking and eating practices. Of course, there isn't one traditional African diet – there isn't one traditional African anything – but there *is* a shared transcontinental approach to cooking, much of which is likely similar to Indigenous communities across the globe.

Local

Traditionally, Africans eat mostly based on what is local to them, that is, the crops that grow well in their locale. As Ruth K. Oniang'o, editor in chief of the *African Journal of Food, Agriculture, Nutrition and Development*, states, 'Even with globalisation... for most populations in Africa, food is still very locale-specific, especially in the rural farming areas where it is produced.'[23] Staples, which tend to make up the bulk of the diet, are typically a root crop like yam or cassava or a grain like maize or teff. When you visit towns and villages across Ghana, you'll notice regional differences in what they consume more of based on what the communities grow. In addition, different communities are known for producing certain foods. Whenever my friends and I head out of town for a break (we always go to the beach, and we always go west), without fail we'll stop at Mankessim to buy pineapples. I'm not exaggerating when I say that Mankessim pineapples are the best I've ever tasted. Maybe it's in my head or maybe it's because these families have been farming the same crop for years, decades or longer.

Mostly Plant-based

Being vegetarian or vegan in Ghana isn't that difficult – but *explaining* that you're vegetarian or vegan in Ghana is. In response to saying I'm vegetarian (I'm not, but I eat a mostly vegetarian diet, following the guidance that comes later in this chapter), I've been offered chicken (because it's 'not meat'), turkey (because it's 'soft') and 'just smaaaallll' meat (because how can you have light soup without meat?). In the Diaspora, whether we're cooking soul food or a Jamaican feast, it feels somewhat incomplete without meat. The consumption of chicken, mutton, goat, beef and, for some, pork has become so standard in our cuisines that it's easy to believe that it's always been that way. But our traditional diet is actually mostly plant-based, rich in vegetables, pulses and beans, herbs, spices and grains. However…

Celebration and Ceremonial Slaughter

To say that Africans traditionally didn't eat meat would be untrue, unless you're looking far back in time to when we hadn't yet figured out fire. We have whole nomadic communities who are known for rearing cattle and utilising them for everything from dairy products to leather goods to, yes, meat for consumption. And imagine asking a South African to give up their shisa nyama! It would be more accurate to say that, before recent times, in many meat-eating communities it was an occasional rather than multiple-times-a-day addition to their diets and made up a smaller proportion of the plate than it does today. For many communities, the consumption of red meat only happened in conjunction with celebrations and ceremony, with seafood and poultry being eaten more often. There is a misconception that animal sacrifices involve the barbaric slaughter of animals that are then discarded. More typical is the slaughter of animals in ceremony, followed by preparing and cooking the meat, and enjoying it as a family or community. So, no, my great-great-grandma probably wasn't vegan, but she probably also only ate meat occasionally.

Traditional Cooking Methods

When I think of traditional African cooking, I think of cooking outside. I know this to be true in many West African countries, and my research shows that it's the case across the continent. I dream of having an outdoor kitchen and cooking my meals in unnecessarily large pots, stirring with a wooden spoon the size of a walking stick, as my stew bubbles and spits over crackling firewood. As I reflect on cooking with my grandma, I realise, real African cooking is hard work! I have memories of sitting on the porch outside my grandma's house and complaining that my arm was tired from fanning the flames of the portable outdoor stove while watching the red-hot embers fly off the charcoal. As a child, I loved waking up to the 'dun, dun, dun' sound of fufu[i] being pounded with the Ghanaian version of a pestle and mortar, mainly because it meant that my arms would be spared the workout. Some other cooking styles I've yet to try my hand at but have definitely enjoyed the labour of are the steaming of food wrapped in banana leaves (for example, kenkey[ii]), the roasting of

---

i   Pronounced as it looks, with the emphasis on the second 'fu'. A dish enjoyed across Africa with slightly varying ingredients and cooking methods but always ending in a solid but tacky ball of starchy goodness eaten by hand with a soup. An example of a 'swallow' food.

ii   Pronounced KEN-keh-y. A Ghanaian food made from fermented maize steamed in banana leaves. Usually eaten with fish and a sauce of freshly ground pepper and onions.

food in sand (for example, groundnuts), and the smoking of fish. These cooking methods are, yes, very hard work. But they're also much better for us than the fast and easy methods we find in modern kitchens today, since they allow food to retain more nutrients and don't typically involve the addition of oil.

Not just this, they also produce food that *tastes* better. This is, of course, my opinion but it seems to be a popular one. Whether it's the time put into the cooking process, the love and care transferred from cook to food or the chemical difference of cooking with materials like wood, sand and steam rather than gas, metal and radiation, food cooked with these traditional methods simply doesn't compare to the more modern ways.

MODERN-DAY MYTHS

A phenomenon called 'nutrition transition' – the change in a people's diet from more nutrient rich to less nutrient rich, driven by modernisation and economic growth (read: Westernisation) – shows that African countries have moved away from diets rich in fibre and nutritional value and low in salt, sugar and fat to, well, exactly the opposite. Studies have found that this, unsurprisingly, correlates with increased levels of obesity and conditions like Type 2 diabetes in African countries. This diet transition can also be seen among Black people who live in the Diaspora, whose diets are less healthy than their counterparts in rural Africa.

While some of this change on the continent can be attributed to people there increasing their intake of processed and junk foods, there is also a lot to be said for the systematic shift from fresh and local foods and ingredients to 'convenient' imported goods. The arrival of fast-food giants like KFC and McDonald's in non-Western countries always elicits a doomsday reaction, but the truth is a huge proportion of the population won't be able to afford to eat there, and many wouldn't want to anyway. The more insidious attack is happening in people's kitchens. Western companies have flooded the market with highly affordable goods with a long shelf-life, and these products, far from being convenient, often bring little to no nutritional value to the table. While products like Frytol and other such highly processed vegetable oils, Maggi cubes and similar stock cubes filled with MSG (monosodium glutamate, a high-salt flavour enhancer) and tomato paste products aren't so bad in isolation, the issue is that they have replaced locally farmed produce or locally made alternatives, which are better for our health and better for Africa's economies. In Black homes across the world, huge tubs of vegetable oils sit in the cupboard next to our kilo bags of rice, those little cubes of flavour and their bright red and yellow packaging are a permanent fixture in many of our cupboards, and I'm sure every second-generation teen has experienced the woe of eagerly opening a Neapolitan ice cream tub only to see frozen tomato paste staring back at them. In both Africa and the Diaspora, these types of products have made their way into our traditional dishes and embedded themselves in our pantries – and our psyche – through excellent marketing and low prices while offering no nutritional benefit in return. So even when we cook our traditionally healthy meals, the *way* we cook them has changed, making them less nutritious.

Both in Africa and its Diaspora, the constant availability of meat products, as well as its unconscious association to wealth and status – a relic of the colonial era – has made it such that dishes that might have been naturally plant-based 100 years ago – red red[iii], kontomire[iv] stew, thieboudienne[v] – are now often served with not one but a variety of meats. As Oniang'o puts it, 'Consumption of animal products especially milk and meat increases with income and urbanisation.' With increased industrialisation,

---

iii   A Ghanaian dish of black-eyed beans cooked in red palm oil and spices, served with fried ripe plantain.

iv   Pronounced kon-TOR-me-reh. A leafy green from the cocoyam plant.

v   A Senegambian dish of rice cooked in spices and a tomato sauce. It's low key and the original (and maybe best) jollof since it's actually a dish of the Wolof people, but as they're not claiming the title, we'll just pretend it's not true. Please note my lack of pronunciation cues; despite much practice, I myself can't pronounce it well, so how can I teach you?

the quality of our meat has deteriorated too. We no longer get grass-fed, free-range goat from local rearers. Now, the meat we purchase is likely to have been mistreated, undernourished, pumped full of chemicals and flown across the world before making its way onto our plates. It's not that meat is bad. But high consumption of meat, especially red meat, has been linked to conditions like high cholesterol and cancer. From a purely nutritional perspective, fish, poultry and red meat have value and should be enjoyed – but the emphasis should be on fish for those brain-boosting omega-3 fatty acids, with poultry and meat taking a firm back seat. The movement to meat becoming the star of each meal rather than a side chick, along with a decrease in its quality, has contributed to the nutritional depletion of our diets.

To put it plainly, whether we're on the continent or not and whether we eat mostly traditional food or not, our diets are not serving us well. Not as well as they used to, and not as well as they have the potential to.

Future Ancestor: Bryanne Hackman

Bryanne is an African nutrition and agriculture expert and coach of Fante and Ga heritage. In 2014, she founded *Best Body by Bry*, a blog on a mission to share African health and wellness knowledge with a global audience. This blog grew and transformed into Best Body Africa, a nutrition and weight management company established in 2020.

Bry says, 'Our foods, at their core, are some of the most nutritious foods one can consume. For example, Western nations praise blueberries as the king antioxidant-rich fruit. Baobab fruit, which is grown in Ghana and other African countries, contains the highest antioxidant content of any fruit; however, this is not commonly known. It's important that people learn more about the power in our foods, especially for our health.'

'Clean Eating' and the Whitewashing of Healthy Eating

For those of us who have already accepted the idea that our diets aren't serving us, we are likely to have also been sold the dream of healthy eating. This dream involves skinny white women laughing with unfiltered joy as they chew on iceberg lettuce and accidentally get yoghurt on their noses. Or it might be the dream that shows the young, metropolitan African who 'upgrades' his diet with supplements from Western companies (whose raw ingredients probably came from underpaid farmers in his country).

Whichever dream it is, they all seem to share a checklist of themes. The Western view of healthy eating is:

- Clinical – What could be more clinical than taking living, breathing, healing herbs and turning them into a capsule?

- Restrictive – Stop eating carbs! No, stop eating meat! No, stop eating sugar! No, stop eating dairy! Western diet culture centres around the demonisation and subsequent restriction of a particular food group, almost always backed up with 'scientific evidence'. The same scientific evidence that years later proves the opposite to be true.

- Morality-based – Your diet isn't just a diet. It determines what kind of person you are. If you eat 'dirty' food, you must not be as good, trustworthy or committed as someone who eats 'clean' food, right? It's this same black-and-white thinking that contributes to fanaticism around certain foods deemed to be 'super'.

- Ethnic... but not too ethnic – White chefs, influencers and brands are forever putting a 'twist' on Indigenous people's dishes that ain't nobody asking to be twisted. The message is clear: these dishes aren't good or healthy or clean enough as they are. Here, we fixed them. There are even whole articles online dedicated to indigenous foods that white people have ruined – from Vegemite sushi to *that* Tesco's jollof recipe.[vi]

For Black people – and other people of colour – this leaves a choice. Either eat your culture's dishes and be unhealthy, or deny yourself the flavours that tie you to memories, to family and to your community in the quest for physical health. Bry says, 'A common misconception about Ghanaian [and other Black] foods is that they can't play a key role in a healthy diet. Many people believe that "healthy food" is synonymous with "Western food". As a result, when people attempt to make healthier choices, especially if the main goal is to lose weight, they tend to gravitate towards "health foods" which are not produced and processed on our soils and aren't even healthier than our traditional foods.'

Our socialisation to associate healthy eating with the Western view of clean eating is only one side of the problem, one that has a greater effect on those of us living in the Diaspora or living a highly Westernised life on the continent. For more rural communities in Africa and other indigenous lands, the problem is at the other end of the supply chain. While Westerners 'discover' superfoods to add to their clean-eating routine, the communities who have been working with these foods and plant medicines for centuries suddenly find themselves simultaneously underpaid for supplying these products as raw materials *and* priced out of purchasing the goods for themselves. And that's before we get on to the topic of the environmental impact of sudden spikes in demand, from deforestation to the death of traditional farming practices.

Wellness companies have made millions by cashing in on the incredible properties of ingredients like cocoa (or cacao), turmeric, matcha and quinoa. You would think that the communities known for producing these

---

vi In case you missed it, in 2014 Black people across the UK were enraged by a recipe on the Tesco (a popular grocery store) website, claiming to be jollof rice. The image of plain white rice adorned with some limp sweet red peppers and the senseless removal of tomatoes from the recipe was unforgivable. Tesco promptly removed the recipe and released an apology.

foods would be rolling in the riches too. But despite increasing demand of limited supply sometimes leading to increased prices, the farmers still only earn a tiny fraction of what these Western companies – and the Western processing companies that often act as the middle person – go on to make. To add insult to injury, the increased price of the raw material, though insignificant to the Western buyers, often makes something that was previously a staple too expensive for some locals. When I lived in Ghana as a child, one of my favourite breakfasts was avocado (or pear as we call it here) spread on sugar bread. It was a dish I firmly associated with being in Ghana, as I never had it, or even saw it, in the UK. Chale,[vii] if only someone had told me that 15 years down the line people would be willing to buy 'avo toast' for £15 a pop, I could have made my millions by now!

The Westernised concept of healthy eating isn't good for anyone. It creates shame (an emotion that the industry feeds off, pun intended), especially for people of colour around their indigenous dishes. It encourages restriction instead of balance, which is dangerous and can increase the likelihood of disordered eating. It shows complete disregard for the place of superfoods in their Indigenous communities. And, most importantly, it emboldens people like Jamie Oliver to add cherry tomatoes, coriander, parsley and a lemon wedge to jollof rice.[viii]

FOOD AND WELLBEING

We eat for nourishment, that much we all know. But it's also key that we enjoy our food, and that we have a cultural connection to it: a 1970s study[24] found that these factors can even have a positive impact on the

---

vii Pronounced cha-LEH. Ghanaian slang for 'friend'.

viii The British chef decided that one jollof scandal wasn't enough. Unlike Tesco, he did not apologise, claiming it was his 'twist' on the dish; however, today the recipe is nowhere to be found on his website.

nourishment we gain from what we eat. But the benefits of eating well – in the broad sense – extend far beyond simply absorbing nutrients.

Belonging

One of the dishes I cooked most when I was at university was jollof rice. Even though it never tasted as good as my mum's, my grandma's, my aunt's or really, anyone else's (sigh) it was always a comfort to eat. For Black people and people of colour, eating the dishes that we've shared with family or experienced while visiting our countries or even learned from YouTube helps us feel connected, feel like we belong. In fact, every aspect of our food journey is an opportunity to connect. When we purchase produce from local farmers or food items from nearby small businesses, we are connecting with our community. When we cook dishes that our mothers, fathers, grandmothers, cousins and friends taught us, we're reconnecting with them and the memories we made together. When we eat together, we're deepening our bond and sharing a moment in time that will never come around again. Food is a medium through which we can connect with our community, our culture and even ourselves.

Chronic Condition Management

Diabetes. Hypertension. High cholesterol. These are some of the chronic conditions that disproportionately affect Black people – and all of them relate to our diet. I heard the ideal description for genetic predisposition to diseases in a documentary once. The doctor said that a condition that runs in the family is like a loaded gun in your DNA. It's a very real threat – but if the gun never gets fired, it won't make any difference to your life. Lifestyle and environmental factors can end up pulling the trigger, one of those factors being diet. In other words, just because diabetes runs in your family doesn't mean you should accept that you'll be diagnosed with it someday. By being mindful of our diets – our intake of salt, fat and sugar, our portion sizes, our intake of fruit and vegetables – we can stave off these conditions or at the very least manage them well once diagnosed.

Mental Health

We often think of our diet as something that affects only our physical health, but it has a material impact on our mental health too. What we eat and how we feel exist together in a symbiotic relationship. When we eat well, we feel good, and when we don't, we don't. The difficulty arises when we are already experiencing poor mental health. In this state, it becomes harder and harder to make healthy choices, the choices that might help us move towards better mental health. This is why it's so key that we make good mental health practices part of our routine – something that's much easier to implement when we're already in a healthy frame of mind. To promote good mental health, we should maintain a balanced diet with plenty of fresh fruit and vegetables and drink lots of water.

READY TO RETURN?

Healthy eating doesn't have to be boring or painful, and Black foods don't have to be bad for us. There is another way! Let me get this out of the way straight up – I do not think a vegan diet is the ideal diet for all Africans, or even for all people. There, I said it. I know there's a particular group of African wellness gurus that will come for me, but I said what I said! As noble a cause as saving the planet is, that is not the main function of our diets. Our diets are intended to nourish us – nourish our mind, body and soul. At the point where you become intensely attached to a specific aspect of your diet as a marker of your identity or morals – whether it's veganism or overconsumption of meat because you're a 'typical African man' – its impact on your body becomes an afterthought.

This means that, as well as feeling good about what we eat and how it impacts the environment, we are also meant to enjoy what we eat, maintain good physical health and nutrition, and feel connected to our food. It's important that we remain open to change around what we eat and listen to the guidance of our bodies. Dogmatically sticking to a vegan diet even though you've developed anaemia due to a vitamin B_{12} deficiency makes no sense. Neither does refusing to cut down on red meat despite suffering from high blood pressure.

The right diet is going to be different for each of us, and is going to change throughout our lives, especially if we move locations. Conditions like IBS, diabetes, even insomnia are literally the body *begging* for change. We need to become better at listening to it.

FOOD PRACTICES FOR THE MODERN AFRICAN

Look to Tradition

Some of the characteristics of the traditional African diet described earlier in this chapter can easily be replicated today:

- Buy local – Commit to making local produce a larger proportion of your diet and avoid purchasing things that are out of season.

- Grow your own food – It's no secret that across the West, organic health food shops are often found only in affluent areas while communities with higher proportions of non-white residents are plagued by food deserts – areas where shops are filled with processed, low-nutrient, convenience foods and there's a Morley's or Taco Bell on every corner. In this case, growing your own food can be a method of taking back control; we'll come back to this in the next chapter.

- Eat less red meat – There's so much conflicting information about how much meat to eat, but what most seem to agree on is that too much red meat isn't great for us. According to the NHS, if we're raging carnivores, we should immediately try to limit our intake of red and/or processed meat to 70 g a day... but since most of us eat portions closer to 140 g at a time (for example, an English breakfast with two sausages and two rashers of bacon), it makes sense to aim for a maximum of about three portions a week. They recommend consuming fish at least twice a week, with at least one of those portions being a fish high in omega-3 (examples are West African favourites mackerel, salmon and sardines). There's no guidance on how much poultry to consume, just that we should, as with red meat, opt for lean varieties. If this is sounding impossible to you, a good first step is only eating one meat product at any given meal (goodbye 'assorted' noodles and 'special' fried rice), and then eating fish or meat at only one meal per day.

• Choose healthier cooking methods – While you might not have the time, energy or tools to regularly employ traditional cooking methods, their modern application might look like opting for steaming and baking over boiling and frying, for example.

Cook with Community

On my travels in Senegal, I stayed at a gorgeous, remote guesthouse called The Little Baobab in Abéné. The owner, Khady, and her family instantly made me feel at home. Not just because they gave me a Senegalese name (Mariama Bintu Fall, if you must know) but because we ate all our meals together, from one huge dish. Bringing an element of community into your cooking could look like:

• doing 'Come Dine with Me'[ix] with a group of friends

• cooking your favourite cultural dishes with friends or family

• cooking the dishes that your family members taught you

• eating together without distractions

---

ix A popular TV show in the UK where a group of strangers go to each other's homes for dinner, and score how each person did.

Adjust Your Mindset

There was a time in my life when, if a meal didn't have meat in it, it wasn't a real meal. No matter the portion size, I would still be 'hungry' afterwards. Can you relate? A huge part of improving our diets is overcoming certain mindsets we have about food. Some examples are that meat is a must-have on every plate, that you need to feel physically stuffed to be satisfied, that you must eat junk food whenever you feel sad or that you don't like vegetables. I'm sorry, but as an adult human, you cannot dislike *all* vegetables and if you do, hopefully you like your life enough to just eat them anyway. To improve your mindset around food:

• Take some time to identify what mindsets are informing your diet.

• Question whether they are really true and whether they are serving you.

• If not, what can you do to change each mindset? If it's a pervasive pattern, you can implement one day a week where you intentionally resist the pattern. For example, going meat-free on Mondays. If it's a response pattern, come up with an alternative response. For example, if you reach for cake whenever you're lonely, decide that your new response will be to go for a walk or call your best friend instead.

Mindset work is hard work, but the first step is always identifying what you want, what you *need*, to change and taking steps to make it happen.

Practice Mindful Eating

Mindfulness is a state of heightened awareness, devoid of judgement and filled with compassion. It has become a bit of a buzzword in recent years and is often confused with meditation. But mindfulness is not something you do, it's something you are. To understand mindfulness, it helps to think of its opposite. When it comes to eating, mindlessness looks like forgetting to eat, making unhealthy, last-minute choices, allowing yourself to get to the point of extreme hunger before eating, being so absorbed in something else as you eat that you barely taste your food, eating too much and only realising you've done so 10 minutes later, fork still in hand... any of these sound familiar?

Mindful eating is about being more intentional in the planning, preparation and consumption of your food. It could look like:

- taking time each week to plan and/or prep your meals, especially important if you have a busy lifestyle – meal prepping can help you avoid too many takeouts or processed meals

- turning your cooking time into a ritual: pay attention to what you're cooking, set the mood with music, sing as you cook, be present throughout the process

- keeping a food diary to track how different foods affect you

- eating with no distractions (no phone, no TV, etc.) and really focusing on your meal

- learning to become aware of and listening to your body's thirst, hunger and fullness signals

MINDFUL MORNING EXERCISE

Here is a simple mindfulness exercise you can do each morning as you make your first cup of tea, coffee, lemon water or whatever it is you start your day with. Give yourself enough time to dedicate 10–15 minutes to this exercise before you rush into your day.

1. While the kettle is on, instead of scrolling through your phone or rushing around the house, stay in one place, focused on the exercise.

2. Place your tea/coffee/herbs/lemon in your mug. Notice the sound it makes as you do this. Take in its appearance, noticing the colours

and textures. Bring the cup to your nose and breathe deeply, taking in its aroma.

3. Set an intention for your day and speak this intention to your cup as if you're adding it as an ingredient into your drink.

4. Add your hot water, milk and/or honey, noticing the changes in the colour and texture of your drink.

5. Again, take a deep breath inhaling the aroma.

6. As you wait for the drink to cool down enough for your first sip, feel the warmth radiating into your hands and repeat your intention to yourself.

7. Finally, close your eyes, take a deep breath and then take your first sip, fully focused on the taste of your drink.

8. If you can, maintain this level of mindfulness until the very last sip!

Reduce Oil and Use Healthier Choices

Oil has gotten a bad rap, especially with the rise of the oil-free cooking movement, the proponents of which usually pair their derision of oils with recommendations for oil-free cooking 'essentials' that could pay my rent in Accra for one year (okay, one month, but still).[x] However, oil isn't the problem, our use of it is. We can instantly make our diets healthier by cooking stews with a tablespoon or two of oil instead of free pouring until an inch-deep pool forms at the bottom of the pan. We can also swap highly processed oils for cold-pressed oils, and swap oils labelled as 'vegetable oils' for coconut oil, sesame oil, avocado oil, or any other oil that is specific. Don't forget that raw shea butter can be used for cooking too! Red palm oil, a favourite in West African dishes, is good for us in

---

x   Accra rent is notoriously high!

moderation, and olive oil is best used at low to medium temperatures. As with everything, buy local or from ethical small businesses if possible. My favourite oils are locally made red palm oil, coconut oil and groundnut oil.

Reduce Added Sugar

We all know that too much sugar is bad for us, so here are some simple swaps you can make to reduce your intake:

- Cut down on processed and prepackaged food. Whether it's a pasta sauce or soy sauce, anything that's premade almost definitely has sugar in it, even if it's savoury. Try to cook with fresh ingredients as much as possible.

- Fruit juices are high in sugar, so balance them out with eating actual fruit or drinking smoothies.

- Make your own snacks! You'll have more control over how much sugar goes into them.

- Swap sugar for honey, which doesn't cause your blood sugar to spike as severely as sugar and, since it's sweeter, you're likely to use less.

Use 100 Per cent Natural Herbs and Spices

I often wonder whether the Swiss use Maggi cubes with the same vim that West Africans do. Probably not. The fact is that, despite their cons, these little cubes do pack a flavour punch. In their place, we can of course use the fresh and dried herbs we're all familiar with. However, the taste profile that the seasoning cubes add to foods is the umami flavour, something that isn't quite replicated by regular herbs and spices. To get this umami flavour, good alternatives are dawadawa (also called ogiri or iru) and ground crayfish. For those in the Diaspora who might not be able to access regular dawadawa, dried and powdered versions are a good option.

Control Your Portion Sizes and Plate Proportions

Honestly, for a lot of Black people, it's not even the type of food we eat that is killing us but the portion sizes! In Ghanaian families, and I'm sure many other Black homes, there seems to be this narrative that the 'man of the house' has to eat out of a dish that the rest of the family would typically use as a serving bowl. And that serving bowl must be filled to the brim with meat and carbs. Often, when we lead with the good intentions of improving our diet and switch to smaller portions, we find ourselves feeling hungry and soon switch back to the portion sizes our body has become accustomed to. Here are some tips for reducing your portion sizes and getting the balance right on your plate:

- Start by reducing starchy carbs and grains and increasing vegetables so that the size of the total plate remains the same. Once you've become accustomed to this, slowly start to reduce the size of your overall plate, if you feel you need to.

- As you reduce your portion sizes for main meals, be sure to keep healthy snacks (nuts, fruit, occasional sweet treats) on hand for when you inevitably feel hungry between meals.

- Be sure to drink enough water throughout the day. The recommended amount varies but generally sits around two to three litres. Make water your first port of call when you're thinking about a snack – a lot of us confuse thirst signals for hunger signals.

- Learn to interrogate your mind's hunger thoughts. Sometimes, when we think we're hungry, we're actually just thirsty, as mentioned above, or bored.

- Be patient and compassionate with yourself, recognising that it takes time for us to adjust to change.

So what size is the right portion size? This is a tricky question to answer as it's different for everyone, and this is why it's important to practise mindful eating and follow your body's signals. In terms of the proportions on your plate, a good guideline is half vegetables, quarter protein, quarter starchy carbs and/or grains.

Add African Superfoods to Your Diet

I mentioned earlier that the sudden spike in demand of superfoods caused by an endorsement from the wellness industry can cause problems for Indigenous communities. However, these foods can and should be purchased and consumed in a responsible way. Adding African superfoods to your diet will boost your health while keeping you connected to African flavours. Here are some examples:

- Teff – This grain grown in Ethiopia and Eritrea is packed with nutrients, high in fibre and naturally gluten-free. It is the key ingredient in Ethiopia's most well-known dish, injera.

- Fonio – This is another delicious grain, this time grown in West Africa. It's a good alternative to rice or couscous and has less of an impact on your blood sugar than these foods, making it a great option for those with diabetes.

- Baobab – The African Tree of Life produces a versatile fruit that boasts many health benefits. It is most easily consumed in powder form and can be added to smoothies, juices and baked goods. If you live somewhere where baobab grows, fresh baobab juice is a must!

- Amaranth – The grain of amaranth is similar to quinoa and contains even higher proportions of protein and iron. Amaranth leaves can be eaten raw or cooked and are similar to spinach.

- Tamarind – The fruit of this tree makes a delicious, naturally sweet juice and is a great digestive aid.

- Coconut – The humble coconut is so underrated! Consumed alone or as an ingredient, raw or cooked, in a sweet or savoury dish, this versatile gift of the gods should be a regular in all of our diets.

- Cocoa – Another extremely underrated health food, raw cocoa powder is great for heart health. It's also the ideal coffee replacement!

- Superfood herbs moringa, neem and hibiscus were discussed in the previous chapter.

To purchase these superfoods and other food products responsibly, consider these things:

- Buy from indigenous brands instead of Western brands. Purchasing from local brands better supports the local economy.

- Buy the raw rather than processed version. As well as being better for the environment, purchasing raw or less processed products means a higher percentage of what you pay is going to the farmer and you're more likely to be supporting a local business – for example, buying fonio grain rather than a preseasoned fonio mix.

- Buy in bulk rather than small packs, especially if you're buying imported goods; buying in bulk is more sustainable.

- Get friends and relatives to bring items from the source. I can't believe I'm actually recommending this, having experienced the shame of pulling sacks of gari[xi] and yam tubers out of my overweight suitcase at the airport check-in desk more times than I care to remember... but doing this allows you to buy local African goods more easily if you live in the Diaspora.

---

xi Cassava that is grated, fermented and then fried or roasted.

GOING BACK TO MY ROOTS

With Black people being overrepresented in the incidence of conditions like diabetes, high blood pressure and high cholesterol, it's time we had a diet revolution that embraces our culture and tradition rather than demonising it. On the continent, we can interrupt the pattern of nutrition transition with small changes that make a big impact, and in the Diaspora we can enjoy a healthy diet without denying our roots. Future Ancestor Bry has shared her favourite recipe to get you started.

BAKED KOOSE/AKARA
BY BRYANNE HACKMAN

Koose is a West African spicy bean cake packed with protein, which can also be found across the Diaspora. In Ghana, it is typically eaten at breakfast with Hausa koko (a spiced millet porridge) or as a snack. It's usually deep fried but this recipe presents a healthier, baked version that tastes just as good as the original! The recipe makes eight to 10 muffins.

Ingredients
350 g raw black-eyed peas
1 red onion
2 spring onions
1 or 2 scotch bonnet/red chillies
Salt to taste
Tiny splash of water for blending
Coconut or other oil

Method
1. Wash and soak your raw beans in water overnight.

2. The next day, peel your beans by rubbing them between your fingers and allowing the skins to fall off. (If you're feeling lazy, you can skip this step but the texture of your koose won't be as smooth).

3. Add your beans to a blender with your chopped onion, chillies, salt to taste and a tiny splash of water.

4. When blended into a smooth paste, mix in chopped spring onions.

5. Brush the holes of a muffin tray with your chosen oil.

6. Add your blended mixture to each muffin tray.

7. Bake for 20 minutes in your oven at 180°C/350°F/Gas mark 4.

8. Allow to cool, then enjoy!

Chapter 9

NATURE

*'Nature is our greatest teacher – the divine
mother Gaia teaches us one of the most important
sacred laws as healers; that things happen
in Rhythms and Cycles and thus there is a
cosmic order in all that we do as healers.'*

Gogo Dineo Ndlanzi

As I write this chapter, I'm sitting on a porch overlooking the Volta River,[i] surrounded by a variety of plants, trees and flowers, with a view of lush green mountains and a soundtrack of playful birds and insects. Simply being present in this space has healing power. The clean air, the interaction with the plants, the absence of city noise. This kind of environment has become a retreat, somewhere to escape to, for so many of us. But nature isn't supposed to be a place we go to – nature is home. It's easy to forget this with the modern lives we live, centred around buildings and transportation and machines and *things*. And when we need our 'nature fix', we go camping or hiking or to the beach or somewhere outside of our normal stomping ground. In reconnecting with Mother Earth, though, we would do well to remember that nature extends beyond her remit.

---

i A river in Ghana that runs the length of the country, exiting on the coast of the Volta Region

The African conception of nature is the entire cosmos and all laws of nature, from the movement of celestial bodies to the law of cause and effect. Our ancestors didn't live 'in tune' with nature, they lived as part of nature. They recognised that, while humans have free will, we are not immune to the laws of nature as some like to think. Their reverence of natural forces is evident in their mythology and spiritual traditions. In the Yoruba tradition, the Orishas are personifications of natural energies; Oya is the wind, Sango is the thunder, Oshun is the river. Across Ghana, abosom or deities are found inhabiting waterfalls, mountains, lakes and rocks. Our ancestors were deeply connected to other natural beings, including celestial bodies. Through this connection, they knew which trees they could turn to for shelter. They knew which fruits and plants they could pick for sustenance and at what times. They knew when to fish and when to leave the waters be. They knew when to explore and when to rest. We can reconnect to our true nature and our position in the cosmic order of life by remembering the importance of Asase Yaa and her children – plants, animals, other humans – in our lives, while also honouring all other elements of the cosmos. To live well, we must reconnect with nature as part of ourselves, as home.

NATURE IN TRADITIONAL AFRICA

Nature is all-encompassing and, for the traditional African, every aspect of life paid respect to the natural laws. To exemplify this, I'll focus on just three areas: architecture, agriculture and cycles.

Traditional buildings across the continent were examples of what is today called African vernacular architecture. This involves using materials found on the land on which you're building or locally and assembling buildings using traditional methods. Examples of materials used include bamboo, mud, timber and palm. Typically the actual construction process would be a community activity, with jobs assigned by gender and age. In his study[25] of the traditional architecture of the Igbo people, Godwin Chikwendu

Nsude notes that the men usually did the bulk of the construction, with women and children supporting, a pattern he recognised among other ethnic groups, including the Kikuyu of Kenya and the Tongo of Ghana. Ritual formed an important part of the building process, with specific rituals performed before breaking ground and before a family moved into their new abode. Dancing, singing and chanting would also accompany the work, invoking the support of deities and Ancestors. Building in this manner shows respect to the land you're building on, celebrates community and produces structures that are in congruence with their surroundings. While the tradition of constructing in this way may be dying out, buildings of this style can still be found across Africa, including in many villages and beachside spots here in Ghana; although today, the value of the tradition is lost, with this form of architecture usually being chosen purely as an affordable (or the only) option.

Africans have been farming for literally thousands of years. Estimates for its advent in the region of West Africa sit at 3000BC. In terms of animal agriculture, there are communities who are known as cattle-rearing or fishing communities and have been for generations. For example, the famous Maasai of Kenya are believed to have been cattle rearers for over 400 years, while the community in Elmina on the coast of Ghana is reported to have been fishing since the 1400s. As with traditional architecture, these practices were infused with ritual. One tradition that has stood the test of time in Ghana is the rest day for farmers, associated with the 'birthday' of the land goddess. Farmers do not work the land on Thursday in the Asante and Akuapem regions (where they revere Asase Yaa, Yaa meaning born on Thursday) or on Friday in the Fante areas of the Central and Western regions (where they revere Asaase Efua, Efua meaning born on Friday). A similar tradition for fishermen in various locations across the coast of Ghana is the ban on fishing on Tuesdays, also viewed as a show of respect to the sea deities. Perhaps as a result of their connection to ritual and spirituality, traditional methods of fishing and farming were more sustainable. There were no harmful chemicals or damaging machinery, and workers respected the spirits of the land and water rather than viewing them purely as resources to be extracted from until there's nothing left to take.

Our ancestors also respected the many cycles that rule our lives. Day and night, cycles of time, seasons, moon cycles. Even as far back as Kemet, we see how they recognised and respected these patterns. During this civilisation the oldest known sundial was created, estimated to be from 1500BC, and there is evidence that the Egyptians tracked the seasons based on the flooding patterns of the Nile. These seasons informed their agricultural practices and their New Year celebration, which also coincided with the emergence of the Sirius star in the sky after a long period of apparent absence. Similar harvest/New Year festivals can be observed across the continent today – for example, Homowo and Odwira festivals in Ghana.

The depth of our Ancestors' knowledge of the universe around them is demonstrated by the mythology of the Dogon people of Mali, which boasts specific details of the Sirius star system, such as the existence of a tiny yet incredibly heavy star that orbits Sirius. This star, now known as Sirius B, was only 'discovered' by modern astronomy in 1862, and proven to be a white dwarf (i.e., incredibly heavy) as recently as 1926. Dogon artefacts depicting this knowledge are estimated to be at least 400 years old.

MODERN-DAY MYTHS

We have fallen out of sync with nature and the worst part is that often we call this progress. What could possibly be progressive about further and further detaching ourselves from life itself? Maintaining our focus on architecture, agriculture and cycles, the degree to which we've fallen out of favour with nature is clear.

Vernacular architecture can still be seen in Africa, as mentioned, mostly in villages and less wealthy communities. In urban areas, mud, timber and bamboo have been replaced with cement, metal and other – usually imported, often expensive – materials. As is the general theme of post-colonial Africa, it is the misconception of these Western-style buildings as better and more modern that has contributed to their pervasiveness rather than them being fit for purpose. It's true that cement sometimes requires less regular maintenance than mud; however, these cement buildings bring problems of their own. The traditional style of building and its materials is much better suited to hot temperatures than cement buildings. The solution for cement buildings is fans and air conditioners. So, clearly Western-style buildings are less friendly to the environment and to the bank balance, and yet they are here to stay.

The question isn't how we go back to the traditional ways but how we firstly disabuse ourselves of any untruths surrounding their inferiority and secondly bring the energy of traditional architecture into our modern homes. Nsude states that 'the symbolic value of traditional art, and that includes architecture, has been under steady erosion, and with this erosion has come a significant depreciation in its communicative quality [while] on the other hand, the myth of Europeans' cultural superiority has continued to grow stronger'. The value of traditional architecture includes what Nsude encapsulates as 'co-operation with nature as opposed to entire subjugation or isolation from natural forces', as well as the community and ritual elements of construction. Award-winning architect Diébédo Francis Kéré – the first Black person and the first African to win the prestigious Pritzker Prize[ii] – is setting an example of how we can bring these elements back to modern community building, as shared in his 2013 TED talk 'How to Build with Clay… and Community'. Companies like Hive Earth and Kasa Konsultants are constructing eco-friendly buildings across Ghana using the ancient rammed-earth method, bringing it into the modern age with a mixture of more durable – but still locally sourced – materials. One of

---

ii   The most prestigious award in architecture, bestowed annually on individuals whose work demonstrates talent, vision and commitment.

my friends Kwaku (@livetolearn_learntolive on Instagram) literally built his own home, with help from friends and the community, and is using it as a base for teaching people from around the world how to live from and with Mother Earth. But we're not all able or willing to build clay homes in Africa (although, just so you know, I'm manifesting a clay-built home and wellness centre near the coast in Ghana – I give myself five years and I hope you'll come visit!). Later in this chapter, I'll share how, even in a 10th-floor flat in East London, you can inject the traditional approach of our ancestors into your home.

As with architecture, traditional agriculture has been supposedly projected into the future while decidedly leaving farmers behind. In a push for globalisation after a wave of independence, African countries – heavily encouraged by Western powers – pushed for large-scale commercial agriculture to overtake small-scale indigenous farming practices. Farmers were encouraged to switch from traditional intercropping to monoculture farming, complete with fertilisers and machinery to scale up production. In his work 'The Wisdom of Traditional Farming in Tropical Africa',[26] professor David A. Iyegha describes how this led to widespread unemployment and poverty among small-scale farmers, while for those farmers who took up the task of industrialising 'these new methods [led to] negative outcomes, including rapid depletion within a few years of the soil that was wisely protected for hundreds of years under the traditional mix-cropping system'. To add insult to injury, the deteriorating condition of the soil meant that the outcome for many African countries was actually *lower* agricultural output, not higher, leading to increased importing of goods such as rice and other crops that should have been entirely home grown. Decades down the line, this has kept African countries and their farmers poor while Western countries continue to enjoy the riches of billions in export revenues while their farmers reap the benefits of subsidies – subsidies that African governments are restricted from offering their farmers due to shady trade deals and the ever-pervasive imbalance of economic power. To avoid going off on a tangent, allow me to redirect you to a couple of insightful documentaries: *Tomatoes and Greed: The Exodus of Ghana's Farmers* and *The Great African Scandal* (both available to watch on YouTube at the time of writing. As with almost all documentaries on Africa, expect undertones of saviourism).

Okay, so to summarise, agriculture isn't what it used to be. But another issue is how far removed most of us have become from the agricultural process. Can you confidently say that you know where your food comes from? Many spiritual traditions agree on the idea of life force, the vital essence of a living being. It is this life force that nourishes us, transferring from the food we eat into our bodies. And it is this life force that steadily drains out of food items the older they get. So when a pineapple is freshly farmed it contains a good amount of life force energy and will be highly nourishing. That same pineapple a week later isn't quite going to pack the same punch. This might all sound a bit strange to you, but it's essentially just an energetic perspective on the decay of food. Now with this perspective, think about the energetic quality of food that you've purchased from Farmer Jordan down the road. Or eggs you've collected from chickens in your garden. Or a chicken you've just slaughtered (sorry, chicken), prepared and cooked all in a matter of hours. In comparison, reflect on the energetic quality of the food you buy in the market or the grocery store. How many days pass from when it is plucked, harvested or slaughtered to when you purchase it? How many hands does it pass through? How many *countries* does it pass through?

Laresh Jayasanker captures this change in our produce in his book *Sameness in Diversity* by saying, 'An apple a day is only recently possible – after all, in the 1960s, a grocery shopper in Detroit or D.C. was hard pressed to find an apple in the dead of winter. Now she can eat a Braeburn in February, "fresh" off a six-thousand-mile marine journey from Chile.' The importance of buying local was discussed in the previous chapter; here, my focus is more on our *connection* to the food we eat. The greater our physical and temporal disconnect from the food we eat, the more likely it is to have endured processes that strip it of its life force. Fruits and veg that have far to travel are often harvested early, then stored at varying temperatures to preserve and then artificially ripen them just before they hit supermarket shelves. The more connected we are to the source of our food – growing it ourselves, knowing the farm where it came from, or in the case of processed foods, knowing the small business that produces it – the more likely it is to be good for us. We need to educate ourselves on what we're actually eating, where it comes from, and what impact it has on the world around us. The greater interest we take in the full life cycle of our food, the more likely we are to make choices that are better for the environment and better for us, choices that favour fresh, organic foods that haven't been manipulated and processed to the point of being dead food in nice packaging.

So we've messed up our architecture, we've messed up farming – but we couldn't possibly mess up cycles, right? Let me tell you a little story. A few years ago, I took a trip with a friend to Lake Bosomtwe,[iii] the Lake of the Fallen Star in the Asante region of Ghana. We stayed in a small village on the banks of the lake. One evening, we were making our way back from town to where we were staying, and I couldn't see. I mean that quite literally, I could not see. I'm not sure if you've ever experienced sunset in Ghana but, to this day, it takes me by surprise. It's daytime one minute and then, it feels like you blink and suddenly there's darkness all around. So the sun went down as we were walking home on a path surrounded by trees on both sides. There were no streetlights and no lit buildings around... and I couldn't see. However, my friend, who grew up in a small town outside Accra, could see perfectly and his stride didn't falter. I legit had to stop, call him to come back and get him to hold my hand and guide me, hobbling across the uneven dirt road like Bambi, until we got back to

---

iii   Pronounced bor-som-TCHWEH. The only natural lake in Ghana, and one of only six meteoric (i.e., the result of a meteor hitting the Earth and leaving a crater) lakes in the world. In Asante mythology, this is where the souls of Asante people travel to after death before making their transition into the next realm.

the village. This was a stark expression of how much we abuse artificial light. I say abuse because we use it improperly to our own detriment. My body was so used to constant light that my eyes couldn't adjust to the darkness – not dead-of-night darkness, 7 p.m. darkness. This might seem trivial, but our circadian cycle – the internal system that manages our sleep-wake cycle – looks to cues such as light and dark to determine when and if we sleep, among other things. As someone who suffered with chronic insomnia for years, I can't stress enough just how vital it is to protect this cycle. Living in artificial light after sundown and staring at these light-emitting devices as we do, has a material impact on our wellbeing (and, apparently, our night vision). There are now all kinds of innovations to help counteract this – blue-light glasses, smart lighting, night mode apps. Just like the air conditioning in cement buildings, though, it strikes me that we keep inventing things to counteract the negative effects of the things we invented before instead of just returning to nature.

The cycle of day and night isn't the only one we've fallen out of sync with. On an individual level, many of us ignore or attempt to override instead of work with our hormonal cycles (yes, men have hormonal cycles too). On a collective level, our hyperproductive, always-on approach teaches us that the only cycle that matters is the one where we keep pushing, pushing and pushing until we burn out, rest, reset and do it all again. These days, the importance of celestial cycles and their effects, from agricultural seasons to our quality of sleep, is largely dismissed. We even celebrate the new year on a date that, frankly, makes no real sense – at least not in terms of nature's cycles. According to professor Johnson Ozoemenam Urama, 'For thousands of years, observations of the cosmos have guided communities in practical and spiritual ways, from agriculture and navigation to religion and ritual. Indigenous communities were the keepers of a rich body of astronomical observations and knowledge, sometimes encoded in the myths and folklore passed down through generations. Yet over the centuries, this connection to the skies has been lost.'[27] Finding this connection isn't about living life based on your daily horoscope. But perhaps by reconnecting with cycles and the cosmos as a whole, we can find a little more meaning and a little more magic in our lives.

Future Ancestor: Gogo Dineo Ndlanzi

Gogo Dineo is a sangoma and a gobela (a trainer and an initiator of other healers) of Nguni and Ndau heritage and an iThongo elimhlophe (initiate), a path exclusive to those who have a Xhosa bloodline. Having been mentored in many spiritual paths, from Christianity to Rastafarianism to Buddhism, she has a deep understanding of spirituality and is committed to helping Africans awaken their Divinity through African spirituality. Speaking about nature as a teacher, she says, *'How the elements of nature interact with each other is complementary instead of competitive. Bees do not compete with flies because they understand their role. You will not see the sun chasing the bees away or the sunflower running away from the bees because it understands that in order to pollinate it needs the bees. We can learn from this idea of complementarity over competition.'*

NATURE AND WELLBEING

Before we delve into the benefits of reconnecting with nature, let's take a moment to discuss what nature is according to the Oxford Dictionary. It states that nature is 'the phenomena of the physical world collectively, including plants, animals, the landscape, and other features and products of the earth, as opposed to humans or human creations'. Within this definition lies part of our problem – that humans are seen as separate to nature rather than a part of it – but we'll forgive that for the moment so we can explore how interacting with nature affects our wellbeing without opening the Pandora's box of human relationships (that's for another book!). Many scientific studies have shown that time in nature can boost physical and mental health, providing benefits ranging from lower blood pressure to reduced stress, but a study from the University of Exeter[28] put a number on it: 120 minutes a week. That's how much time we need to spend in nature to reap the benefits. But, as already mentioned, sitting among the trees isn't the only way to connect with nature and it's not the only way to reap benefits.

Empathy

Seeing ourselves as connected to the universe around us makes us more empathetic towards it. By being more in tune with ourselves as nature, we might be less likely to act in ways that are destructive to the planet and more likely to demand fairer practices from the companies and governments who hold more power to make impactful change. This empathy isn't just good for the planet and those around us, it helps us build better relationships, manage our emotions and cultivate a sense of – here comes my favourite word again – belonging.

Inspiration

The cosmos is awe-inspiring. Whether we're thinking about the forest, the seasons, the moon or anything else, it's difficult not to feel struck with wonder and inspiration. Inspiration helps us to see the bigger picture, which can take us out of the minutiae of everyday life, relieving us from stress. It also boosts creativity, which is, in turn, good for us, as we've explored in Chapter 6.

Self-esteem

Have you ever experienced the immense pride of eating a delicious meal and knowing that you grew, cultivated and harvested everything on the plate? No, me neither, but I imagine it would be a huge boost for your self-esteem! When I visited my friend Kwaku on his land, he taught me how to harvest cocoyam and kontomire, which we later used to make our dinner. I was extremely proud of myself, even though all I did was swoop in at the last minute and pull a few things out of the ground. But it felt good to work for my meal, and to really know where my food came from. Whether you start your own vegetable garden, raise chickens, or even just support a local farmer, you'll feel so much better about what you're eating and the impact it's having on you, your community and the environment at large.

Sleep

Spending time in nature promotes good sleep as it reduces our stress levels. But there's another way to beat insomnia too and that is by working with rather than against the cycle of day and night. Melatonin is an important hormone for sleep, inducing drowsiness and signalling to the body that it's time for rest. Light is a critical indicator for the pineal gland, which produces melatonin, so traditionally it knew to produce more melatonin when the sun went down and less when it was up. These days, artificial light and the constant presence of screens has thrown off our melatonin production. By aligning your environment – lighting and devices – with the natural cycle of day and night, you can realign your melatonin production and have better sleep.

READY TO RETURN?

What image comes to mind when you think of people returning to nature? Is it a hippie commune? People living off-grid in a semi-cult? Do you hear the self-righteous preaching of the zero-waste brigade begging you to use beeswax wrap instead of cling film? These are all totally fair imaginings, but you don't have to be a bona fide tree-hugger to embrace natural living. And it's not an all-or-nothing commitment. Whether your main concern is detoxifying your body, saving the planet or spiritual growth, every little helps.

NATURE PRACTICES FOR THE MODERN AFRICAN

Bring the Elements into Your Home

So you don't fancy living in a house made of mud? No problem! There are other ways to bring the natural elements into your home:

- House plants – In addition to looking nice, house plants can also purify the air in your home. Even if you don't consider yourself a plant person, try putting at least one plant in each room and see how it feels. Worried about killing them? I've been there, and my fears have been realised. Here are some good starter plants that are (almost) impossible to kill; snake plant, spider plant, aloe vera and cactus. Beyond simply shoving the plant in a corner and watering it when it looks sad, it can be beneficial to build a relationship with your plants. Name them, talk to them, move them to a different spot if they look unhappy; they are living beings after all...and research shows that talking to your plants makes them grow faster!

- Natural furniture – Swap out those Ikea flat packs for more natural-looking furniture with pieces made from bamboo, cane, raffia or slabs of wood.

- Get a water feature – Running water is soothing and also helps to purify the air. You don't need to have a garden to get a water feature – small, indoor features are a thing but, heads up, they're also quite pricey.

- Open the windows – This may sound super obvious but, especially if you live in a hot country, you might find yourself conditioned to reach for the fan or the AC remote instead of opening your windows. Save on electricity and improve your indoor air quality by making windows your first port of call and only switching to a cooling device when absolutely necessary.

- Light a fire – If you have a fireplace, a fire is a wonderful way to warm the home. If outdoor space allows, a bonfire is always magical, and a great excuse to invite some loved ones over. On a smaller scale, lighting candles indoors, while it is absolutely not going to warm you up, does set a nice ambience and help to relieve stress, especially if you opt for a scented candle.

Make a Herb and Vegetable Garden

Getting green fingers is a great way to spend time in nature and to better connect with your food. If, like me, you don't have a garden, you can still grow! I have a wheelbarrow on my balcony for growing herbs and have attempted to grow some vegetables in regular plant pots.

To save money and do some recycling at the same time, you can grow your herbs or vegetables in plastic bottles – simply cut them in half and use the base. If you have the time and patience, you can also grow from your groceries instead of buying seedlings. After all, almost every piece of fruit or veg you buy to eat has the potential to grow into a new plant. You can germinate the seeds or, in the case of herbs, propagate some cuttings, then plant them.

Once you have an abundant natural grocery, be sure to share your spoils with your community. Whether that means giving some goods to friends or to a homeless shelter, it's always important that when Mother Earth blesses us, we share the spoils.

Schedule Time in Nature

As per the study mentioned earlier, two hours a week should do the trick. It doesn't have to be two hours all at once; it can be split into several occasions. If you don't schedule it in, it probably won't happen, so take some time to think about how you're going to make time in nature part of your routine. If you already go for a run a few times a week, can you alter your route so you stop off in a park? If you already see your niece and nephew every week, can you decide to take them to the beach instead of playing indoors? Can you read, write, work, meditate, work out, eat in the garden, park, beach or forest instead of inside?

Respect Cycles of Nature

Stop trying to outwit nature. Life is much easier and more enjoyable if you work with rather than against it. Here are some ideas:

- Use low, warm lighting in the evening – I hardly ever turn on my lights. I have fairy lights in my living room that I use after the sun goes down, or sometimes I use candlelight. Warm bulbs are less disruptive to your melatonin production than harsh, bright lights, so they are a good choice for your lamps and bedroom lights.

- No screens before bed – The ideal time to stop using screens is two hours before you want to be asleep but even 10 minutes is better than nothing, so just do what you can. I'll share a bedtime ritual with you in Chapter 12 with some ideas of what you can do while you're separated from your beloved phone.

- Put your devices on night mode if no screens isn't an option – most devices have a night mode option, which reduces the amount of blue light (that's the worst one for sleep) coming through your screen. You can set up an automatic transition to night mode on most phones, tablets and computers – mine are all set to go into night mode at the same time the sun goes down, and to turn off when the sun comes up.

- Notice and work with your personal cycle – If you have a menstrual cycle, take notice of how it affects your body and your mood at different stages. Whether you have a menstrual cycle or not, take notice of your daily fluctuations. With some awareness, you might find that you're particularly creative in the mornings or that you have a better workout in the afternoons, or that your presentation skills improve during ovulation. When you're knowledgeable about your personal cycles, you can make them work for you.

- Use moon cycles, eclipses, solstices and equinoxes for personal growth – Whether you believe that these celestial events have a material impact on us as humans or not, you can use them as a guide for reflection and growth. Moon rituals are discussed in Chapter 12. Think of eclipses as a time for revelations and major change. Use solar eclipses to reflect on what new beginnings you want to bring into effect, and use lunar eclipses to make decisions about what needs to make a swift exit from your life. Your view of the solstices and equinoxes may differ depending on if you're in the Global North or South, but, for me, they represent the genesis of a time for resting and making plans (December solstice), a time for taking action (March equinox), a time for enjoying the fruits of your labour and reflecting on what has or hasn't worked (June solstice) and a time for refocusing, then winding down (September equinox).

Embrace Nontoxic Living

When it comes to living well, there are so many things to think about. Climate change, the water crisis, fair trade, fast fashion, recycling, animal rights... the list goes on. It's truly overwhelming and entirely unrealistic for any one person to tackle. I've found it helpful, instead of trying to adapt every area of my life for each of these causes, to focus on just one: nontoxic living. By doing my best to reduce my personal intake of toxins, I inevitably end up making choices that are also better for the environment, better for small businesses and better for me. Some examples are:

- Diet changes – I eat less meat, less packaged food, and more fresh, local produce.

- Natural toiletries – For the most part, I make my own toiletries (black soap, shea butter, ACV[iv] or coconut oil are the basis of almost all of them), and those that I buy come from small businesses with ethical practices.

- Less plastic – In the UK, I fill up my reusable bottle with tap water, but in Ghana, drinking tap water isn't really an option for me. Instead, I have a clay water filter, which means I avoid buying water in plastic bottles.

- Fewer new clothes – I get almost all my clothes second-hand from thrift stores or as hand-me-downs from my very fashionable friend Belle. New clothes I get handmade by local tailors or buy from Black-owned brands.

- Fewer toxic people – The better I become at avoiding toxic relationships, the more present and nurturing I can be in other relationships, and that includes my relationship with you, dear reader! If my life had gone in a different direction, influenced by different people, I wouldn't be writing this book.

I want to be 100 per cent clear: I'm not saying I've succeeded in removing all toxins from my life... and that's not even my goal because it sounds both unrealistic and unbearably tedious to me. Some say that sugar is a toxin, but a life without baked goods is not a life worth living (chocolate melty-middle is my fave). Some say that alcohol is a toxin, but wine-drinking Sardinians are among the longest-living people on the planet (I'm on an eternal hunt for Black-owned vineyards so, if you know any, hit me up). Some say that mainstream media is toxic, but I'm mildly obsessed with MCU (Marvel Cinematic Universe to the uninitiated). My point is that my approach to nontoxic living is to do what you can and take incremental steps. Doing a small something is better than doing nothing at all.

---

iv Apple cider vinegar. A favourite of anyone who loves DIY toiletries.

Be a Custodian of the Planet

A trend I've noticed in recent years is that people choose 'saving the planet' as their cause, whether through veganism, reducing their carbon footprint or going off-grid – and it's a noble cause – but then subsequently develop an air of self-righteousness and judgementalism that I just don't see with other causes. In addition, causes relating to the environment and animal rights appear overwhelmingly white. The refrain of 'I'm making sure we have a world to pass on to our great-great-grandchildren' especially gives me pause. Because, to be honest, I wouldn't *want* to hand this world to my great-great-grandchildren. And I'm not sure any person of colour would. I'm not saying we shouldn't attempt to save the planet (though, let's be honest, what the planet needs saving from is humans) but by fighting for environmental causes without also trying to make the world a better place for marginalised people, all you're really doing is preserving the current system in which we live. Which is wonderful for your white descendants but not so good for my brown ones. Focusing on saving the planet gives people a pass on doing the deep and difficult inner work of reckoning with their role in the system that continues to oppress and degrade certain groups of people – a system that we are *all* complicit in upholding. Instead, all you have to reckon with is your past carbon footprint or the fact that you used to eat animals when you were 'less evolved', neither of which carry particularly burdensome levels of residual guilt. I propose that instead of trying to 'save' the planet as it is, we each view ourselves as custodians of the planet, including everything, every*one*, on it. What might that look like?

- doing the necessary work of recognising our privilege and identifying how we can use it for good

- unlearning hatred, discrimination and prejudice

- uplifting the voices of people of colour in environmental activism

- spotlighting and fundraising for Indigenous-led conservation initiatives – after all, Indigenous people are the original environmental activists – instead of starting our own

- not being judgemental about what we perceive to be people not 'pulling their weight' in the fight for climate change. Some people are so tired from the daily fight to simply exist as a Black, brown, queer, disabled, neurodiverse, unemployed or chronically ill person that they can't care about using a KeepCup or taking a tote bag to the grocery store. Not they don't care, they *can't* care – they have no reserves of energy or emotional capacity left with which to care.

If we each step into our roles as custodians, starting with these actions and doing the best we can, we can truly say we're on the path to leaving a better world behind for all future generations instead of just some.

SHEA BUTTER BABY

Our movement away from nature, away from the cosmos, away from ourselves has not served humans well. Our internal environments are ravaged with disease, stress, death and destruction. Our external environment is ravaged with disease, stress, death and destruction. We have attempted to contort and control the world around us and its patterns to fit our flawed vision of progress. We describe activities that should be inherent to our daily lives – rest, sleep, time in nature – as luxuries. Things may look pretty dire, but the good news is that nature will always be home. It hasn't left us because it is of us. So, whenever we're ready, we can take steps to return to Mother Earth, to return to the family that is nature.

It's true, I do dream of hippie life in my future, living in my clay house, shopping in my garden instead of a grocery store and spending my evenings sitting by a fire. But that's far from the only way. Even with a simple commitment to get to know yourself better, you're already making your way back home. So are you ready for the journey?

Part IV
MAGICK

Sesa Wo Suban – 'Change your behaviour.'

*When you change your behaviour, you change
your life. We have the capacity to create magick,
to create transformational change. But to do so,
we have to be willing to confront our thoughts,
confront our beliefs and confront our behaviour.
When we commit to change, anything is possible.*

Chapter 10

STORYTELLING

'Stories are the palm oil
with which wisdom is swallowed.'
Usifu Jalloh

When Europeans came to Africa, they said we didn't have an education system. The truth is, we had a system of learning that far outshines – and in some cases informs today's Western educational system. For example, the earliest known mathematical artefact, the Lebombo bone, appears to show evidence of people (most likely women) tracking the moon cycle. Found by South African archaeologist Peter Beaumont in the 1970s, it features 29 distinct notches carved into a baboon's fibula. The bone is estimated to be between 43,000 and 44,000 years old and was found in the Border Cave area, between the places we know today as South Africa and eSwatini. Another example comes from the Yoruba tradition, where their Ifá divination system, through which babalawos support people with everything from illness to job hunting, is founded upon a complex system of mathematics. In their book, *Religious Beliefs and Knowledge Systems in Africa*, Toyin Falola and Nicole Griffin state, 'This system of divination has been studied as a mathematical permutation that involves the binary multiplication of the Ifa figures to produce the 256 Odu [literary corpus of Ifá]… The Ifa divination system has been proven to have some similarities with the coding system of computer science.' These examples show how Africans gained knowledge through practical application rather than the Western concept of classroom-style learning. As the birthplace of civilisation, it should come as no surprise to us that African communities throughout time have been far more advanced than modern whitewashed history would have us believe. We learned through rites of passage (more on this in Chapter 12), through shadowing our elders, through guiding young ones and through applying knowledge to everyday life. The African system of learning was about gaining knowledge through experience, knowledge that would help each person live a good life – a life worth emulating. And one educational tool that continues to espouse knowledge is storytelling.

Storytelling is truly unrivalled as a form of both archiving and educating. This age-old African wisdom – the power of storytelling – is often shared today as if it is new and revolutionary information. There are countless articles and seminars designed to teach you how to use storytelling to teach, to sell, to make your brand memorable and so on. What Africans have always known is that storytelling elicits emotion, and emotion is what creates experience, and experience is what transforms information into knowledge. Storytelling creates transformational change; it is a tool for making magick.

You'd be forgiven for thinking that African storytelling only takes the shape of folk tales, but storytelling manifests itself in every area of our lives. Proverbs are a form of storytelling, as are many languages in and of themselves. The conversations we have with others – and with ourselves – are a form of storytelling. The modern expression of stories includes literature, film, TV, plays, songs and even social media content. All of these things shape who we are and shape the world around us. With intention and positive direction, we can use all forms of storytelling to create the change we want to see in the world. As the face of storytelling changes, how can we keep its spirit alive?

TRADITIONAL STORYTELLING IN AFRICA

'Once upon a time...'

'Time time.' In Ghana, this is one of the modern-day call and response phrases that opens a storytelling session. Another, which seems to be present in West Africa and parts of the Diaspora, is:

'Story, story.'

'Story.'

'Who born your mama?'

'Story.'

'Who born your papa?'

'Story.'

A traditional Twi opening is 'Anansesemsesow'. Ancestor and legendary sangoma, writer and artist Vusamazulu Credo Mutwa started his Zulu tales with 'Indaba, my children'. No matter what words are used to open a story, though, the remainder of the experience bears resemblance across Africa. Stories were traditionally told in the evening, around a fire, by an elder or the community storyteller. Stories were typically either cosmological in nature – for example, creation stories – or fables designed to share life lessons, often through the personification of animals. One of the most popular characters from African storytelling is Kwaku Ananse, a mischievous but highly intelligent trickster who is most often portrayed as a spider.

Anansesem, the collection of stories featuring Kwaku Ananse as a protagonist, which many children across the world, from Ghana to Jamaica, grew up with, is an excellent study on the power of African storytelling. Each of these stories features most, if not all, of the following things:

- God as a character – Belief in a higher power is presented as a given rather than a question.

- A moral lesson – The stories instil the community values in those who listen.

- Humour – The stories are entertaining as well as educational.

- Flexibility – Aside from those stories told only by healers and chosen elders, traditional African stories belong to the community. There is no ownership of the stories and, due to our oral tradition, the same story can be told in different ways. Gifted storytellers turn each story into a truly communal activity, whether through the incorporation of drumming, singing and dance or call and response.

- The incorporation of music and dance – Traditional African storytelling is almost inseparable from drumming, singing and movement. As mentioned in previous chapters, music and dance tell a story, and in the same way, storytelling is done through music and dance, not just words.

With the Westernisation of the continent, traditional storytelling doesn't hold the same place in our lives that it once did. Young people often move away from the places where they grew up to the big cities, so not only are they listening to the stories less, but they also lose out on the opportunity to retell the stories, which is really the best way to cement them in your memory. Even for those who stay in their communities, storytelling around the fire has been replaced with watching TV, going to the local hangout spot or any other number of activities that are seen as more modern or fun. Of course, times are supposed to change, so this isn't necessarily a bad thing and, as we've already mentioned, storytelling appears in many forms. So the question we have to ask ourselves is what stories – in other words, what lessons, morals and values – are being taught in place of the traditional ones.

Traditional African storytelling did find its way to the Diaspora but, since the pastime was unlikely to find us in a community or school setting, experiencing them relied heavily on our (exhausted, overworked and underpaid) parents – and on our willingness to listen to an Ananse story with no visual aids rather than having 'The Very Hungry Caterpillar' read to us for the thousandth time. In addition to this, stories being read to us seemed to be something that should be reserved for young kids. As soon as the mpaninsem[i] kicked in, we would read our own bedtime stories, thank you very much. My faves were anything by Jacqueline Wilson, classic young adult series *Nancy Drew* and *Sweet Valley High* and the OG *Are You There God? It's Me, Margaret*. All excellent stories and all decidedly lacking in Black characters. In fact, the only substantial Black characters I remember reading are those created by the legendary Malorie Blackman. Just a handful of books in a whole childhood of bookwormery. Now, as an adult, I love discovering new Anansesem tales (even though I can never remember them afterwards, so please, when you see me, don't say, 'Tell me an African story'), reading Zulu mythology and devouring all the African literature I can, but I can't help feeling like I'm trying to play catch-up when the true moment has passed. So then the question becomes, Even if we can't go back in time to how storytelling used to be, how do we keep its essence alive for ourselves and for the generations to come?

Future Ancestor: Usifu Jalloh

Usifu, also known as the Cowfoot Prince, is a storyteller and educator who describes himself as an architect for social change and cultural awakening. Born in Sierra Leone, he is of Fulani and Limba heritage, currently living in the UK, but his work is truly international, taking him everywhere from Argentina to South Korea to Kenya. Unsurprisingly, Usifu

---

i   Pronounced mm-PEH-nyin-SEM. An Akan word for a child who thinks they're grown.

has a way with words. When we discuss storytelling as an educational tool, he says, *'The African way of education starts by opening up the emotion, and the emotion opens up the brain. The European starts with the brain and often stops there too, never progressing to emotion.'* This is why *'even in its simplest form, storytelling can carry the most complex, intricate information to help design and recreate a person or community'*.

He encapsulates the immense power of storytelling with one sentence: *'The success or failure of every person, family, community, organisation or country is entirely dependent on the narrative that they conceive, that they perceive, that they believe, that they accept and that they eventually act upon.'*

MODERN-DAY MYTHS

A while back, I was having a conversation with my new friend kobby ananse (remember him from Chapter 5?) about tradition. I was lamenting the difficulty we face at times in our quest to rediscover and learn knowledge that was once so integral to our Ancestors' lives – for example regional myths and libation prayers – and his response is something I think about a lot, especially when sitting down to write this book. He said that he had shared a similar sentiment with one of his elders, and they said to him, 'You are the new elders.' Yes, kobby ananse shared, it is important to understand and, as much as possible, protect and archive the traditional ways. But it's also our job as the next generation to build upon this knowledge and create *new* traditions, practices and tools that will keep the knowledge alive.

A similar sentiment was expressed by the elders I visited at the National Folklore Board, a government department charged with protecting and promoting Ghanaian folklore, including storytelling. I went to them to seek permission to use Adinkra in my oracle deck. Honestly, I was pretty scared they would say no. But they loved the idea and were thankful to have a young person interested in preserving the culture… and to actually have someone seek their counsel instead of just using the symbols willy-nilly. They also said it was up to us 'young ones' to modernise traditional knowledge so that it doesn't get left behind.

So as it was told to me, I am now telling you. *We are the new elders.* That's not to say we can just throw tradition out the window and create a whole new one but rather that, with a foundation in understanding, respecting and celebrating our traditions, we can – actually, we *must* – build new manifestations of them.

The Stories We Tell

This sentiment of us being the new elders applies to every area of this book and to every area of life. In storytelling, it takes many forms. It makes me so happy to see:

- my niece and nephew reading children's books with illustrations that look like them and featuring characters like Ananse

- platforms like Owari Kids reimagining edutainment (entertaining and educational) content for preschoolers to normalise Afro-Caribbean cultures

- the rise of the African magical realism genre in literature; important because it acknowledges that many of these magical stories are not pure fantasy but rather rooted in the spirituality and, yes, magic that exists within our communities, our histories and our futures

- platforms like kweliTV that give us ownership of our content

- the ever-increasing ability to get African and Diasporan news and current affairs from African and Diasporan publishers and content creators

- the global popularity of modern African music – from Malian chill to Kumerican drill – that tells African stories.

Whenever we are telling a story, we must be clear on our intentions. Usifu reminds us, 'You have immense responsibility, so be clear on what imprint you want to leave on the memory of your audience.' The examples above show a clear intention of reclaiming the narrative. For so long, our stories have been told for us. Even as we have gained the power to speak for ourselves, our work is somewhat shaped by what the industry wants to hear from us, from what 'sells'.

And it seems like, more often than not, what sells is either Black trauma or Black exceptionalism. While it's important for us to remember and respect the traumas we have experienced and continue to experience as a people, I think we can all agree that there is a wealth of content centring on that aspect of the Black experience. Not just this but also, it tends to be the *same* trauma that we're retelling – and therefore reliving – time and time again. Slavery, sexual abuse, crime, poverty, racism. Many of our other struggles remain unexplored and largely ignored. Why can't we see a middle-class Black woman struggling with depression? Why can't we see more stories of Black people navigating queerphobia?

On the other side of the spectrum, it seems that in our attempt to tell stories of more than just trauma, the go-to counter-narrative has become, 'We are descended from Kings and Queens.' While that's a nice sentiment and all, chale, some of us are descended from carpenters, fishermen, batikers, herbalists and village drunks. And that's okay! We don't have to be royalty to be worthy – that's what white supremacy would have us believe. I love stories of Black Excellence – but we don't have to be excellent to be worthy either.

Did you ever watch *The Incredible Jessica James* on Netflix? I did, and I LOVED it. Not just because LaKeith Stanfield was in it, although let's be honest, how could you *not* love anything that features him? And not because it's a particularly great film – it's feel-good, but it's not a masterpiece. I loved it because it was a film with a Black female protagonist… that wasn't *about* her being a Black female. It was about her being a slightly awkward, slightly lost, slightly arrogant twenty-something trying to navigate life and love. These are the stories I love to see. Too often Black characters exist because of their Blackness, whether it's in a Black film or TV show, or they're playing the Black character in a white film or TV show. We need more stories of us just living, where we have full, complex stories and instead of doing 'Black things' we just do… things.

The Future of Storytelling

Even though stories of trauma and stories of excellence might seem to be on opposite ends of the spectrum, they both stem from the idea of scarcity. Whether it's a woman racing against time to get a man and/or baby, men hustling to 'make it' or families with more secrets and drama than the *Real Housewives*, scarcity is the common thread. Even the apparent stories of abundance – which tell us that the only rich Black people are criminals, royalty or from a fictional country – reinforce the idea of scarcity, because they tell the story of the exceptions, or those who made it 'against all odds'.

This is especially disheartening because Africa is literally the land of abundance. Just like other Indigenous communities, our Ancestors weren't concerned with ownership and individualism. We lived in communion with each other and with the land, safe in the knowledge that there is always enough to go round because Asase Yaa is the sustainer of life. A scarcity mindset – which is the driving force behind ideas of ownership and individualism – is a Western import that we've internalised as our truth. It's time for us to do the work of returning to the abundance mindset that is our nature, and stories can help us do that. Usifu says, 'We must create stories that tell of abundance – an abundance culture is the true culture of Africa. Scarcity culture came from the West. We cannot any longer accept the narrative of "let's lift Africans out of poverty". Instead we must look at how we as Africans develop the wealth we already have, the wealth that is here on our land.'

Of course, an abundance mindset alone isn't going to make the very real challenges we face as Black people simply disappear. It's not so easy to believe in abundance when you're facing a system that is literally designed to keep you broke, fearful, underpaid and undernourished. Or when the main form of abundance you see is your leaders chopping[ii] the same money that's supposed to be building your country. But with these stories of abundance we can at least have access to concepts and ideas that show a different way of living. A story about the joys of growing your own fruits and vegetables, a story about connecting with your community, a story about coming together for susu – these are all stories of abundance that can inspire Black people around the world instead of feeding us the same stories of infidelity, struggle and poverty.

Future Ancestor: Maïmouna Jallow

Maïmouna is a Spanish-Gambian storyteller of Fulani and Wolof heritage. Currently residing in a small village in Spain, she grew up mostly in Togo and the UK but has also spent time living in São Tomé and Kenya.

She reminds us that we shouldn't sacrifice truth by aiming to tell only positive stories: *'It's not about telling positive stories, it's about telling truthful stories; the good and the bad. We're pulled towards telling positive stories because of the Western gaze, because we're so aware of how, for so long, they have told our stories and portrayed us in a negative light that we don't want to start airing our dirty laundry so they can say*

---

ii   Pidgin term meaning 'eat', often used in reference to spending money, as heard in the classic P-Square and Akon song 'Chop My Money'.

> *"aha, you see!" For me, the main thing is to forget about them as an audience, I'm not talking to them. We're talking amongst ourselves, and we know the truth. We know that when we say something bad it doesn't mean that everything is bad. When we say something good it doesn't mean that everything is good. We can have a deep and nuanced conversation.'*

We are slowly but surely doing the work of reclaiming the narrative on Africa, Africans and the global Black population. Whether it's publishing a book with Hay House or having Netflix as a sole distributor for a film, Black creators are gaining more opportunities to tell our own stories on leading platforms – but often we are reliant on these non-Black platforms to get the level of access, funding, scale and reach our content deserves. There's still a long way to go in terms of full ownership. Companies like Farafina Books, aftown and iROKOtv are leading the charge in shifting this reality, but the truth is, we can't tell our stories and *own* our stories without money. Black creators, Black platforms, Black distributors – we all need to get paid in order to create, produce, publish and distribute freely and to the scale needed to really get our stories out there. We've all heard time and time again that the Black pound or Black dollar or Black whatever currency you get paid in is powerful (okay maybe not the Black cedi, but stay with me). We like to spend money and what we choose to spend on as a people grows! To this day, I'm praying for someone to start a Black-owned version of Hennessy because the way they are raking in our hard-earned cash just ain't right. TikTok, MAC, hell even Supermalt. These brands are where they are today because Black people love them… but none of them are Black-owned.

Remember, I'm not about dogma, so I'm not saying we should *only* buy from Black-owned brands. But we must as a people become way more intentional about how we spend our money, time and attention. And supporting Black storytelling doesn't have to cost money. On social media, engagement turns into opportunities and money for Black content creators. New, brave, Black-centric platforms need us to be early adopters so they can raise capital and establish their brand. Distributors need our support through promotion and, if we can afford it, patronage if they are to compete in the market. In December 2021, the UK's first ever Black bookshop announced its closure after 55 years operating in North London, not just as a bookshop but as a true icon and cultural centre for Black people across the city. Unsurprisingly, the community was devastated and rallied together to support a crowdfunding campaign. New Beacon Books achieved their initial target of £35,000 in just 24 hours and went on to raise a total of £81,122. Not only has the physical space remained open, at the time of writing they are in a position to consider moving to a larger premises and scaling up their publishing and events arm, which would further enable them to support young creators. This is just one example of the power of us putting our money where our mouth is. Another success story – after being noticed by 'Humans of New York', the crowdfunding campaign started by Ghanaian photographer Paul Ninson raised $1 million in 24 hours, money that will build Africa's largest photo library in Ghana. This is the kind of transformational change – magick – that we can create when we come together as a community. To secure the future of Black and African storytelling, we need to support Black and African storytellers.

The Stories We Don't Tell

In addition to the stories we share and consume, there's a whole world of stories that we reserve for ourselves. Some of them are conscious and others unconscious, but all of them drive our actions and have a huge impact on our lives. Our actions are a manifestation of our beliefs, and our beliefs are a product of our thoughts. The thoughts that we entertain – and accept – about ourselves, others and the world around us shape our reality. When we're continuously exposed to harmful or negative thoughts, whether they originate from us or from others, they can contribute to a wide range of issues. Poor mental health is both a cause and an effect of repeatedly telling ourselves harmful stories. If you're reading this book, then you're already aware of the importance of us taking care of our mental health. But for Black people, this is a point worth labouring because the potential dangers of poor mental health are greater for us.

We're More at Risk

The statistic that's most commonly quoted when it comes to mental health is that one in four of us will experience a mental illness this year. This is the figure quoted in the UK and at a global level from the World Health Organization. However, since racism and discrimination are risk factors for poor mental health, Black people – particularly those in non-majority Black countries or areas – may be more at risk.

Institutional Racism

In addition to facing a higher likelihood of suffering poor mental health, the Mental Health Foundation[29] states that, in the UK, Black men are more likely to have experienced a psychotic disorder in the last year than white men, and Black people are four times more likely to be detained under the Mental Health Act than white people. Black people, in their most vulnerable moments, are more likely to be treated like nuisances at best or criminals at worst instead of receiving the care and compassion they need.

Community Stigma

In Black communities around the world, a stigma persists around poor mental health. In some communities it's seen as a 'white man's disease', in others as a spiritual affliction and in others still evidence of witchcraft. This makes it much more difficult for some to seek the help and support they need.

Poor Access to Support

We've already discussed in Chapter 7 some challenges around pharmaceutical access in Africa and institutional racism in the healthcare systems of the Diaspora. When it comes to therapy, the first barrier is stigma. It's seen as a white person's activity, a waste of money or a way of shaming the family by going to spread your business. What we don't realise is that by moving away from our traditional practice of spending time with elders and visiting healers when we had emotional or spiritual problems, we've left a gaping hole in our lives that therapy can contribute to filling. Therapy saved my life. Therapy has saved the lives of many. As a community we have to stop shaming people for thinking about or seeking therapy, for seeking something that has the potential to save them.

Once we get past the stigma though, there are still a few other hurdles to jump. Firstly, therapy is expensive. Even if you're in a country like the UK where healthcare is 'free', you have to face barriers like doctors trying to put you on pills before offering you therapy or the months-long waiting lists between referral and first session. Once you've made it past the barriers to entry and you're able to have therapy, another challenge is finding the right therapist to work with. On the continent, the main issue is having so few therapists to choose from in the first place. Here in Accra, everyone I know who has a therapist is seeing one of two names that keep coming up. Many of the mental health professionals we have work in a clinical setting as that's where they're most needed, leaving few options for outpatient therapy, especially for those who fear being seen entering a psychiatric institution. The situation is so dire that after having had an introductory call with a couple of therapists and not vibing with them and being given a months-long waiting list by the one she *did* like, one of my friends had to turn back to the UK to find a virtual therapist. Very few people have this privilege. In a UK or Western setting, while there are more therapists, there is still a limited number of Black therapists to choose from and, owing to this relatively low number, they're in high demand. Having a therapist who doesn't understand your cultural context can do more harm than good. However, while the obvious answer might seem to be getting a therapist with the same background as you, that isn't necessarily a guarantee for success, and within the profession the focus is more on training culturally sensitive therapists and adapting therapy frameworks that are traditionally Eurocentric.[30]

My best experience with therapy was with a white therapist, Kubi May, the therapist I'm referring to when I say therapy saved my life. My initial impression was, 'How does this posh hippie white woman think she's going to fix me with art therapy?' In fact, I told her straight up to keep the art therapy and woo-woo business to a minimum and focus on 'normal' therapy, whatever that is. Tell me why a few sessions later I'm doing, 'Yes, the feeling has the colour yellow', and holding back tears as I doodle the things that are too painful to speak. My time with Kubi was absolutely transformational and I believe that without her I wouldn't be here writing this book.

So what made Kubi and I connect despite very obviously coming from different backgrounds? At the most basic level she was culturally sensitive, understanding some of the unique challenges associated with being Black and being from an African family, and she was willing to explore them with me rather than avoid issues of race owing to her own discomfort, as many white therapists have admitted they do. But more than that, it was her nonjudgement and compassion that made our relationship work. Now, you might think, 'Isn't every therapist supposed to be nonjudgemental and compassionate?', and the answer is yes. But the fact is therapists are human and they can't leave all their humanness outside the door. From the other two therapists I've worked with, I felt judgement, dismissiveness and condescension. I've heard from other people of colour that, when getting a therapist of the same race, they felt like they were talking to a judgemental auntie rather than an impartial professional. So yes, we do need more Black mental health professionals, and it can be useful to opt for a Black therapist – my newest therapist is a Black female I found through the BetterHelp app – but most important is that you connect with and feel totally safe with whoever you decide to work with.

STORYTELLING AND WELLBEING

You might not instinctively link storytelling to wellbeing, but it plays a huge part in our mental and emotional growth both as individuals and as a society. The books we read, the programmes we watch, the music we listen to, the conversations we engage with – all of these stories we consume have an effect on us. One example of this is something that many scientific studies have found – reading fiction makes us more empathetic. Some studies have gone so far as to show how specific books – like Harry Potter for example – make us more empathetic generally but also more tolerant of minoritised groups. A 2015 study[31] published in the *Journal of Applied Social Psychology* found that reading the wizardry series made children of various ages more empathetic towards immigrants, refugees and the LGBTQ+ community (It's a shame it appears not to have had the same effect on its author). When we think of storytelling as the stories we tell ourselves in terms of our self-talk and our ingrained beliefs, these impact everything from our self-esteem to our relationships. So whether we're referring to the act of creating stories, consuming stories or managing the internal stories we tell, how can these things affect our wellbeing?

Belonging

Gathering together around a fire to share stories obviously instils feelings of belonging. But this can also be achieved even when you read a book at home by yourself. When we recognise ourselves in the characters we are reading about, hearing about or watching, we feel seen. Being an observer as someone who looks like us navigates the same challenges we struggle with day after day shows us that we are not alone. This is why (nonstereotypical or nontokenistic) representation in literature and other mediums is so important.

You may have noticed that most protagonists are flawed in some way. They might have the mischievousness of Brer Rabbit, the self-centredness of Joan in *Girlfriends* or the impulsivity of Zélie in Tomi Adeyemi's *Legacy of Orïsha* series. These characters are purposefully created as flawed beings because *we* are flawed beings. In order to connect with the characters and the story – which is, in my opinion, the only way we can learn anything from it – we have to be able to relate to the characters. None of us would find an entirely perfect individual relatable. However, these flawed beings usually go on some kind of hero's journey. As the story progresses, they grow and they do better (it could be argued that Brer Rabbit simply becomes more cunning, but intelligence too is good, abi?[iii]). So, far from these stories giving us a free pass for being mischievous, self-centred or impulsive, they often show us that we can be better.

Creative Outlet

We already know from Chapter 6 that creativity is good for our wellbeing and storytelling is a creative exploit we all engage in, whether we consider ourselves storytellers or not. Sending a juicy voice note, bigging yourself up in an interview, curating the perfect caption – all of these are forms of storytelling. When we can create more spaces for this kind of creativity to flow through us, we experience all the benefits of creativity, from improved self-expression to better relationships.

Humour

This one is pretty self-explanatory – laughter is medicine!

---

iii   Emphasis on the second syllable. A Nigerian pidgin term that equates to 'right?'.

Self-esteem and Mental Health

In cognitive behavioural therapy (CBT), a form of talking therapy, the main objective is to recognise and address distorted ways of thinking in order to drive behavioural change. In other words, it's all about identifying the damaging, often incomplete stories we tell ourselves, and replacing them with more realistic, more nuanced and more positive stories. Just as continually telling ourselves stories where we are the victim, the bad guy, stupid, worthless, unlovable and all the rest will have a negative impact on our sense of self and overall wellbeing, telling ourselves stories where we are deserving of love, care, respect and joy – in other words, truthful stories – can improve our self-esteem and overall mental health.

Social Order

Different cultures and societies have different norms and expectations. To thrive in whatever community you find yourself in, it's important to understand and to navigate these norms. In the olden days, stepping out of line would most definitely lead to death. To be ousted from your community meant to be left without shelter, without protection from predators, without tools for hunting and without human contact. These days, the punishment for being rejected isn't as harsh but it *feels* about the same. Studies have shown that when we experience rejection, some of the same areas of our brain become activated as when we experience physical pain.[32] That's how essential community and belonging are to our lives. If you don't understand the social norms of a community, it's pretty easy to get yourself shunned. Luckily, the values and societal norms of a culture are interwoven in their stories. They are an excellent tool for instilling and reinforcing these values and norms in the community and, for outsiders, provide a useful insight. This is another reason it's essential that more stories exist that reject white supremacy, patriarchy, homophobia, ableism and all other hate-based conditions that affect us as a society.

READY TO RETURN?

New African stories are being written and told every day. They are taking the form of books, short stories, songs, TV shows, poems and plays. If you are a Black person and you bring stories to life, whether through writing, rapping, directing, producing or anything else, you are part of the new generation of African storytellers. But of course there are also the stories that play out in our personal lives rather than on a stage, and these have as big an impact on us and the people around us. In whatever form they come, stories have a transformative power, and this is what makes them an ideal tool for wellbeing. Whether your storytelling level is Ava DuVernay or 'the only stories I tell are to get out of doing the dishes', I have some ideas on how the tradition of African storytelling can inspire your wellbeing journey.

STORYTELLING PRACTICES FOR THE MODERN AFRICAN

Read and Listen to Stories with Intention

Whatever it is you're going through – poor mental health, a break-up, disordered eating, redundancy, addiction, simply trying to be a better person – allow the lessons and experiences of others to firstly assure you that you're not alone and secondly support you on your journey of growth. Some ideas:

- Consume content focused on the challenges you're experiencing. True stories of how others have overcome will be especially helpful.

- As important as it is to engage with stories about people who aren't like you, it's also vital – especially for Black people and people of colour – that we see and hear stories about people who are like us, both positive and negative.

- Recognise the importance of the stories children consume. Whether you're raising children who are Black or not, it's imperative you expose them to content that centres and celebrates Blackness in its many shades.

Use Proverbs for Direction and Motivation

Proverbs are essentially aspirational short-form stories. These little nuggets of age-old wisdom remind you of the kind of person you want to be and the kind of life you want to live. They're kind of like the old-school version of positive affirmations, and they give you the advice of an elder when there isn't one around. According to Ancestor and philosopher Kwame Gyekye, 'We should... use our wisdom constantly and bring it to bear on practical problems of life [to] enhance our well-being.' You can connect with the power of proverbs by:

- sticking them on your mirror or around the house

- having them as your phone background

- putting a proverb in your email signature so you see it repeatedly while working but also share its magick with others

- choosing a different proverb each week or month to focus on.

Working proverbs into your everyday life will provide direction, motivation and connection with your heritage. Here are some of my favourites – and some new ones I discovered while writing this book – to get you started:

Obanyansofoɔ yɛbu no be, yɛnnka no asem. (Akan)
The wise is spoken to in proverbs, not plain language.

Kwaterekwa se ɔbɛma wo ntoma a tie ne din. (Akan)
If a naked man promises you a cloth, listen to his name.

Mgbo aga egbu onye ya na Chi ya di. (Igbo)
Bullets will not kill a person who is with his Chi [God/personal deity or god/spirit].

Ijiji na-enweghi onye ndumodu na-eso ozu ala n'inyi. (Igbo)
A fly that has no counsellor follows the corpse to the grave.

Gbogbo alangba lo d'anu dele, a ko mo eyi t'inu nrun. (Yoruba)
All lizards lie flat on their stomach; it is difficult to determine which has a stomachache.

Bi aba so oko soja ara ile eni ni ba. (Yoruba)
He who throws a stone in the market will hit someone he knows.

ከማን ጋር እንደምትውል ንገረኝ አንተ ማን እንደሆንክ እነግርሀለሁ. (Amharic)
Tell me who you are staying with and I will tell you who you are.

Gishiri na yi wa man kaɗe ɗariyar rana, ran da ruwa ya zo gishiri ya ji kunya. (Hausa)
Salt laughs at shea butter while the sun shines, but when the rain comes, it is ashamed.

Huba inaondoa unyonge. (Swahili)
Love removes misery.

Use Sacred Symbology for Reflection

The Adinkra of West Africa are often referred to as a group of symbols, but this does an injustice to their wisdom and importance. Adinkra is better understood as an ideographic writing system of the Akan people, with each symbol being imbued with deep knowledge that remains relevant today, a couple of centuries (by estimation) after its inception. Adinkra is just one example of this kind of writing system. There is the Samai of the Ga people, symbols of the Ewe people, Nsibidi of Igbo and other peoples in Southern Nigeria, symbols of the Bantu people, vèvè of Haiti and, of course, Medu Neter of Kemet. These writing systems offer us a tool for reflection and spiritual development. By pondering the meaning of each symbol (or in the case of vèvè, the spiritual energy encoded within each symbol) and how it shows up in our lives, we can uncover new information about who we are and how we show up in the world, as well as identify any changes we might want to make to become more of who we want to be. You can connect with these sacred symbols in the same ways suggested for proverbs above. You can also:

- use a card deck like my *Adinkra Oracle Deck* or Ancestor Simone Bresi-Ando's *Adinkra Ancestral Guidance Cards*

- look at the items in your home with fresh eyes – do you spot any Adinkra or other sacred symbols?

Many of us are used to seeing Adinkra symbols – though we may not be aware of it – in art, architecture, clothing and jewellery, but their magick goes far beyond just the aesthetics. It was this knowledge – and my Ancestors – that led me to create an oracle deck based on Adinkra. Even as everything was coming together, I never could have imagined just how powerful these cards would be. Based on my own experience and that of others who've shared with me, the deck provides such deep wisdom and guidance that is so on point that sometimes it's actually a bit scary. You've already been introduced to a few of the Adinkra throughout the book so far; here are a few more, my three favourites:

Dwennimmɛn – 'Ram's horns'
Meaning: Strength in humility

Nea ɔnnim no sua a ɔhu – 'One who doesn't know learns, and then knows.'
Meaning: Continual learning, knowledge

Sankɔfa* – 'Go back and get it'
Meaning: Learn from the past.
*This teaching has two popular associated symbols so I wanted to share both.

Practise Compassion and Self-compassion

We don't reserve stories for works of fiction and for entertainment. We are constantly telling stories about ourselves and others, whether it's through that voice in our head, how we present ourselves to others or doing konkonsa[iv] when we think nobody else can hear us. Maïmouna reminds us, 'If you tell someone the same story about themselves over and over again, they'll end up believing it. You are the story that people build about

---

iv Akan word for 'gossiping'.

you and that you end up creating about yourself. So how do we create an embrace of positive stories around each other?' Here are a few ideas:

- Speak to others, especially children, with kindness and compassion. If you tell a child repeatedly that they are stupid, naughty or ugly, they will come to see themselves as exactly that. Equally if you affirm to a child that they are capable, loved and beautiful, they will internalise these stories instead.

- When you need to have a difficult conversation with someone, make bullet points of what you want to say. It will help you communicate without going off track and using potentially hurtful language.

- Practise active listening, especially in times of conflict. To do this, listen fully when the other person is speaking rather than formulating your response. Then, when they've finished, allow a pause (take a breath) before responding thoughtfully.

- Use self-compassion in self-talk. My favourite definition of self-compassion is 'knowing the difference between *doing* something wrong and *being* something wrong'. The language of self-compassion is, 'This thing didn't work, and I am sad/upset/angry, but also here's what I learned and here's how I can move forward.'

- Practise self-compassion phrases. Two phrases that have helped me not spiral into negative self-talk are, 'and I love myself anyway', and, 'and that's okay'. For example, 'I completely messed up that presentation...and I love myself anyway' or 'It's 19th January and I've forgotten what my resolution was supposed to be...and that's okay.'

The more we can tell stories that are compassionate to ourselves and others, the more we will feel the safety and belonging that allows us to truly thrive.

Go to Therapy

Therapy can be prohibitively expensive. Here are some ways to access some or all of the benefits of the service without the high price tag.

- Search for pro bono and reduced-price sessions – Many therapists offer a limited number of these.

- Attend group therapy and support groups – These are often more affordable and sometimes even free. You can usually find a group specific to your demographic or the challenge you're working through.

- Make use of DIY content such as online courses and videos from trained professionals – This can't replace one-on-one support but it can be a good starting point that you can access instantly.

- Check if your workplace has an Employee Assistance Programme (EAP) or anything similar in your benefits package – This will give you access to free-of-charge therapy sessions.

- Talk to trusted friends and advisers – While they aren't trained professionals and any advice they share shouldn't be followed blindly, simply having the space to talk through what you're experiencing can make a world of difference. On the other side of this, it's up to all of us to do what we can to make this kind of safe space available to our friends and loved ones – they need to feel sure they can come to us for help before they'll do it.

- Confide in your elders – If you're privileged enough to have elders to sit with, take advantage of it while you still can! Time spent with elders is never a waste, and sometimes the wisdom they share with you is so well wrapped in humour and stories that it's only after serious reflection that it slaps you in the face, right when you need it.

If you're able to access one-on-one therapy, here are some tips to ensure you select the right person:

- Research the different types of therapy and see which one you feel will work best for you.

- Go digital. A new app called Talk2Me has recently launched in Ghana to help address some of the barriers people face in accessing therapy and to help match individuals to the best therapist for their needs. Versions of this app exist in other markets too – for example BetterHelp, which I mentioned earlier, and Talkspace.

- Always start with an introductory call or session. This is usually free or lower-priced than the full sessions and is designed for you to get to know the therapist. This is your opportunity to see if you connect with them and if you trust that they will be able to help you. Be sure to ask them if they have experience working with clients who have a similar background or similar challenges to you. And remember, you are not obligated to move forward if you don't feel like they're the right therapist for you. You don't even need to know why – if you don't feel it, you don't feel it!

- Don't select a therapist just because they look like you. Be open to working with someone of a different race or gender to you, but be sure to use the intro session to decide whether you feel they will be best suited to support you.

Write Your Own Stories

Whether you consider yourself a writer or not, writing your own stories can be a therapeutic task. By no means do you need to write the next bestselling novel, and your writing doesn't need to be seen by anyone but you. Different styles of writing can help us at different points in our healing journey.

- Journalling – Recording your thoughts, feelings, experiences and challenges as and when they happen is an excellent way to process everything. Spending time journalling first also makes it much easier to communicate your thoughts and emotions to others later.

- Creative nonfiction – Writing a story about your personal experience is something I find particularly healing and empowering. In creative nonfiction, you use creative writing tools to bring your story to life, whereas journalling is more about recording in plain language. I believe it helps to have some distance from what you're writing about. Turning a fresh break-up into an engaging story while you're in the midst of it wouldn't be much fun, but writing about it a year or so down the line could help you to see it from a different perspective or at the very least find humour or guidance in a situation that once elicited only pain.

- Fiction – Drawing on your own experiences to create fiction can be extremely empowering, whether you're reimagining an alternative past or creating your ideal future.

As well as writing stories, you can express yourself through writing songs, making audio recordings, video, visual art or any other medium that you connect with. Draw on the power of intention to guide you. There are a thousand ways to tell the same story, so how do you want to tell yours?

Be an Advocate for Community Healing

Whether your community is your family, a group of friends, your business partners, local mums and dads or anything else, active, intentional storytelling can aid you in coming together as a group for healing and deeper connection.

STORYTELLING EXERCISE

Maïmouna shared a powerful exercise with me that I would encourage you to practise with a group of people you trust and would like to bond with more deeply.

1. Create cards or pieces of paper, each with a different word on them. The words can be completely random – anything from 'red' to 'tree'.

2. Each person can take anywhere from three to five cards.

3. For each word, start a sentence with, 'I remember...' and tell a (true) story that incorporates this word. Try to build each 'I remember' statement, and therefore, each word, into the same story if possible.

WHAT'S THE 411?

The stories we tell shape the world in which we live. This means that, as storytellers – and make no mistake, we are *all* storytellers – we have the power to inspire true transformational change: in ourselves, in our families, in our communities and in the world. We can look to the African tradition of storytelling as a tool for education and community building. We must each take ownership not just of the stories we share, but also of those we tell ourselves. A safe and healthy internal environment is essential for creating the same energy in our external environment. Taking inspiration from the wisdom of those who came before us as we step into our role as the new elders, we can tell better, more intentional stories – stories that hold the power of transformation. These stories are not just a memory of the past but also a wish for the future. So what kind of future do you want to build?

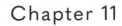

Chapter 11

ANCESTORS

'Every ability, every talent, every trait you have traces back millions of years to millions of individuals, so you are not just a single entity.'

Dalian Adofo

Talking about the Ancestors might be where I lose some of you, but stay with me for a moment. If we want to take a logical view of things, we literally wouldn't be here if not for those who came before us. I wouldn't have written this book and you wouldn't be reading it. So at the most basic level, we have our ancestors to thank for our existence, our being. While we can agree on that, some might find it a step too far to believe that they have any real providence or power over our lives right now, or even feel that it's blasphemous to pray to or call on these beings. Those people would be both correct and mistaken. It *would* be blasphemous to worship or pray to Ancestors as if they are God…and that's why nobody does that, or at least not if they're following tradition.

Indigenous communities around the world revere their Ancestors, but in the Black community we've come to see this as evil or wrong, and that's largely due to misunderstanding. By educating ourselves on the truth of Ancestors, we can build a transformational relationship with them that suits our religious and cultural beliefs. Connecting with those who came before you, in my opinion, is not about magic but it can create *magick*, transformational change. To tap into this, we first need to understand what it actually means to be an Ancestor, why and how you can honour them (no matter your religious or spiritual beliefs) and – since we're all about community and paying it forward here – how to ensure that you have earned the title of Ancestor when the time comes to make your transition. What, you didn't think you were gonna get a free pass, did you?

ANCESTORS IN TRADITIONAL AFRICA

You may have heard about ancestors, thought about ancestors, even spoken to ancestors – but have you ever really thought about who they are and what their role is in our daily lives? In African belief systems, any reference to community refers not only to the living. Both the Ancestors and the children as yet unborn are understood to be part of the community. Ancestors hold a special place because they, like elders, possess a huge amount of knowledge and are greatly respected. You'll notice that, when referring to the purely biological definition, I write 'ancestor' fully in lower case, while when referring to Ancestors in the African worldview, I capitalise. This is to mark the difference – the capitalisation is a sign of respect and honour to those who have earned the title of Ancestor.

In the African worldview, death is not the end; it is simply a transition. We can see this from looking at how the Kemetic people treated their dead. Their funeral rites were extensive and believed to be entirely necessary if the individual was to be allowed entry into the afterlife. Specific prayers and incantations, commonly referred to today as the 'Book of the Dead', had to be recited and items had to be placed with the dead to help them in the next world. These items ranged from the most basic necessities, like bowls and combs, to more luxury items, such as money and jewellery, but they all had the same purpose – to help the individual in the next life. The commitment to ensure loved ones' safe entry into the afterlife may seem like a noble practice, and it is – but it was also done in the belief that those in the afterlife could bless – or curse – those still in the living world. As we move through time and across Africa, we see a similar dedication to the transition of our dead. For example, in their paper 'Funerals Among Akans', Samuel Adu-Gyamfi et al. state that 'the Akan people hold a general belief that death is but a transition into a next world termed locally as *Asamando* (Asante/Akuapim) or *Samanadze* (Fanti) and not necessarily the end of mankind'.[33] As a result, the deceased are buried with adesiedɛ, burial gifts, such as pieces of cloth, rings and money, often accompanied by a prayer to the dead or a message to pass on to other Ancestors. Observations are usually made on the eighth, forty-second and eighty-fourth day after death, followed by annual memorials. So, far from being the end, death in the African worldview is a continuation, just in a different realm.

In many African cosmologies, Ancestors are considered to be messengers of the Most High. They can be relied on to petition the Creator for blessings for those who invoke, respect and venerate them. Others believe the Ancestors have autonomy and the power to either bless or wreak havoc on the lives of those who they left behind. In either case, Ancestral veneration is a necessary part of African life. It's important to note that Ancestral veneration isn't about worshipping the Ancestors as gods. We must do away with this misconception that African spiritual paths reject the idea of an all-powerful Creator in favour of worshipping smaller or lesser gods. As Olusegun Oladipo puts it in his paper 'Religion in African Culture', 'The Supreme Being in African culture is regarded as the ultimate reality... the Supreme Being, called Onyame by the Akans, Chukwu by the Igbos, and Olodumare by the Yoruba, to cite a few examples, can be regarded as the ultimate point of reference.'[34] Ancestors are not worshipped as gods. Rather they are honoured in their own right and understood to be useful to us in matters of spirit, just as we can be useful to them in matters of this physical world. The relationship of an African to their Ancestors is a symbiotic one. Ancestors have walked on this Earth and know the pleasures of food, drinks, family and community. Our role is to continue to 'feed' them these things though they have passed to the Ancestral realm. This is why you'll see people offering everything from food to cigarettes to alcohol to their Ancestors. In return, the Ancestors can feed us with knowledge and spiritual guidance, and pass messages on to the Creator on our behalf. However, in some belief systems, not all who die become Ancestors – no matter how many rituals their living do on their behalf. To make it to the Ancestral realm, a good life is as important, if not more than, a good death.

To be considered an Ancestor, an individual must have lived a life worth emulating. Like living elders, Ancestors are supposed to be those who you would turn to for help, advice and support. While some cultures recognise Ancestors only as those in your bloodline, others believe that Ancestors can be from your bloodline, someone you knew or were connected to in another way, or even inspiring community members and leaders. Ancestors are those we look up to and whose example we wish to follow. And by this belief, each of us has access to even more role models to call on in times of need. Examples of individuals we might think of as 'community' Ancestors are Yaa Asantewaa, Kwame Nkrumah, Chadwick Boseman, Vusamazulu Credo Mutwa, Mary Prince, Cicely Tyson, Bob Marley, Virgil Abloh and Mary Seacole.

MODERN-DAY MYTHS

According to science, an ancestor is simply someone from your bloodline who is no longer living. A few years ago, I came across an Instagram post from @lyricalzen that used numbers to bring this meaning to life. The post read:

ANCESTRAL MATHEMATICS

In order to be born, you needed:

2 parents

4 grandparents

8 great-grandparents

16 second great-grandparents

32 third great-grandparents

64 fourth great-grandparents

128 fifth great-grandparents

256 sixth great-grandparents

512 seventh great-grandparents

1,024 eighth great-grandparents

2,048 ninth great-grandparents

*For you to be born today from 12 previous generations, you
needed a total of 4,094 ancestors over the last 400 years*

By this scientific definition of ancestors, in the last 400 years, approximately 4,094 people had to live, die, love, fight, come together and be in the right place at the right time to make you possible. Four thousand and ninety-four ancestors, four thousand and ninety-four lives. And that's only if we look at the last 12 generations, including your own.

Modern science has long acknowledged that every one of those lives has an impact on our lives today, but this has typically been in reference to genetics that affect us physically, such as our appearance and hereditary diseases. In recent years though, more and more evidence is pointing towards the idea that mental and emotional events can affect our DNA too. In other words, experiences and their effect on us can be transferred to our descendants. In their review of a number of studies on the topic, Rachel Yehuda and Amy Lehrner state that 'On the simplest level, the concept of intergenerational trauma acknowledges that exposure to extremely adverse events impacts individuals to such a great extent that their offspring find themselves grappling with their parents' post-traumatic state. A more recent and provocative claim is that the experience of trauma – or more accurately the effect of that experience – is "passed" somehow from one generation to the next through non-genomic, possibly epigenetic mechanisms affecting DNA function or gene transcription.'[35] So, what does this mean about our ancestors? It means that, as well as giving us life, they may also have given us trauma. Some go so far as to say they also passed on their fears and phobias or, importantly, knowledge. All of which are encoded in our DNA. So, if you have a strong aversion to a particular food, it might be because that very food was taboo, harmful, or even a cause of death to one of your ancestors. All this to say that, even when we look only at the scientific explanation of ancestors, we cannot deny the huge impact they have on our lives, and the huge amount of respect and reverence they deserve.

However, the idea of paying your Ancestors any more attention than a moment of remembrance on their birthday has been wrongly associated with witchcraft, black magic and other dark and mysterious things that no godly person has any business exploring. Even if you don't think of Ancestral veneration as evil, you're probably likely to associate it with a certain headwrap-wearing, 'ah-shay'-saying, 'white Jesus'-denouncing group of individuals (of which I may or may not be part). And you wouldn't be wrong. But there is so much more to Ancestral veneration than all-white ceremonies at Cape Coast Castle and seven-day candles burning at altars. Making time for our Ancestors can, of course, be a spiritual practice, but it is also a *cultural* practice, one that can and should be available to you whether you are Christian, Muslim, Jewish, Bahá'í, Rastafarian, agnostic, atheist… you get the picture. Recognising and honouring our Ancestors may conjure images of pouring libations or creating an altar but, while these are both powerful practices, they're not the only way. Even if you don't connect with the supernatural idea of Ancestors, you can still honour them in a way that works for you.

Future Ancestors

Unsurprisingly, almost everyone I interviewed had something to say about connecting with their Ancestors. Here's a selection of quotes:

Nangamso (Chapter 4): *'It can be confusing when you might be using on your altar a herb that wasn't necessarily used by your community, but it's readily available, so now you're using the wrong herb. So I'm trying to find out for example, Did my Ancestors use sage or lionshead or raspberry leaf? But then we have to understand that intention is the most important thing, and our Ancestors relate to intention. So whether I use sage or raspberry leaf, if I have the right intention that alone is big enough.'*

kobby ananse (Chapter 5): *'It is an homage to our Ancestors for us to be able to tap into our creativity.'*

Gogo Dineo (Chapter 9): *'New Age spirituality perpetuates subtle white supremacist philosophies. It tells you your pain is an illusion, it's your ego. My pain as an African is not an illusion. It is an inherited ancestral generational wound and trauma that was inflicted by the colonisers. So I cannot affirm life if I haven't dealt with my grandmothers' and grandfathers' wounds, my ancestors' wounds. That which I've come to heal is not only my own.'*

Joy (Chapter 12): *'Our Divinity is not our Ancestors – they are our support team. It's important not to fall into dogma. But you can connect with them through your dreams, so learn the language of your dreams, the language of your Ancestors.'*

> **Verona** (Chapter 12): 'When it comes to healing, the foundational point I share with every person I meet, regardless of what spiritual faith they follow, is Ancestral reverence because, by doing it, you're honouring your own being, your own sacredness. You will start tuning in to aspects of yourself that allow you to receive insight and guidance on how to move forward in your life.'

ANCESTORS AND WELLBEING

So what do our Ancestors have to do with our wellbeing? As well as influencing our biology, our Ancestors can support our emotional, mental and spiritual health. Through cultivating belonging by bringing to life the image of those who came before us, feeling held by speaking with our Ancestors safe in the knowledge that, in one way or another, they are with us, and allowing ourselves to be inspired and motivated when we remind ourselves of the feats – both small and great – they achieved in their time, we can make our Ancestors a valuable part of our wellness routine.

Belonging

Recognising the huge web of beings that make up your lineage can be emotional, humbling and quite comforting. If you're unable to trace your blood ancestors or have a difficult relationship with your family, the practice of connecting with community Ancestors can help to fill that void. Look at the qualities and gifts that manifest through you. Which Ancestors have shown the same qualities and skills? Identify them, get to know them, and adopt them as Ancestors. One thing about being an African is that you can never be alone. No matter what has happened in your physical life, the spirit world is always here for you. The Ancestors are always here for you.

Clarity and Direction

One of the hallmarks of African life is the presence and importance of the elders. In African communities across the continent, you will find the practice of seeking advice, counsel and the blessing of elders embedded in everyday life. Elders are seen as wisdom keepers. Not only are they those who have lived and experienced, they are also closer to the spirit world, as they near Ancestorhood. As we've discussed already in the book, parallels have been drawn between the modern practice of therapy and the ancient custom of sitting with elders, and the traditional healer – often an elder – in African communities was usually not just a medicine man or woman, but someone who could be relied on for physical, mental, spiritual and emotional support. Leaning on those who have more experience, knowledge and wisdom than us is a timeless practice, and one that helps us to feel fully supported. Think about a time when you've gone to an elder for advice, whether it be a parent, grandparent or elder in the community. Something about the time spent with them has a very different impact and energy when compared with the support we seek from our peers. As well as the transfer of useful information, we feel the energy of their wisdom, their unconditional love and their certainty that, whatever the issue, we will prevail. We feel supported, loved and motivated to take action

While the Ancestors might not be in this physical world with us any more, we can still connect with these feelings by going to them for guidance. The act of simply talking through our challenges already helps us to process our thoughts and feelings and see things from a different perspective. This act of connecting with a power beyond ourselves, whether through prayer, meditation or speaking with Ancestors, has also been shown to help relieve stress and anxiety, boost mood and even affect our long-term behaviour by making us less reactive, less negative and just overall healthier, happier people.

Gratitude

The practice of gratitude helps to reduce stress and improve our mood. What can inspire more gratitude than meditating on the many people who have paved the way for you to be who you are today. There is nothing blasphemous or demonic about taking time out to reflect on and be grateful for the many lives that have shaped yours, the many people who have shaped our current reality, and the many loved ones who have passed everything from their wit to their smile to their talents on to you.

We live in an unjust, unequal world. At times, the weight of this truth can lead us to feelings of helplessness, despair or apathy. But, no matter how bad things are, we have to give thanks for the people who made change in generations past. When we're able to take a step back and show appreciation for the freedoms that we do have, we're energised to keep fighting for those that we don't.

Inspiration

Calling on specific Ancestors for help in different areas can also help to provide just the energy and insight we need. Whether you're experiencing creative block, relationship troubles or a moral dilemma, identifying a specific Ancestor who has the skills, knowledge or character needed to help you work through the situation is key. Far from being simply supernatural, this is an exercise in inspiration. For example, if you are facing oppression and you know that the answer is to stand up for yourself and fight, you might look to Yaa Asantewaa for inspiration.

Nana Yaa Asantewaa was the Queen Mother of Ejisu in the Asante Kingdom at a time when the British were infiltrating their turf in the Gold Coast, modern-day Ghana. The Asante Kingdom was founded on the Golden Stool, a sacred stool believed to hold the soul of the kingdom. In the late 1800s, the British demanded the stool be handed over to them. Fearful of the consequences of declining, the men of the kingdom were ready to hand it over, but Yaa Asantewaa proudly and firmly stood in their way. It is believed she gave an impassioned speech, reminding the men of the importance of the stool, and challenging them to let the women go to war if they were too scared. Needless to say, that jolted the men into action. When the war came, Yaa Asantewaa stood on the front lines with the men. Unfortunately, the war was won by the British, and both Yaa Asantewaa and the king, Prempeh I, were exiled to the Seychelles. The Golden Stool, however, was never handed over to the British, and continues to be the pride of the Asante Kingdom to this day. Despite the outcome, the courage, leadership and pride shown by Nana Yaa Asantewaa changed the course of history. We don't have to pour libations or say invocations in order to take inspiration from this story and motivate ourselves to develop the same characteristics as our heroine.

READY TO RETURN?

There are endless ways to give thanks and honour to those who paved the way for us. As you know if you've made it this far in the book, I don't believe that there is a 'wrong' way for us to do these things. Yes, there may be a traditional way, but – far from disrespecting tradition – we have a responsibility to create new traditions. These are some ideas to get you started, but don't be afraid to pave your own way – and share it with others to inspire us!

ANCESTOR PRACTICES FOR THE MODERN AFRICAN

Do Your Research

The simple act of learning who your Ancestors are and what they did while they were walking on this Earth is an act of veneration. Look through old photos, make a family tree, ask your relatives about your Ancestors and maybe even search through the internet or books to see what you find. Many cultures believe that a person only truly dies when nobody remembers them. So keep your Ancestors alive simply by remembering them.

Keep Their Names Alive

In many African belief systems, Ancestors are said to return in spirit through their descendants, often to continue on the same or a similar Nkrabea, and so those descendants are given the Ancestor's name. Adopting this practice of renaming is a beautiful way to honour Ancestors. Reflect on the kind of traits you want your child to grow up with. What kind of spirit do you sense in your child? What kind of place do you want them to hold in this world? Thinking about these things, you can select an appropriate Ancestor's name to bestow on your child. Remember, Ancestors don't have to be from your bloodline.

As well as naming children after our Ancestors, we can name other creations of ours too. Books, businesses, works of art, buildings, initiatives… as long as it is thoughtful, intentional and appropriate, any of these things and more can be named after our Ancestors as a way of showing respect and invoking their blessings on whatever it is we have named after them.

Practise Ancestral Healing

I mentioned earlier that even modern science confirms that trauma is carried across generations. Ancestral healing is the practice of identifying this trauma, recognising patterns, and doing the work to heal these wounds so that they don't pass down to your descendants. There are healers who specialise in leading people through this work – like Joy Mogami, who you'll meet in the next chapter – but here is a basic exercise to get you started.

ANCESTRAL HEALING EXERCISE

1. Create a safe and comfortable space where you won't be disturbed.

2. Write a list of the major challenges you are experiencing/have experienced in your life.

3. Looking at the challenges, identify which themes come up repeatedly – for example, financial issues, substance abuse or unhealthy relationships.

4. Reflect on which of these patterns you have seen repeated with your parents, your grandparents, your siblings, your children and your grandchildren.

5. Tackling one pattern at a time, dedicate yourself to healing that pattern. Tools that can typically help are meditation; educating yourself through books, courses and online content; joining communities; working with a therapist or coach; making changes to your relationships; changing your diet; etc.

As with any healing work, this isn't something that can be done with a quick fix. But as you work through Ancestral trauma, not only are you healing yourself, you're also healing your family – those living, those come and gone and those yet to come.

Set Up an Ancestor Altar

An altar is so familiar as it's a feature of many, if not all, spiritual beliefs and religions. At its most basic level, an altar is a physical space where a particular energy is honoured. Setting up an Ancestor altar doesn't mean you're worshipping your Ancestors. It simply means you're creating a space that shows them how much you love and respect them. It can be as simple as a photo of an Ancestor next to a vase that you keep fresh flowers in. However, it is important to specify who you are honouring/inviting to the space; as mentioned earlier not all ancestors are Ancestors. And the fact of the matter is, just like there are certain family members you avoid, there are certain ancestors you wouldn't want to connect with. You can specify by name, or you can do what I do and say, 'All Ancestors who love me unconditionally,' whenever inviting or invoking. If you want to create a more elaborate altar, you can do that with:

- A private space in your home that won't get too much foot traffic – Some healers advise against drawers and cupboards, but if that's the only space you have, I believe you should still use it. The only place I would avoid is the bare floor as it seems a bit disrespectful to shove your Ancestors there.

- A white cloth – This is to lay on the table, shelf or wherever you decide to set up your altar.

- A photo – If you're lucky enough to have images of your Ancestors, you can lay them at the altar. If you'd like to honour some of our community Ancestors, you can print photos of them from the internet. Just ensure that none of your photos include anyone who is still living!

- A list of names – If you don't have photos, you can also write a list of the names of the Ancestors you would like to honour and place this on the altar.

- Water – Keep a fresh glass or bowl of water at your altar. You should change it every few days.

- Elements – If you'd like to, you can place an item to represent each element. I like to use shells for water, feathers or incense for air, crystals for earth and a candle for fire.

- Candle – Some say that the flame at your altar should never go out. Again, for me, it's all about energy and intention. I prefer to light a candle every morning. When it goes out, it goes out. If you intend to light a candle once a week, then do that. Whatever you decide, just be sure to commit to it and make it part of your routine.

- Food – In many African cultures food is offered to the Ancestors at the start of every meal. If you have an altar, this offering can be placed there, but it doesn't have to be. You can simply set aside a small plate of food in the kitchen or eating area, or if you're outside, place some on the ground.

- Offerings – Other offerings such as tea, coffee, fruit, jewellery, fresh flowers and anything else your Ancestors might like can also be made at your altar.

Remember, your altar is about your relationship with your Ancestors. It's not about doing things 'right' or the way everyone else does them. You could do two things on this list or everything on this list; both are correct. Just be true to yourself and follow your intuition. Your Ancestors will surely let you know if you do anything they don't like, as long as you're open to listen.

Talk to Your Ancestors

Start a conversation. It doesn't have to be anything wild; just tell them what's going on in times of joy, confusion, stress or doubt. Talk to your Ancestors as if you're talking to a friend. You can do this by literally talking out loud or, if you would feel more comfortable, you can write a letter to them. Whether you believe that they can actually hear you (or read the letter) or not, this will help you work through whatever you're feeling. You might feel like you don't know *how* to talk to your Ancestors. I'm sure different people have different approaches, but I say just be yourself! When I talk to my Ancestors, I use my fake American accent, laugh at my own jokes and say 'giiirrrrll' just like I do when I'm talking to people

IRL.[i] The important thing is that you're building a relationship with them and sooner or later, whether through your intuition, synchronicities, or through other people, you'll start to feel that they are not just listening but also responding.

Stand in Your Power

One of the most impactful means of honouring your Ancestors is to step into and stand in your unique power. A lot of people had to endure a lot of struggles for us to be here today. When we think of the pain, torture, fear, degradation and endless suffering of our people, it can weigh us down. But if we remember the sheer determination, resilience and strength it must have taken for them to endure so that we could be here today, the only response is to make sure we take up space. The space our Ancestors carved out for us with their blood, sweat and tears, but also their skills, efforts and victories. Playing small, doubting ourselves and allowing others to take our power is an insult to our Ancestors. So the next time you're thinking about shrinking or staying silent, remember the force of Ancestors waiting for you to make them proud and ready to have your back.

Live a Life Worth Emulating

Death alone does not make an Ancestor. To be considered an Ancestor, you must have lived a 'good' life. The trouble is, good is subjective. In some cultures, being married and having children are non-negotiable aspects of a good life and are necessary criteria for becoming an Ancestor. In the modern world we recognise that the meaning of marriage has evolved and producing children has become less of an obligation. Some may disagree with this, but I believe that marriage and children as a path to Ancestorhood can have a broader meaning.

---

i   In real life.

What is true marriage other than commitment? In the African worldview, marriage is not even about two individuals. Community and family are at the heart of African life, and it is no different in marriage. This union is about a union of families, a commitment to carry on the family name, traditions and work. Traditionally, African families lived in large compounds with multiple generations represented in each household. Even today, when an African introduces someone as their mother, father, daughter, son, sister, brother, cousin… you cannot assume that they mean that in the biological sense. Aunts call their nephews sons, cousins call each other siblings and even close friends might call each other brother or sister. With this view, in my opinion, marriage in the modern day can be broadened out as a commitment to the community. To the growth, protection and uplifting of the community. That community might be your family, your town, your country, Black people across the world, or even humanity as a whole.

What about having children? Again, there will be many who believe that there is no loophole here – if you don't have children, you cannot be an Ancestor. But when I think about some of the incredible souls who left a mark on this world – but no reported offspring – I can't conclude that they would be denied entry to the realm of the Ancestors: Rosa Parks, Langston Hughes, bell hooks, George Washington Carver and Gisèle Rabesahala to name a few. When asked why she did not marry and have children, Gisèle Rabesahala – a leading force in the fight for independence in Madagascar, and the country's first female minister – said she preferred to 'serve [her] country, rather than one person'. All of these people birthed change into this world, whether through activism, art or invention. I believe that to be an Ancestor, you must birth something positive into this world – something that will continue to have impact after you are gone – but I don't believe that it has to take human form.

If you can do these two things – commit to your community and birth impact – in fact, if you can simply work towards these two things, never mind if you actually 'make it', I believe you'll be living a life worth emulating.

N.E.R.D

Even if you consciously think that Ancestral veneration is wrong (in which case, you perhaps understand it as the worship of Ancestors rather than reverence for them), chances are you're actually already practising it in one way or another. Perhaps you recognise the anniversaries of your parents or grandparents passing, or have their picture on the mantlepiece next to some flowers. I hope that in this chapter I've helped to undo some of the misconceptions around this practice and, as a result, given you permission, whatever your faith, to start or continue building a relationship with your Ancestors.

Not only can a commitment to Ancestral veneration create magick for us, it also enlivens us to create magick for those to come by living a life worth emulating. So how do you know if you're living the life of a Future Ancestor? Take some time to reflect on the future. What do you want your descendants to call on you for? Centuries into the future, what kind of traits do you want to inspire in the young people who read about you and hear stories of your life? Once you know the answers to these questions, you can keep them with you and use them as a guide for how to live today in a way that inspires tomorrow.

Chapter 12

RITUAL

'Ritual was a way of life to us as Africans. This way of life was about revering and connecting to Divinity. Everything we did we were intentional and conscious about, honouring and revering the life force of all living things, for in them we saw source creator. We and them are one.'

Gogo Dineo Ndlanzi

Ritual has always been an ever-present theme in African life, but these days, the word alone can attract fear, judgement and disdain, not least because it might conjure images of a half-naked man expertly slicing the neck of a squawking chicken. To repair our image of what a ritual is, we must first remember what ritual is *for*. Quite simply, ritual is the indigenous science of creating change. I like to conceptualise it with this formula: Intention + Energy = Magick. Intention is the reason for doing the ritual; it is the outcome you wish to elicit from the spirit world (and/or your subconscious). Energy is created by the actions that take place during the ritual and can also be influenced by the occasion on which the ritual takes place – for example the time of year, the phase of the moon and so on. The energy and the intention of the ritual must align in order to create magick. Magick is transformation, intentional change. While ritual in Africa is traditionally associated with community, personal rituals can also play an important role in our lives. Personal rituals tend to be 'small' and it's their repetition that makes them transformational. Community rituals and rites of passage tend to be 'big' and it's their intensity that makes them transformational for the individual, while both the intensity and repetition make them transformational for the community. In short, we use ritual to create magick.

RITUAL IN TRADITIONAL AFRICA

Ritual is an indispensable part of everyday life for the traditional African. In communities across space and time, rituals have been relied on by individuals, families and the community at large. There have been and still are rituals for everything from farming to war to enstoolment of new royals to punishment of criminals. There are many different types of rituals, but the three I want to focus on are life-stage rituals, community rituals and personal rituals.

The understanding of ritual as a way of creating change explains why it has been so often associated with new life stages. In many traditional African cultures, there are rituals for birth, naming, outdooring, puberty, marriage and, of course, death or transition. These are all times of intense change, and their associated rituals are designed to make that change as seamless as possible. Birth rituals support the mother and bring the baby into an environment of love and joy. Naming and outdooring rituals celebrate the new addition to the community and integrate them into this extended family. Puberty rites educate and support individuals in their transition from childhood to adulthood. Death rituals allow the community to collectively grieve a loss while also promoting safe passage of the spirit from this realm to the next.

Community rituals typically mark events such as a change of seasons, new harvest and commemorative events. These community rituals often form the basis for larger celebrations, mostly termed festivals. A festival usually takes place over a full day or multiple days and will likely include a number of rituals. For the purposes of our conversation, I'll use 'community ritual', 'festival' and 'community event' as interchangeable descriptors. In Ghana, an example of this kind of community ritual can be seen in the Akwasidae Festival of the Asante people, which happens every 40 days and is said to both commemorate the appearance of the Golden Stool from the heavens and honour the Asantehenes[i] who have passed into the Ancestral realm. In my ancestral hometown of Elmina, Bakatue is celebrated every July. The ritual pays homage to the deity Benya, who resides in the lagoon, thanking him for his protection and requesting another year of abundance for the fishing community. These traditional community rituals create change in two ways. Firstly, the belief is that adherence to these rituals pleases the deities and the Ancestors, encouraging them to shower blessings on the community. Secondly, there is the creation or maintenance of change within the community. Without these rituals, communities would likely experience less coherence, less pride in their culture, less belonging.

Finally, we have personal rituals. Rather than being triggered by life stage or time of year, these rituals are typically a form of medicine. They are traditionally performed in the event of a personal challenge – anything from ill health to disturbing dreams. The person experiencing this challenge visits their local healer, who performs a sort of spiritual triage, diagnosing the issue and identifying the necessary treatment through the process of divination. The treatment prescribed might include the administering of herbs (as discussed in Chapter 7), instructing the querent to add or remove something from their diet, a sacrifice or offering to a particular spirit, and any other number of actions, and all of these parts form one or multiple rituals. A ritual might be performed with the healer and others might be performed by the querent alone in the days after their visit.

---

i   Asantehene is the ruler of the Asante kingdom. Perhaps the most powerful of the monarchs in Ghana.

Rituals can be understood as a means of communicating with the spirit world. When we look at the traditional use of rituals, we can see that they typically centre around showing gratitude to and/or requesting guidance from God, deities or Ancestors. It makes sense then that symbolism features heavily in rituals, as this is a major tool in communicating with the Divine. Examples of the kind of symbolism used in ritual are burying something in the ground as a way of planting an intention and the use of water for (spiritual) cleansing.

Future Ancestor: Joy Mogami

Joy is a healer of Tswana heritage currently living in Botswana and working with clients internationally. She describes herself as an Oracle, ascension guide and writer, passionate about archiving African experiences and philosophies. She tells me about her connection to ritual, saying, *'Ritual and storytelling have been a big part of engaging with my Ancestry. For those of us who practise African spirituality, we involve ritual in every part of our lives – from the moment you wake up, starting with the way you process your dreams. A large part of my ritual training has been through dreams; the way I work with candles, the way I work with water – these were shown to me in the dream state.'*

About returning to ritual if you haven't been taught tradition, Joy says, *'The idea is not to strive for the ancient template but rather to evolve the ancient template to our time.'*

MODERN-DAY MYTHS

I believe that one of the greatest losses the global Black community has faced is that of the importance of ritual. Our disconnect from cultural rituals has left so many of us lacking in community, lacking in cultural connection, lacking in support, lacking in elders and lacking in direction. Malidoma Patrice Somé encapsulates this loss, saying, 'Because ritual is so deeply connected to our human nature, anytime it is missing there will be a lack of transformation and healing.'

When we look at life-stage rituals and rites of passage, they are decidedly missing from our lives. These days, most of us are left to fend for ourselves. Whether we're going through puberty, getting married or naming our children, aside from a few words of wisdom whispered over dinner with the parents or advice from peers who mean well but are every bit as clueless as we are, we pretty much have to figure everything out on our own (read: with the help of the elder known as Google). Religious communities have done a good job of offering alternatives for this – for example, the Confirmation that many Christian teens go through – but indigenous rituals and rites of passage are dying out, both on the continent and in the Diaspora. In the case of rites of passage, one factor for this may be the unsafe and, to some, unethical practices that can accompany them. Circumcision (across genders), performing dangerous feats and spending nights in the forest with only your prayers and your fighting skills to protect you are some aspects of traditional rites of passage that give many people pause. This has added to the continued demonisation of these traditions as backwards and barbaric. But rites of passage also include learning, pageants, dancing, singing, drumming and immense joy and pride upon completion. Instead of allowing the tradition to die out, we can make necessary changes so that they reflect our current beliefs, as the Zimbabwean government did some years ago by introducing medical circumcision within a healthcare facility (instead of in the ritual space, usually somewhere in nature) as part of the rites.

With life-stage rituals entirely absent, we can be left feeling extremely alone in these times of transition. Whether it's the uncertainties around getting your first period or the cold feet before your wedding day, it can feel like you have to keep these thoughts and fears to yourself because others might not understand, or you feel embarrassed to ask. Traditional rites of passage and life-stage rituals create a space where you know that those around you are experiencing or have experienced similar thoughts and feelings, making it much easier to speak up for advice and support. Imagine if, near the first day of your period, you were gathered with other girls around your age, laughing, gossiping and learning from an older cousin whose aim was to prepare you for what's to come. Imagine if, the day before your wedding, you were surrounded by three or four generations of family and close friends, sharing support and dropping gems of wisdom, as your other half was elsewhere experiencing the same. Rituals and rites of passage are like taking a six-hour road trip from Accra to Busua in a car full of friends, snacks and good music instead of the alternative – six hours of dodging potholes, street hawkers and reckless overtakers in a busted-up car, alone.

As mentioned in the previous section, community rituals like Akwasidae do still take place, but many of them are losing their importance in the minds of the people, especially those who no longer live in their hometown. Equally some of these rituals and festivals are turning more into tourist attractions than the deeply spiritual and meaningful events they once were. There does seem to be, however, a new wave of celebrations that, while they may look wildly different, in my opinion carry the spirit of gratitude, pride and celebration of the traditional community festivals. The Caribbean carnivals that have spread across the world are undoubtedly one of the best examples. But newer events such as Afrochella in Accra, Black Girl Fest in London and Afro Punk around the world also carry the baton. You may not think of these as rituals but, as we'll see in the next section, they tick many of the boxes for modern-day rituals. I want you to think of the last community event you attended, whether virtually or in person. Maybe it was Ghana Party in the Park. Or Notting Hill Carnival. Or a TEDx event. Or a film screening. For me, it was Thursday Lates, an event by Trybe, my friend's business that is dedicated to supporting creatives in Africa. Thursday Lates exhibits the work of a different upcoming artist every couple of months and simultaneously acts as a mixer for the Accra creative community. Just like every time I've attended, I left the latest event feeling inspired, energised and incredibly proud. Proud of my friend and the impact she's having, proud of the artist and their unapologetic talent, proud to see the support of the creative community and proud to count myself as a member of that community. Now, back to you. How did you feel after that community event you attended? Grateful? Connected? Inspired? Energised? If the event did its job, hopefully all of the above. While you may not think of this as a ritual, that's exactly what these kinds of events have the potential to be. Remember, a ritual is intention plus energy that creates transformational change. As Black people living in a white supremacist world, we *need* community events that create transformational change – change within us in the form of healing and belonging, change in our community in the form of healing and opportunity, and change in the world in the form of healing and justice.

On a smaller scale, we can start to reintroduce rituals into our close communities, whether that community is your family, your group of friends, your local neighbourhood or your workplace. Parents can work together to create modern-day rites-of-passage rituals for their children. Friends can come together to create a ritual for grief and loss. Lovers can commit to making their anniversary ritual something more meaningful than posting '5 years <3' on Instagram.

Now when it comes to personal rituals, we're all already doing them. Whether you start your day each morning by scrolling through your phone, take a mini vacation every year on your birthday or buy yourself a gift each time you get promoted, you're practising a ritual. And, whether you're aware of them or not, these rituals are shaping your life. Far from only employing them in times of need, we can employ rituals to actively support ourselves in our continued growth, joy and spiritual development. But only if we are intentional about them. Just as you're probably already engaging in a ritual that's good for you, I'm willing to bet you're also engaging in a ritual that is taking you away from who you want to be. Perhaps you *say* you want to have a peaceful life. But you have a ritual of inviting chaos into your life whenever you're bored. Perhaps you *say* you want to save money. But you have a ritual of deleting/throwing away your bank statement because you're scared of what you'll see. Perhaps you *say* you want to be healthy. But you have a ritual of reaching for the (literal and/or proverbial) cookie jar whenever you're sad (guilty!). In all of these examples, there's a conscious intention. But your *subconscious* intention (which is to stay in the same destructive yet familiar situations) joins together with actions that create a certain energy, and the result is transformational change that is entirely opposite to what you say you want. And you wonder to yourself, 'How did I get here again?'.

By being intentional about the rituals you insert into your daily life, you can interrupt and counteract these self-sabotaging rituals and start to make real change, real magick in your life.

Future Ancestors: Dalian Adofo and Verona Spence-Adofo, Ancestral Voices

Ancestral Voices is an Educational Initiative documenting and disseminating research-based knowledge about African cosmologies and spiritual philosophies. Through their work, Dalian and Verona have helped countless people – including me – learn about and connect with African spiritual knowledge and traditions. A proud Pan-African husband and wife team, Dalian is of Ghanaian heritage, while Verona is of Jamaican heritage, and they currently live in the UK. When discussing ritual, Dalian shared, *'Ritual on a collective level is about bringing everyone within a certain space or within a certain mindset together to work for a singular good or a mutually beneficial good for everyone in that community. Ritual in that regard is like a glue, an adhesive that brings everyone together.'*

Verona continued, *'If we're looking for ways that ritual can benefit our society today, one of the major things that stands out to me is rites-of-passage programmes for young people to address some of the social issues that we are facing. Rituals can help our youth by inviting them into the community, giving them a sense of purpose and reminding them of why they're even here, that life is more than just this physical reality. Ritual can definitely be used to address many of the social issues that we are facing as a community.'*

RITUAL AND WELLBEING

Whether you practise them within a community, alone, or a combination of both, rituals can help boost your wellbeing. A 2020 study[36] focusing on the Indian festival of Diwali found that community rituals not only positively impact social cohesion, affect and health responses on the day(s) of the celebration but also in the run-up to it, as people look forward to what's to come. To truly see the positive effects of rituals, it's important that you really commit to them. A morning ritual you do for three days and then forget about probably isn't going to be life changing, but stick with it and, within weeks, you'll notice a change in your energy and you'll wonder why you didn't start this ritual earlier!

Belonging

It's clear to see how gathering with friends, family or even strangers for a common goal breeds a sense of belonging. Smaller group rituals can intensify these feelings of belonging as they tend to encourage sharing of more intimate thoughts, feelings and experiences, deepening your connection with your fellow ritual goers. Personal rituals can cultivate belonging when you know and feel that you're part of a larger group of interconnected spirits observing a particular event or celebration, and they can also help you feel more connected to your Ancestors or to God.

Faith

The outcome of ritual is transformational change. Whether that change is internal (for example, less anxiety and better sleep) or external (for example, a new job) the realisation of this change helps us to keep our faith alive. It might be faith in God, faith in your Ancestors, or faith in yourself – whichever it is, a deep sense of faith promotes good mental health and helps us stay on the path of wellbeing even when times get tough.

Self-esteem

In a similar vein, recognising that, with the help of the Divine, you've created real positivity in your life through your commitment to ritual forces you to acknowledge that you truly do have the power to create the kind of life you want and deserve.

Cultural rituals act as a tool for archiving and preserving culture. When we participate in these kinds of rituals, we feel connected to our roots and the sacred wisdom of our Ancestors. And when we lead these rituals we recognise our roles as custodians of the culture. Both of these experiences boost our sense of self.

Self-reflection

While not all rituals involve specific self-reflection activities like journalling, the nature of ritual causes you to be self-reflective. This is because you are either repeating the same ritual at different points in time or, for one-off rituals, have a clear sense of life before and life after the ritual. Naturally these situations will cause you to compare your life, mental state, level of satisfaction and other markers of change. It could be a birthday ritual that causes you to reflect on how life has changed over the year, a morning ritual that feels so much easier than when you started it three months ago or a grief ritual that helped you move from a place of sorrow to peace. Regardless of the specifics, rituals have a way of making us more aware of who we are and how we're growing (or not).

READY TO RETURN?

Ritualising my life has been the single most transformational tool in my spiritual and personal growth in recent years. At first, I was definitely held back by worrying about doing things wrong or feeling that I needed to find a teacher to show me the way. But I'm so glad I pushed past that doubt and just started. There are certain rituals that probably shouldn't be attempted alone – please do not invoke spirits you have no business invoking just because you read about them on the internet – but to get started with some basic rituals, all you need is a clear intention. And remember, we are the new elders. It's much better to create new rituals based on what knowledge you do have rather than do nothing because of the knowledge you don't have. Here are some ideas to get you started – this is by no means a prescriptive list nor is it an exhaustive list, but I hope it gives you the inspiration and confidence you need to bring the magick of ritual into your life.

RITUAL PRACTICES FOR THE MODERN AFRICAN

Build Your Community and Attend Community Rituals

Ritual and community often go hand in hand, and we are a reflection of our communities. Some communities I consider myself a member of are my extended family, Accra creatives, Ghanaian 'returnees' (as much as I dislike the phrase), LGBTQ+, global healers, Pan-African, Black British, Black writers, nineties babies, people with 'rasta' hair who aren't Rastafarian….

Each of these communities and the many more I didn't mention shape who I am but also my ability to achieve my goals. Some of these communities I was born into, but others I have found my place in as a result of the kind of life I want to create for myself and the kind of world I want to live in. So now let's see if your community reflects who you are:

1. Take some time to think about the kind of life you want to create. Do you want to live the fast city life, a quiet country life or a mixture of both? What kind of work do you want to do? What kind of impact do you want to have? What kind of enjoyment is your kind of enjoyment? What are your political views? What causes are close to your heart? What change do you want to see in the world?

2. Write out a list of communities that you belong to. Does this align with the kind of life you want to create? Where are there gaps? How can you fill them?

    For example, perhaps this book has convinced you that African-centred wellness is the path for you. But when you look at your list of communities, there are none interested in personal growth and wellbeing, or none who take pride in African heritage, or none who are Black, in which case, you've found a gap. To address this gap, you could cry into your gari soakings[ii] and decide to just dash your dreams since it's too much hard work. Or you could…

3. Address this community gap by putting yourself in (virtual or physical) spaces where you will meet people who share this dream. Or you can create the very community you desire through hosting your own events or connecting with people on social media.

---

ii   A delicious but apparently 'poor man's' dish made of gari, sugar and milk. When money is flowing, you might add groundnuts and/or chopped banana. When times are hard, just gari, sugar and water.

Joy says, 'If you find you are alone, either search for and join existing communities that resonate with you or create your own.' However, especially when searching for spiritual communities, it's important to keep your wits about you. When the yearning for connection and answers is so deep, it's easy to get sucked into something that isn't truthful, is dangerous or just isn't right for you. So, as important as community is, continuing to develop your own intuition and trusting in yourself is even more so. Dalian reminds us that 'this is also the call to spirituality – to be able to find the power within yourself to trust yourself and know yourself to the degree that you're able to filter and practise good discernment'.

Once you're clear on the communities that align with who you are and who you want to become, look for rituals and events happening in those communities and get involved! Whether it's attending a wellness retreat, joining a career bootcamp or getting more involved in your church/mosque/spiritual centre's activities, joining rituals that are already taking place is one of the easiest ways to get started.

Identify Your Existing Rituals

How do you start your mornings? What do you do to prepare for bed? How do you spend your days off? What do you do in times of intense joy or pain? Reflect on your existing rituals and ask yourself – do these rituals reflect the kind of life I want to create? For any that don't, it's time to…

Create New Rituals

Intention + Energy. Using this formula, you can create your own ritual for anything! Some things to bear in mind:

- Setting – The location of the ritual matters. It's always super healing to perform a ritual outside in nature, but if it's inside, ensure the room is clean and tidy, well ventilated, and made to feel like a space of healing with plants, incense, candles or whatever else feels right for you.

- Structure – In my opinion, a ritual should always be opened and closed with a prayer. The opening prayer should set the intention and the closing prayer should be one of gratitude (templates below).

- Solitude – Whether you're doing a personal or community ritual, it's important that you won't be disturbed. Be sure to avoid distractions by having phones put away and, if being done at home, informing others that you're not to be disturbed.

Example opening prayer – I call on God/Allah/Spirit/the Most High, Mohammed/Jesus Christ/[specific deity or Saint name], the Ancestors, and my Higher Soul to be with me in this space as I embark on this ritual. I start by sending you gratitude for [whatever you want to express gratitude for – for example, health, bringing everyone safely to the space, etc.]. I come to this ritual with the intention of [state intention]. I ask for your protection, love, guidance and support throughout, and as I ask, I already know it is done. Ameen/Amen/Àṣẹ/And so it is!

Example closing prayer – I close this ritual by giving thanks to God/Allah/Spirit/the Most High, Mohammed/Jesus Christ/[specific deity or Saint name], the Ancestors, and my Higher Soul for being with me in this space. I thank you for the love, healing and insights I have gained and ask for your continued guidance in helping me integrate these learnings into my life. Ameen/Amen/Àṣẹ/And so it is!

These prayers can, of course, be adapted to groups also, reflecting a collective prayer, using 'we' instead of 'I', 'our' instead of 'my' etc.

Ideas for Rituals

The rituals below are a combination of those I have used in my own life and others I have outlined based on my experiences and research but have yet to practise – for example, the outdooring ceremony.

Naming and Outdooring Ceremony

Intention: To introduce a new baby to their community and announce their name.

Occasion: Traditionally done 8–10 days after the baby is born. This ritual should be the first time they are taken outdoors (hence the name 'outdooring').

Actions:

• All guests should wear white.

• The ceremony should be conducted by a chosen elder.

• The elder should announce the name of the baby. (If allowing elders to name the baby, this will be the first time the parents hear the name.)

• A spiritual leader should perform a prayer or libations for the baby.

• 'Introduce' the baby to the guests, starting with the elders.

• Drumming or other music, dancing and general celebration.

• Guests can present gifts to the baby.

Puberty Rites of Passage

Intention: To support adolescents in their transition from childhood to adulthood.

Occasion: I believe this should be at the discretion of the parents but is best done before puberty hits its peak. It should take the form of individualised sessions run over a longer-term period – for example, weekly sessions over three months.

A note on gender: These rites of passage are traditionally specific to gender. One basis for this is that children with a recent or upcoming shared experience – for example, menstruation – will be taught and guided by an adult who shares that experience. While there is huge value in this, it must also be noted that the idea that these rites teach you how to 'be a man' or 'be a woman' can be damaging to the initiates' ideas of gender and identity. My solution is that the groups not be split by gender, or at least only be split for sessions where absolutely necessary. And honestly, the world would be a much better place if fewer men were scared of periods.

Actions:

- Each initiate should be paired with a mentor from their community (ideally not someone in the same household as them and perhaps someone of the same assigned gender who can advise on bodily changes). The mentor should be older but still relatable – probably someone in their twenties or thirties. The role of this mentor is to support them even beyond this rites-of-passage process, to be a buddy and a role model.

- Perform an opening ceremony to set the intention for the rites of passage and to bring the group together, along with elders and mentors.

- Conduct regular lessons that cover important topics such as sex education, community values, mental health, confidence building and other topics that you've identified as key for your youth. Sessions should be led by mentors, elders or, where necessary, trained professionals.

- Provide physical experiences, ideally out in nature, such as hiking, camping, trips to the beach, etc. These help to bring the group together as well as allowing them time in a healing environment.

- Hold a sharing circle, giving initiates an opportunity to share their thoughts, feelings, concerns and what they've learned from the experience. This should be led by the mentors and/or elders.

- End with an initiation ceremony where they 'pass' and are celebrated by their parents and the wider community. The ceremony should include:

  - prayer or libations

  - presentation of something to the initiates that commemorates the occasion – for example, waist beads, a piece of jewellery, a cloth, anything more imaginative than a certificate!

  - drumming or other music, dancing and general celebration.

Remembrance Ceremony

Intention: To mark the anniversary of a loved one's passing.

Occasion: In my culture, we typically do this at one year, five years and 10 years, and it forms a large family gathering. This idea can be adapted into a smaller community ritual or a personal ritual, done annually.

Actions:

- Wear white.

- Set up an altar with a photo of the departed on a table covered with a white cloth. You can add flowers, candles, water and anything else you like.

- Prepare a feast and offer the first plate of food to the Ancestor at the altar.

- If a community ritual, share stories of your favourite memories of the Ancestor.

- Drumming or other music, dancing and general celebration.

Community Empowerment Event

Intention: To create a space of healing, belonging and support for the community.

Occasion: Anytime! This could be anything from an annual in-person event to a virtual monthly series.

Actions:

- Healing – Whether it's a meditation session, a fitness class or the opportunity to speak with a therapist, dedicate a portion of the event to intentional healing.

- Education – This could be peer-to-peer learning, a talk/workshop from an expert or learning a new skill.

- Opportunity – To ensure the event has effects that last beyond the few hours guests are there, create some element of opportunity. It could be networking, a careers fair, free headshots or an open mic.

- Empowerment – A good community ritual should leave guests feeling proud and inspired. This can be done through anything from a motivational speech to vision board creation.

- Celebration – Food, drinks and enjoyment!

Forgiveness Ritual

Intention: To gain closure on a matter and forgive yourself or someone else.

Occasion: Can be done at any time, as a community or personal ritual. Especially powerful at the Full Moon, as this is a time for releasing what no longer serves us.

Actions:

- For an outdoor ritual, this can be done around a bonfire. For an indoor ritual, have a fireproof dish and matches nearby.

- Write a letter to the person who needs to be forgiven (which may mean writing a letter to yourself). Detail the reason forgiveness is needed, how the event or situation made you feel and your desire to forgive and move on.

- Repeat the mantra, 'I forgive you, I love you and I'm ready to let go.'

- Still repeating the mantra, throw the letter into the bonfire or set the letter alight and allow it to burn in the heatproof dish.

- Still repeating the mantra, sit down, close your eyes and visualise the person you're forgiving.

- Stop repeating the mantra, and in your visualisation see that all is well between you and the other person (or yourself) and send them off with love.

- Stay silent with your eyes closed for a few moments more. Then, when you are ready, close the ritual.

- For an indoor ritual, dispose of the ashes of the letter by throwing them in the wind (outside, of course) or, if putting them in the trash, take the trash to a bin outside your house.

New Moon Ritual

Intention: To set the tone for a good month ahead.

Occasion: On the night of the New Moon or up to three days afterwards. Can be done as a community or personal ritual.

Actions:
- Reflection – How has the last month been? What went well? What didn't go so well?

- Intention setting – What do you want to experience in the month ahead?

- Turn this intention into an affirmation. For example, if you want to experience more joy, your affirmation could be 'I am joyful.'

- Meditate on this affirmation, repeating it softly in your mind and feeling the energy of this intention.

- Write it down and stick it somewhere you will see it every day.

Full Moon Ritual

Intention: To release something that is holding you back.

Occasion: On the night of the Full Moon or up to two days either side.

Actions:
- Reflection – How has the last month been? What went well? What didn't go so well?

- Identifying blocks – What is one thing that is holding you back? It could be a relationship, a habit, a situation or an environment.

- Write down three actions you can take this month to help you release this block.

- Prepare a bucket for a spiritual bath with warm water and salt. You could also add Florida water, Kananga water, or your own blend of essential oils, along with basil, rosemary, prɛkɛsɛ, bay leaf or any other herbs for cleansing. As you take the bath, think about what you want to release, and repeat, 'I am ready to release,' or, 'I am releasing [fill in the blank].'

- After the bath, allow your body to air-dry and wrap yourself in a clean cloth or robe.

- Return to where you were completing the ritual to close it.

Morning Ritual

Intention: To set the tone for your day –You might want to have a peaceful, motivated or joyful start to the day. Decide which it is and choose the appropriate actions.

Occasion: Every morning! Choose a realistic length of time based on when you can wake up and when you need to start engaging with work/family/people.

Actions:

• The first action you should take upon waking depends on what kind of energy you wake up with. You can find my 'Morning Mood' quiz on my website, which will help you figure this out. Once you have your first activity sorted, pick and mix from the ideas below, selecting those that match your intention:

  – A stress-relieving activity: meditation, calming breathing exercises, journalling, slow yoga/dance/tai chi/other movement practice, stretching, playing soothing music, lighting incense or a scented candle, drinking herbal tea

  – An intention-setting activity: planning your day, repeating affirmations or mantras, prayer

  – An energy-boosting activity: fast yoga/dance/fitness/other movement practice, energising breathing exercises, playing energetic music, drinking coffee or an energising tea

  – A joyful activity: reading, a creative activity, a crafting hobby, singing, drinking cocoa

• Select two to four activities and do each for anywhere from 10 to 30 minutes. Try not to look at your phone or engage with the outside world until you've finished the ritual – it would be great if you can get through it without engaging with anyone but, if you have a family, that might not fly!

You might be keen to do the exact same ritual each day but, if not, you may prefer to have set themes and then vary the exact action from day to day, week to week or month to month. For example, perhaps your morning ritual is move, meditate, do something creative. These broad categories allow plenty of room for flexibility.

Bedtime Ritual

Intention: To close out the day and pave the way for a restful sleep.

Occasion: Every evening! It should start anywhere from two hours before you want to be asleep. Not all of us have that kind of time available, so even if your whole routine is 15 minutes, it's still worth doing! Try to start it at the same time every evening (mamas and papas, I see you rolling your eyes at me – that's why I said 'try', oh!).

Actions:

- Say goodbye to the screens! This is a great time to go and put your phone on charge. Experts recommend charging your phone outside your room. I don't do this because I use it to listen to podcasts, audiobooks and meditations. But I also don't have an addiction to scrolling in bed. If you do, I would try the leaving the phone outside the room tactic! Need it as an alarm? Buy an alarm clock or, even better, set your phone volume to loud so that you have to go into the next room to turn off the alarm – you'll never hit the snooze button again.

- Choose some activities that match your need:

  - A mood-boosting activity: your favourite hobby as long as it's not something too active that will prevent you from sleeping. Mine are reading or listening to an audiobook, listening to a podcast, or listening to music (neo-soul is a bedtime favourite).

  - A body-relaxing activity: stretching, self-massage, slow yoga, tension-release meditation, warm shower/bath.

  - A stress-relieving activity: meditation, calming breathing exercises, journalling, planning the next day, lighting incense or a scented candle, drinking herbal tea: prayer, sleep meditation, sleep music.

- Select two to four activities and do each for anywhere from 10 to 30 minutes.

As with the morning ritual, build flexibility into your ritual if it's important to you. Your bedtime ritual might be to read or write, stretch, listen.

POWER

The beauty and importance of traditional rituals must not be forgotten. For those of us with the privilege to have some kind of connection to them, it is a good idea to attend traditional rituals while we can, if not just for the experience, for the opportunity to allow these age-old traditions to inform the rituals that we implement in our own lives.

That said, ritual does not belong only to elders and traditional communities. As Black people, we must reconnect with the energy of ritual to create transformational change in our lives and our communities. With the power of ritual we can provide direction and inspiration for our youth, create opportunities for everything from career progression to healthy relationships for ourselves, and take back the power in a world that, quite frankly, will never stop trying to sell us the lie that we have none.

Part V
INITIATION

Akobɛn – 'War horn'

This is your call to action. What happens next is up to you!

Chapter 13

LIVING WELL, THE AFRICAN WAY

Let me be real with you. The topics that we've covered in this book – I get major impostor syndrome when I talk about these things or post about them on Instagram. So imagine how I feel publishing a whole book on the topic! Thoughts and fears about not being enough of an authority, not having been practising this for long enough, not having enough personal experience, or not having been initiated visit me often.

So it surprised me to realise, as I interviewed the incredible Future Ancestors whose knowledge, guidance and support have brought this book to life, that so many of them shared a story similar to mine. I was raised in a Christian home where our Ghanaian culture was reflected in our food, in the language I learned to understand but not to speak (at least not well enough to deter sniggers and corrections), and sometimes in our clothes. But some of the topics discussed in this book, especially Ancestral veneration and ritual, if they came up at all, would be dismissed or demonised. The vast majority of my emotional, mental and spiritual return home has had to be self-guided. In fact, to be completely honest, I'm certain that the publishing of this book will lead to some uncomfortable but important conversations with close family members.

I heard varying versions of this story time and time again in my interviews. Aside from easing my impostor syndrome somewhat, this brought up two primary emotions.

Firstly, both pride and gratitude to be involved in this global movement of homecoming. To contribute a small part to this huge work of protecting, archiving, modernising and promoting the sacred wisdom of our Ancestors is truly humbling. I'm a firm believer that this book absolutely had to be birthed into the world... but it didn't *have* to come through me. If I hadn't got my act together, the Ancestors would most definitely have channelled it through someone else, a more serious somebody who could handle the work they needed to get done.

And secondly, immense joy to see how far this movement truly reaches, not just forward but backwards. As my generation works hard to rebuild a connection to a past that our parents' and grandparents' generations didn't necessarily have the privilege to build, we also give them permission to do the same, later in life but never too late. Since I dropped my Christian name, my father has followed suit, going only by his Fante name, and my mum has added her local name, also Araba, to her signatures. As I continually uncover new nuggets of wisdom about our culture and, on a personal level, my family history, I share them with Araba Senior and, as long as it doesn't disturb her hyper-Christian sensibilities, she revels in the newfound knowledge with me. This is evident in my healing journey too. Some years ago, I bought my mum her first-ever daily planner to help her get organised with life and personal growth. And now I can honestly say I may have created a monster! Over the years, she's tried out different planners, different goal-setting styles, and now *she's* the one telling *me* which planner to invest in for the new year. I've watched her dedication to reflection and growth expand exponentially, and I'm so proud of the progress she's made in her faith, in her parenting, in her power.

This work that we are doing is not just for us – we are healing generational trauma and uplifting the global Black community as we do. So, what does it mean to live well, the African way? I know I've just written a whole book about this, but I believe it can ultimately be encapsulated by this one sentence, this one commitment:

> *I will do my best every day to honour my heritage,*
> *my faith*, my community and myself.*

*This truly applies to everyone; it could be faith in God, Allah, the Creator, the universe, your intuition, yourself.

Are you ready to make this commitment now? If you are, in the spirit of community, share a post on social media with #returntosource #mycommitment.

Searching the hashtags might connect you to someone in your local area or even reunite you with an old friend! This journey is always easier when you take it with friends. If you're posting on Instagram, you can tag me @araba.oa

Now the thing with commitments is that, even with the best of intentions, if we don't have an action plan, we're likely to miss the mark. How many books have you read that shared life-changing knowledge? And how many times have you actually changed your life after reading? We've all been there! Let's make sure this time is different. Take some time to reflect on the questions below:

- What is my one key takeaway from this book and how am I going to implement it in my life and/or my work?

- Which three to five actions am I going to take in the short-term as a result of what I've learned? For example, creating a morning ritual, buying crafting materials or setting up an Ancestor altar.

- Which three to five actions am I going to take in the long term as a result of what I've learned? For example, planning a community ritual, moving a proportion of spending over to Black-owned brands or growing a garden of healing herbs.

If you're not Black and you've made it this far, thank you for your willingness to engage with and learn from a culture that isn't your own. Thank you for having the patience to stick with something that doesn't centre your experience (most content, especially wellness content, is like this for Black and Brown people). Now, I want to invite you to take the same oath. I truly believe that, whatever our heritage, if we can return to the source of who we are, who we have been, we can unlock a deeper level of wellness than we'll ever recognise with another peoples' path. This commitment applies to you. If you're Indigenous, South Asian, Celtic, Polynesian, Latinx, Arabic, Vietnamese, Hungarian, Italian, Chinese... wherever your roots are, it's time to return. Look before the colonialism, before the slavery, before the oppression and get to the heart of your heritage. Sankɔfa – look to the past in order to move forward. Are you ready to return?

I will do my best every day to honour my heritage,
my faith, my community and myself.

When we think of initiation in the traditional African sense, it centres around rites of passage, ritual, secret societies and religion. But initiation is also the act of starting. It is a new beginning. It is the answering of a call, one that echoes from the depths of your being. I hope that I've done the Ancestors proud by presenting that call within this book. Now it's up to you to decide: Will you answer?

You've made it! Ayekoo! I hope that this is the kind of book you'll come back to time after time. But I also want to encourage you to pass it on once you're done. In the spirit of community, think about who could benefit from the messages contained here and gift this book to them, especially if they are unlikely to have the funds or access to get it themselves. You could also gift the book to your local library. Thank you for reading, and I'm sending you all the vibes for your journey as you return to source.

CLOSING INCANTATION

I give thanks for reaching the end of this book. I give thanks to the author, to the Future Ancestors, to myself and to the Ancestors for this wisdom exchange. I ask the Most High, my Higher Soul and my Ancestors to support me in integrating this wisdom and turning it into action for the benefit of myself and my community. Ameen/Amen/Àṣe/And so it is!

GRATITUDE

Idedicated this book to my mum. I'm going to continue being clichéd by starting my acknowledgements like this... All praise to the Most High God, without whom none of this would be possible. I want to thank my spirit family: my Ancestors for leading me on this path and trusting me with this message, my angels and guides for their protection, and my Higher Soul for never leaving me. I want to thank my blood family who are my biggest inspiration: my mum whose resilience is equal to her kindness, my auntie who is my second mum, my sister who is already changing the world and my brother who is showing me what love and family can be. I want to thank my chosen family, the gworls whose friendship isn't counted in phone calls or messages but in unconditional love, support and laughs: Tiff, Linda, Belle, Agyeiwaa, Yvette, Izzy, and the boy dem who have no idea how meaningful our music and wine therapy sessions are: Temple, Ben and Kwaku. And I want to thank myself for typing through the tears, tantrums and takeouts. We did it!

This book wouldn't have been possible without the help and guidance of so many, some who aren't even aware of the impact they've had! Immense gratitude to my Future Ancestors for trusting me with your words and for believing in the vision. Thank you to family members, friends, experts, random people I accosted for the conversations that helped inform and inspire me in this writing process, especially Uncle Kofi, Uncle Ato, Kwame Adapa, Yaw Makatah, the team at the National Folklore Board, the old guy with great stories in Busua....

Shout-out to the two writers residencies that gave me a month each of focused writing time: Library of Africa and the African Diaspora (LOATAD) and Ebedi Residency. Sylvia Arthur and Dr Wale Okediran, the work you do for African writers (and readers!) is unparalleled. Thank you to the Society of Authors for awarding this book a World of Books Impact award and grant, and for all the encouragement and support they give to writers.

To all the healers, cultural leaders and writers who have paved the way for my work to exist, I thank you, I love you and I hope I've made you proud. There are so many but here I will name a few in the hopes that you will go and engage with their work: Yeye Luisah Teish, Reni Eddo-Lodge, Patrice Malidoma Somé, Vusamazulu Credo Mutwa, Angela Davis, Zora Neale Hurston, Yomi Adegoke and Elizabeth Uviebinené.

Thank you to my aunties Doreen and Yvonne for your commitment to making my return home a success – I couldn't have done it without you. I decided I needed two things in order to be a 'real writer': a MacBook and time spent at residencies. Thanks, Prof, for making both happen. Thank you to my two homes; it's the London in me that gave me the methodical thinking and mild anxiety required to write this book in under two years, and the Accra in me that helped me write laughter into pain.

My route to publishing with Hay House started with reading their books, so I have to thank Louise Hay, the real spiritual OG, and all the other authors that make up the Hay House family past and present. The next step was the Diverse Wisdom mentoring programme. To Jessica Huie and the rest of the team who run it – thank you for rejecting me in 2018... no, really! I now know I definitely wasn't ready. Thank you for accepting me in 2020 when I actually had something to say. Gratitude to my mentor on the programme, Suzy Ashworth, as well as all the other mentees for your support and inspiration. With Suzy's help, I wrote a kick-ass book proposal and that is how we find ourselves here. To the whole team at Hay House, I give thanks for all your work on the book, and for supporting me in making this an all-Black production: George Dorcoo of Ghana for the cover illustrations (though we had to change it, the original was pivotal to the final direction of the cover) and Adaobi Obi Tulton of America via Nigeria for the copyediting. You both brought this book to life!

A huge thank you to my beta readers, the first people to read this book! Your feedback and kind words were invaluable in refining this work into the masterpiece it is today. Thank you Mkutaji, Ama, J, Vanessa and Sarko.

Finally I want to thank anyone who has ever engaged with my work. From my first blog, Working Girl London (it was a name for the times, sigh) to my Self-Care Sunday events in Accra. If you've ever read an article, meditated with me, shared my content, hired me to speak, watched an energy reading, bought a card deck, had a coaching session or liked a photo on Instagram, thank you. And thank you for reading this book!

BIBLIOGRAPHY

Afolayan, F. (2004), *Culture and Customs of South Africa*. Westport: Greenwood Press.

Appiah, A. and Grossman, A.R. (1992), *In My Father's House: Africa in the Philosophy of Culture*. New York: Oxford University Press.

Ashmolean Museum. 'History of the Ashmolean': https://www.ashmolean. org [Accessed 10 May 2022]

Baird, R.P. (2021), 'The Invention of Whiteness: The Long History of a Dangerous Idea', *The Guardian*: https://www.theguardian.com/news/ 2021/apr/20/the-invention-of-whiteness-long-history-dangerous-idea [Accessed 12 May 2022]

Bangura, A.K. (2011), *African Mathematics: From Bones to Computers*. Maryland: University Press of America.

Busia, K. (2016), *Fundamentals of Herbal Medicine: History, Phytopharmacology, Phytotherapeutics* Vol. 1. Bloomington: Xlibris

Deisser, A.M. and Njuguna, M. (2016), *Conservation of Natural and Cultural Heritage in Kenya*. London: UCL Press.

Duvall, C.S. (2019), *The African Roots of Marijuana*. Durham: Duke University Press.

Fu-Kiau, K.K.B. (2002), *Self-Healing Power and Therapy: Old Teachings from Africa*. Baltimore: Imprint Editions.

Gathara, P. (2019), 'Eurafrica and the Myth of African Independence', Al Jazeera: https://www.aljazeera.com/opinions/2019/11/24/eurafrica-and-the-myth-of-african-independence [Accessed 10 May 2022]

Griffin, N. and Falola, T. (2021), *Religious Beliefs and Knowledge Systems in Africa*. Lanham: Rowman & Littlefield.

Gyekye, K. (1996), *African Cultural Values: An introduction*. Accra: Sankofa Publishing Co.

Jayasanker, L. (2020), *Sameness in Diversity: Food and Globalization in Modern America*. Berkeley: University of California Press.

Kamalu, C. (2000), *Person, Divinity and Nature: A Modern View of the Person and the Cosmos in African Thought*. London: Karnak House.

Karenga, M. (2004), *Maat, the Moral Ideal in Ancient Egypt: A Study in Classical African Ethics*. Hove: Psychology Press.

Madowo, L. (2020), 'Silicon Valley Has Deep Pockets for African Startups – If You're Not African', *The Guardian*. https://www.theguardian.com/business/2020/jul/17/african-businesses-black-entrepreneurs-us-investors [Accessed 13 May 2022]

Mattoon, M.A. (2005), *Jung and the Human Psyche: An Understandable Introduction*. London: Routledge.

Mbiti, J.S. (1975), *Introduction to African Religion*. London: Heinemann Educational.

Mbiti, J.S. (1990), *African Religions and Philosophy*. Oxford: Heinemann.

McClellan, R. (2000), *The Healing Forces of Music: History, Theory, and Practice*. Indiana: iUniverse.

Mutwa, C.V. (1999), *Indaba, My Children*. New York: Grove Press.

Ollivier, J.J. (1996), *The Wisdom of African Mythology*. Top of the Mountain.

Painter, N.I. (2020), 'White Identity in America Is Ideology, Not Biology. The History of 'Whiteness' Proves It', NBC News: https://www.nbcnews.com/think/opinion/white-identity-america-ideology-not-biology-history-whiteness-proves-it-ncna1232200 [Accessed 12 May 2022]

p'Bitek, O. and Wiredu, K. (2011), *Decolonizing African Religions: A Short History of African Religions in Western Scholarship*. New York: Diasporic Africa Press.

Perbi, A.A. (2004), *A History of Indigenous Slavery in Ghana: From the 15th to the 19th Centuries*. Accra: Sub-Saharan Publishers.

Somé, M.P. (1998), *The Healing Wisdom of Africa: Finding Life Purpose through Nature, Ritual, and Community*. New York: Jeremy P. Tarcher/Putnam.

Spicer, A. (2019), '"Self-care": How a Radical Feminist Idea Was Stripped of Politics for the Mass Market', *The Guardian*: https://www.theguardian.com/commentisfree/2019/aug/21/self-care-radical-feminist-idea-mass-market [Accessed 13 May 2022]

Taylor, S. (2020), 'Self-care, Audre Lorde and Black Radical Activism'. DissolvingMargins.https://www.dissolvingmargins.co/post/self-care-audre-lorde-and-black-radical-activism [Accessed 13 May 2022]

Valley, G. (2019), 'Decolonization Can't Just Be a Metaphor', Africa Is a Country: https://africasacountry.com/2019/11/decolonization-cant-just-be-a-metaphor [Accessed 10 May 2022]

wa Thiong'o, N. (1986), *Decolonising the Mind: The Politics of Language in African Literature*. London: J. Currey.

Welsh-Asante, K. (2009), *African Dance* (2nd edition). New York: Chelsea House.

REFERENCES

Chapter 1: What Does It Mean to Be African?

1. Global Wellness Institute (2021), 'The Global Wellness Economy: Looking Beyond COVID': https://globalwellnessinstitute.org/wp-content/uploads/2021/11/GWI-WE-Monitor-2021_final-digital.pdf [Accessed 12 May 2022]

2. Nyerere, J.K. (1962), 'Ujamaa: The Basis of African Socialism', *The Journal of Pan-African Studies*, 1: 4–11: www.jpanafrican.org/edocs/e-DocUjamma3.5.pdf [Accessed 1 December 2022]

Chapter 2: The African Worldview

3. Dei, G.S. and Imoka, C. (2018), 'Colonialism: Why Write Back?', E-International Relations: www.e-ir.info/2018/01/03/colonialism-why-write-back/ [Accessed 12 May 2022]

4. Tuck, E. and Yang, K.W. (2012), 'Decolonization is not a metaphor', *Decolonization: Indigeneity, Education & Society*, 1(1): http://resolver.scholarsportal.info/resolve/19298692/v01i0001/nfp_dinam.xml [Accessed 18 November 2022]

Chapter 4: Dance

5. Kitata, M. (2020), 'Sexualising the performance, objectifying the performer: The twerk dance in Kenya', *Agenda: Empowering Women for Gender Equity*, 34(3): 11–21: https://doi.org/10.1080/10130950.2020.1773286 [Accessed 1 December 2022]

6. Vecchi, M., et al. (2022), 'Shall We Dance? Recreational Dance, Well-Being and Productivity Performance During COVID-19: A Three-Country Study', *Journal of International Marketing*, March: https://doi.org/10.1177/1069031X221079609 [Accessed 1 December 2022]

7. Women and Equalities Committee (2020), 'Special Report: Body Image Survey Results': https://publications.parliament.uk/pa/cm5801/cmselect/cmwomeq/805/80502.htm [Accessed 18 November 2022]

Chapter 5: Sound

8. Nketia, J.H. (1958), 'Traditional Music of the Ga People', *African Music: Journal of the International Library of African Music*, 2 (1): 21–27: https://journal.ru.ac.za/index.php/africanmusic/article/view/523 [Accessed 1 December 2022]

9. Heather, S. (2007), 'What Is Sound Healing?', *Wholistic Healing Research*, 7(3): www.simonheather.co.uk/pages/articles/ijhc_article.pdf [Accessed 18 November 2022]

10. Holmes, J.A. (2017), 'Expert Listening beyond the Limits of Hearing: Music and Deafness', *Journal of the American Musicological Society*, 70(1): 171–220: https://doi.org/10.1525/jams.2017.70.1.171 [Accessed 18 November 2022]

11. Goldsby, T.L., et al. (2022), 'Sound Healing: Mood, Emotional, and Spiritual Well-Being Interrelationships', *Religions*, 13(2): 123. https://doi.org/10.3390/rel13020123 [Accessed 1 December 2022]

12. Smith, C., Viljoen, J.T., McGeachie, L. (2014), 'African Drumming: a holistic approach to reducing stress and improving health?', *Journal of Cardiovascular Medicine*, 15(6): 441–446: https://doi.org/10.2459/JCM.0000000000000046 [Accessed 12 May 2022]

13. Akimoto, K., et al. (2018), 'Effect of 528 Hz Music on the Endocrine System and Autonomic Nervous System'. *Health*, 10: 1159–1170: https://doi.org/10.4236/health.2018.109088 [Accessed 1 December 2022]

14. Pereira, C. (2016), 'Effect of tuning fork generated frequencies on cognition in snails (Achatina fulica)', *Journal of Entomology*

and Zoology Studies, 4: 1096–1101: www.researchgate.net/profile/ Contzen-Pereira/publication/309465157_Effect_of_tuning_fork_ generated_frequencies_on_cognition_in_snails_Achatina_fulica/ links/5811e56308ae205f81037794/Effect-of-tuning-fork-generated- frequencies-on-cognition-in-snails-Achatina-fulica.pdf   [Accessed 12 May 2022]

15. Akombo, D. (2013), 'Effects of Community African Drumming on Generalised Anxiety in Teenagers', *Approaches: An Interdisciplinary Journal of Music Therapy*, 5(1): 25–33: https://approaches.gr/effects- of-community-african-drumming-on-generalised-anxiety-in-teenagers- david-akombo/ [Accessed 1 December 2022]

Chapter 6: Creativity

16. Brosowsky, N.P., et al. (2022), 'Creativity, Boredom Proneness and Well- Being in the Pandemic', *Behavioral Sciences*, 12(3): 68: https://doi. org/10.3390/bs12030068 [Accessed 1 December 2022]

Chapter 7: Herbs

17. Kofi-Tsekpo, M. (2004), 'Institutionalization of African Traditional Medicine in Health Care Systems in Africa', *African Journal of Health Sciences*, 11(1–2): https://doi.org/10.4314/ajhs.v11i1.30772 [Accessed 18 November 2022]

18. Duvivier, R.J., Burch, V.C., and Boulet, J.R. (2017), 'A comparison of physician emigration from Africa to the United States of America between 2005 and 2015', *Human Resources for Health*, 15(41): https:// doi.org/10.1186/s12960-017-0217-0 [Accessed 18 November 2022]

19. MBRRACE-UK (2021), 'Saving Lives, Improving Mothers' Care – Lessons Learned to Inform Maternity Care from the UK and Ireland Confidential Enquiries into Maternal Deaths and Morbidity 2017- 19, Lay Summary': https://www.npeu.ox.ac.uk/assets/downloads/ mbrrace-uk/reports/maternal-report-2021/MBRRACE-UK_Maternal_ Report_2021_-_Lay_Summary_v10.pdf [Accessed 1 December 2022]

20. Petersen, E.E, et al. (2019), 'Racial/Ethnic Disparities in Pregnancy- Related Deaths – United States, 2007–2016', MMWR Morbidity and

Mortality Weekly Report, 68: 762–765: http://dx.doi.org/10.15585/mmwr.mm6835a3 [Accessed 12 May 2022]

21. Bailey, D.G., et al. (2013), 'Grapefruit–medication Interactions: Forbidden Fruit or Avoidable Consequences?', *Canadian Medical Association Journal*, 185(4): 309–316: https://doi.org/10.1503/cmaj.120951 [Accessed 12 May 2022]

22. NICE (2021), 'Chronic pain (primary and secondary) in over 16s: assessment of all chronic pain and management of chronic primary pain', NG193: https://www.nice.org.uk/guidance/ng193 [Accessed 18 November 2022]

Chapter 8: Food

23. Oniang'o, R.K., Mutuku, J.M., and Malaba, S.J. (2003), 'Contemporary African food habits and their nutritional and health implications', *Asia Pacific Journal of Clinical Nutrition*, 2003; 12(3): 331–336. https://pubmed.ncbi.nlm.nih.gov/14505997/ [Accessed 21 November 2022]

24. Hallberg, L., et al. (1977). 'Iron absorption from Southeast Asian diets. II. Role of various factors that might explain low absorption', *The American Journal of Clinical Nutrition*, 30(4): 539–548: https://doi.org/10.1093/ajcn/30.4.539 [Accessed 18 November 2022]

Chapter 9: Nature

25. Nsude, G.C. (1987), 'The traditional architecture of the Igbo of Nigeria'. PhD thesis. Thames Polytechnic: https://gala.gre.ac.uk/id/eprint/8750/ [Accessed 1 December 2022]

26. Iyegha, D.A. (2000), 'The Wisdom of Traditional Farming in Tropical Africa: The Nigerian Experience', *Journal of Third World Studies*, 17(2): 73–92: www.jstor.org/stable/45198194 [Accessed 1 December 2022]

27. Urama, J.O. (2021), 'Celestial stories: Rediscovering ancient traditions of stargazing can help to awaken interest in modern astronomy', *The ACU Review: Dialogues of Difference*: www.acu.ac.uk/the-acu-review/celestial-stories/ [Accessed 18 November 2022]

28. White, M.P, et al. (2019), 'Spending at least 120 Minutes a week in nature is associated with good health and wellbeing', *Scientific Reports*, 9, 7730: https://doi.org/10.1038/s41598-019-44097-3 [Accessed 12 May 2022]

Chapter 10: Storytelling

29. Mental Health Foundation (2021), 'Black, Asian and Minority Ethnic (BAME) Communities': https://www.mentalhealth.org.uk/explore-mental-health/a-z-topics/black-asian-and-minority-ethnic-bame-communities [Accessed 1 December 2022]

30. Ade-Serrano, Y., Nkansa-Dwamena, O., and McIntosh, M. (Eds.) (2017), *Race, culture and diversity: A collection of articles*. The British Psychological Society: https://docplayer.net/136539348-Race-culture-and-diversity.html [Accessed 21 November 2022]

31. Vezzali L., et al. (2015), 'The greatest magic of Harry Potter· Reducing prejudice', *Journal of Applied Social Psychology*, 45(2): 105 121: https://doi.org/10.1111/jasp.12279 [Accessed 1 December 2022]

32. Eisenberger, N.I., Lieberman, M.D., and Williams, K.D. (2003), 'Does Rejection Hurt? An FMRI Study of Social Exclusion', *Science*, 302(5643): 290–292: https://doi.org/10.1126/science.1089134 [Accessed 12 May 2022]

Chapter 11: Ancestors

33. Adu-Gyamfi, S., et al. (2020), 'Funerals among the Akan People: Some Perspectives on Asante', *Revista de Etnologie și Culturologie*, 27: 44–53: https://doi.org/10.5281/zenodo.3956748 [Accessed 12 May 2022]

34. Oladipo, O. (2007), 'Religion in African Culture: Some Conceptual Issues', *A Companion to African Philosophy*, 353–363: https://doi.org/10.1002/9780470997154.ch28 [Accessed 18 November 2022]

35. Yehuda, R. and Lehrner, A. (2018), 'Intergenerational transmission of trauma effects: putative role of epigenetic mechanisms', *World Psychiatry*, 17: 243–257: https://doi.org/10.1002/wps.20568 [Accessed 21 November 2022]

Chapter 12: Ritual

36. Singh, P., et al. (2020), 'Time investments in rituals are associated with social bonding, affect and subjective health: a longitudinal study of diwali in two indian communities', *Philosophical Transactions of the Royal Society of London*, Series B, Biological sciences, 375(1805), 20190430: https://doi.org/10.1098/rstb.2019.0430 [Accessed 1 December 2022]

Kumi Obuobisa

About the Author

Araba Ofori-Acquah is a healer, writer, DJ and cultural curator interested in the preservation and reimagining of African tradition. She lives and teaches African-centred wellness, a practice rooted in African wisdom that promotes the wellbeing of the global Black population.

By the age of 25, Araba had ascended to marketing management roles in industries ranging from legal to tech but faced many unspoken challenges as a young executive and often the only Black woman in the room. Her journey to becoming a healer began with herself through experiencing first-hand the power of talking therapies, mind and body practices and meditation. Inspired to create safe spaces for other Black people, Araba studied different healing modalities, including a 200-hour yoga teacher training in India, an NHS-accredited wellbeing coach qualification in the UK and the study of advanced pranic healing in Ghana.

Drawing on her experiences as a Ghanaian-British woman who searched in vain for ways to achieve wellbeing that felt authentic and in alignment with her African identity, Araba's debut book is a timely guide that gives readers an insight into traditional African knowledge, with a view to making it relevant and accessible to Black people of any religion or spiritual belief who simply want to live well.

Brimming with hard-earned wisdom from seldom-reached sources, *Return to Source* is much more than a personal development book. It is an accessible, powerful and practical guide to rediscovery and reconnection for Black people that leads readers through unlocking the power of soul-affirming wellness practices.

 **@araba.oa**

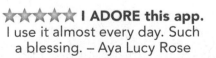

CONNECT WITH
HAY HOUSE
ONLINE

🌐 hayhouse.co.uk   **f** @hayhouse

📷 @hayhouseuk   🐦 @hayhouseuk

▶ @hayhouseuk   ♪ @hayhouseuk

'The gateways to wisdom and knowledge are always open.'

Louise Hay